SHORTY

MISTAKEN IDENTITY OR STITCH UP?

PETER BREEN

Published by:
Wilkinson Publishing Pty Ltd ACN 006 042 173
PO Box 24135
Melbourne, Vic 3001
Ph: 03 9654 5446
enquiries@wilkinsonpublishing.com.au
www.wilkinsonpublishing.com.au

Title: Shorty: Mistaken Identity or Stitch-up?
ISBN: 9781921804717

A catalogue record for this book is available from the National Library of Australia.

Cover design and internal design by Spike Creative
Printed and bound in Australia by Ligare Book Printers

To the memory of John Kennedy McLaughlin AM, KCSG

(1938 – 2023)

doctor, lawyer, judge, friend

CONTENTS

AUTHOR'S NOTE

Murder committed in New South Wales prior to 1990 carried a life sentence unless the trial judge was satisfied that certain mitigating circumstances significantly diminished the prisoner's culpability for the crime. In practice, a life sentence did not mean natural life, as a prisoner could apply to the Supreme Court after eight years' incarceration to convert the life sentence to a fixed term of years. In 1990, the average life sentence served for murder was between 13 and 15 years. Thanks to a vote-catching policy initiative on crime and punishment, the State government changed the law in 1990 so that a life sentence now means for the remaining term of a prisoner's natural life. The new law served no useful purpose other than to trade justice for votes, effectively abolishing restitution and rehabilitation for life prisoners, as well as removing any opportunity for parole.

Approximately 250 lifers indicted before 1990 applied for fixed-term sentences to replace their life sentences and 225 of them were successful. Another ten prisoners who committed murder prior to 1990 were the subject of retrospective special legislation in 2001 which effectively quadrupled their judicial sentences—should they live so long. In other words, the Labor government of the day did not want any of the ten convicts to apply for fixed- term sentences to replace their life sentences. Premier Bob Carr dubbed his sentencing statute 'the cement law' since the object of the legislation was to cement the ten life prisoners in their cells and effectively deny them parole.

Two of the ten targeted prisoners in the 2001 cement law, Bronson Blessington and Matthew Elliott, were juveniles aged 14 and 16 years respectively at the time of their crimes in 1988. They abducted, raped and murdered bank teller Janine Balding. Blessington and Elliott were accompanied by two lesser offenders, Wayne Wilmot and Carol Arrow, aged 15 and 18 years respectively. A fifth older boy convicted of the crimes against Ms Balding, Stephen 'Shorty' Jamieson, always claimed to be innocent. The four young people gave evidence at trial that the Shorty who was with them when they committed the crimes against Ms Balding was not Shorty Jamieson.

During the first trial of Blessington, Elliott and Jamieson in 1989, Justice James Wood was concerned that police had arrested the wrong Shorty and dismissed the jury. Crown prosecutors convinced the jury of a second trial in 1990 that Jamieson was the right Shorty. In sentencing Blessington, Elliott and Jamieson to life for the crimes against Janine Balding, a new judge described the wrong Shorty allegation as *a tissue of lies*. It was the first time in Australian criminal law that DNA evidence was used to help convict the accused. From 2001 onwards—when the cement law came into force—I began to wonder whether DNA test results and other evidence in the case should have acquitted Shorty Jamieson, not convicted him.

Chapter 1

BRONSON BLESSINGTON

Goulburn city rests in a hollow of the Great Dividing Range, 2000 feet above sea level, a prison town whose colonial administrators once flogged convicts at the triangles and hung their bodies from the gibbet to remind passers-by of the respect due to British justice. By the standards of such brutality, today's government may appear soft on crime, yet prisoners are still abused to promote executive government authority, and I fear some wounded part of the legal system remains deeply attached to our convict past. A correctional officer once told me that prisoners always go down when they arrive at Goulburn—a reference to convicts doing time and serving long sentences—but also referring to the location of the city on a wide plain surrounded by outcrops of the east coast mountain range.

The first thing you see as you drive into town from the north is a shiny new cemetery with its bright flowers and fresh-cut lawns, and then across a dry gully on a grey grass hill, the gloomy red brick jail suddenly appears. Two more cemeteries flank the jail: one is the Anglican burial ground of St. Saviour's consecrated in 1830; the other is the resting place for long-suffering Celts, including Irish Catholics who made up nearly one-third of the local population in the early days of the penal colony of New South Wales. I count my ancestors in the ranks of those forlorn convict Micks, including one William Davis transported to the colony for his part in the Irish Political Movement of 1798.

It was just past midday, peak summer in the New Year after the first bushfire-black Christmas of the new millennium, and the correctional officer who greeted me at the jail's main gate wanted to know if I was the politician visiting Blessington. The officer was wearing dark blue serge pants, polished black loafers, and mid-blue shirt, open at the neck. His wispy grey hair, receding at the temples, was brushed straight back. Prison staff were not permitted to address prisoners by their first names.

Yes, Bronson Blessington. He's the one.

A patient man, the correctional officer arched a grey eyebrow and stared at me through weathered eyes. I followed him through a series of steel and toughened-glass doors, finally presenting at a counter where he made a discreet inquiry of a redheaded woman processing a long line of visitors from behind a glass screen. The officer soon delivered the bad news—there would be a short delay gaining entry to the visitors' enclosure.

"Blessington's seeing his family," the officer said. "You can wait in reception till you're called." With that, he directed me to a visitors chair and headed back to his main-gate post.

Seated in the expansive reception room, I opened my lever-arch folder and read over Bronson Blessington's unsolicited letter—especially the paragraph that had brought me to the jail.

> *To tell a Man the only Hope in Life He has of getting out of prison is hoping He gets Cancer or something just as hideous is a huge mistake on the part of the Government. The Law is a wonderful thing, as long as it punishes, rehabilitates, and forgives once the sentence is given. My Father wrote to Me just after He heard about this new Law.*

He said that it would have been more Human for them, meaning the Authorities, to have hung Me when I was 14 years old. When all hope is taken away from someone by the Law, what is there to live for? I am extremely remorseful for My part in the Crimes I committed... But to leave Me with nothing to hope for in this Life is ten times more severe than a death sentence.

The prisoner wrote to me following a vote on the cement law in the upper house of the Parliament of New South Wales where I was elected on a platform of law reform. At the time of the vote, I knew nothing about Blessington except that he was the youngest person sentenced by the parliament to effective life without parole since transportation to the colony of New South Wales ended in 1840. I argued against the new law from the crossbench, pointing out to my fellow legislators that sentencing was a job for judges, not politicians. I lost the vote when major party members voted together to change the law to ensure that Blessington and his co-offenders were never released from jail.

Perhaps the redheaded woman behind the glass screen shared my Irish convict roots, although it was not a question to ask someone admitting me to prison. After I'd waited for about half an hour and listened to a litany of complaints from those visitors standing in the queue, the woman called me to the glass screen and glanced at me over the rim of her glasses.

"Blessington's free now."

I doubted it, but I was not about to give the woman any more trouble. She checked my paperwork and directed me through a door-frame metal detector and then to a holding area where another prison officer searched me with a hand-held metal detector and then asked me to stand on a wooden box while he checked the soles of my shoes. Finally, I received the all-clear. A metal door clicked open, and I reached the main visitors centre, which consisted of an open reception area with two separately caged areas on either side, one for 'Islanders and Whites' and the other for 'Kooris and Lebanese', according to large cardboard signs on the walls. Inside the two cages, inmates in white boiler suits sat around white laminate tables with their friends and families—the victims of crime you never read about in the daily newspapers. Most visitors were mystified by the segregation of inmates and the complex sentencing laws.

Three more correctional officers gave me a long hard look. Contrary to his facial expression, one of them—a moon-faced fellow with greying temples—turned out to be very sympathetic. He directed me down a narrow corridor with small cages known as 'box cells' on either side. At the end of the corridor, he ensconced me in a cell about three-metres square, a space designated for legal visits. It was sparsely furnished with a laminate table and two plastic chairs. I placed my folder of papers on the edge of the table, not knowing what to expect from a man who'd spent the last half of his life in jail. There was always a feeling of apprehension before meeting a convicted felon—most crime lawyers had experienced it. You never quite knew if an inmate was about to pour out their soul or attempt to inveigle you into a complex web of deceptions intended to minimise their crimes.

As I contemplated bolting, I realised that the moon-faced correctional officer was standing in the cell doorway with an unassuming young man in a white boiler suit. I stared at both of them for a moment before realising I'd nothing to worry about. Bronson Blessington had straight brown hair, parted to one side, fair complexion with noticeably flushed cheeks, and dark blue eyes. He looked physically strong in an unthreatening sort of way, of average height, with a respectful demeanour.

The prisoner placed his own folder of papers on the table next to mine and thanked the moon-faced officer for allowing us the privacy of a 'legals' cell. The officer pushed the cell door open as far as it would go and then left without a word. My apprehension persisted for just a moment longer before seating myself at the table in the plastic chair nearest to the cell door. As we began talking, I was struck by the prisoner's unusually frank disclosures, and his apparent willingness to accept the full measure of responsibility for his crimes. We agreed that nothing he said or did could make up for the loss of Janine Balding's life—even to ask her family for forgiveness was traumatising and deeply offensive for them.

He handed me what he called his 'Little Red Book', an NIV edition of the New Testament. The pages were well read, the text highlighted and underlined. Most of it he knew by heart, he said, so I tested him on a few passages I pulled out of thin air, having no idea whether the references he gave me were right or wrong. He told me he'd been conducting Bible classes in jail for the past ten years. He handed me another red book, a Collins Debden accounts book, with entries going back several years. The record indicated more than 5,000 prisoner attendances at several hundred Bible classes. When I asked about further restitution for his crimes, he showed me a copy of a letter he sent to the State government offering to assist other Christians in prison. He received no reply.

The young man produced from his folder of papers a letter from the High Court informing him that any appeal against the severity of his life sentence must be filed in person at the registry. The words *in person* were underlined. Attached to the letter was 14 pages of procedural guff about applications to the High Court. Bronson Blessington was well and truly stuck in the legal procedural bog. I asked about medical evidence.

In answer to my question the prisoner handed me two reports, both dated in July 1987—just 14 months before the murder of Janine Balding. A clinical psychologist from the Royal Far West Childrens Home at Manly reported that Bronson needed counselling—aimed at making him aware that his parents' divorce was final. There was no chance of their reconciliation. The other report was an assessment from a Manly psychiatrist describing Bronson as a badly behaved 13-year-old with the emotional development of a much younger boy. *The boy has found it very difficult to cope with the splitting of his family, the failure of reunion of his parents, the interposition of two partners with his parents, and his inability to live with his mother whom he is clearly missing.*

I asked whether these medical assessments were tendered in evidence at his trial, and he said the lawyers were unable to use them because initially he pleaded not guilty. By the time he changed his plea to guilty, the judicial horse had well and truly bolted. Already I could see that the young man was the archetypal juvenile offender: the product of a broken home, poor academic record, and emotionally disturbed.

And then there was the additional problem that politicians

going into bat for the perpetrators of crime rather than its victims was a bad news story. The media was likely to fly into a rage about the waste of taxpayer funds. For me, it was difficult to ignore the injustices the young man's case seemed to involve: the failure of the court to hear medical evidence of his mental age (nine to ten years) at the time of his crimes; the fact of his physical age (14 years); the brutality of the trial judge's recommendation that juveniles should never be released; and the passing of the cement law by politicians, breaching every sentencing principle in a fair and reasonable judge's bench book.

I asked the prisoner about his two co-offenders, Matthew Elliott and Stephen 'Shorty' Jamieson, who were also serving life sentences for the crimes against Janine Balding. Elliott was aged 16 at the time of the crimes and the ringleader of the criminal cohort. Jamieson was an older boy aged 22 who suffered from foetal alcohol spectrum disorder.

"Jamieson wasn't a co-offender," the inmate said matter-of-factly. According to the jury and the sentencing judge, Jamieson was guilty as charged with eight offences against Ms Balding including abduction, robbery in company, sexual intercourse without consent (four counts) and murder, crimes for which he was now sentenced by the parliament to life imprisonment.

"The Shorty who was with us that day was Mark 'Shorty' Wells, not Shorty Jamieson," Blessington insisted.

Of course, some prisoners will say they're innocent even when faced with overwhelming evidence against them. I mentioned the backpacker killer, Ivan Milat, who drove the authorities to distraction with his false pleas of innocence and police corruption.

"I'm telling you, Brother," said the prisoner, "Jamieson wasn't there."

After I summoned the moon-faced correctional officer, the three of us walked back down the corridor between the box cells. In the general visiting area, the prisoner shook my hand and thanked me for visiting him. He urged me to do anything I could to help Shorty Jamieson.

"Jamo's twice the person I could be," he said. "He's been punished for the way he looks since the day he was born, but he's a man with no malice, and no desire for revenge. He only wants his freedom."

For me, an adult convict serving a natural life sentence for crimes he *did not* commit was no more or less troubling than two children serving natural life sentences for crimes they *did* commit. The juveniles could be in jail for 60 or 70 years when the average sentence for comparable adult crimes at the time of their offences was less than 15 years. The idea that politicians would re-sentence children by adding perhaps 50 years to their fair and just judicial punishments beggared belief.

The moon-faced prison officer nodded his head as though reading my thoughts.

"I hope you can do something for Blessington" he said boldly, no hint of embarrassment at taking up the cause of the prisoner. "It's quite wrong to lock up a man for the rest of his life for something he did when he was just 14 years old."

Chapter 2

JACK BEGNELL

I wanted to talk to Blessington's family, hoping I might understand what turned a troubled teenager into a rapist and murderer. I began by contacting the clergyman, Jack Begnell, who was not strictly family, but seemed to have guided the young man since his days as a juvenile inmate. Jack lived on the mid-north coast at Port Macquarie with his wife and a procession of visiting grandchildren. When I caught up with him in the backyard of his blonde brick suburban house, his life revolved around the local church, and Bronson was the sole remaining connection to his former prison ministry. Tall and dignified, ageing gracefully, likeable and optimistic, Jack was surprisingly tolerant for a man who held every word of the Bible as literal truth. He told me that his prison ministry began with regular visits to Minda Juvenile Remand Centre to pray with inmates and teach them the Bible.

"Like the prisoner Jesus," Jack said, "all prisoners are familiar with suffering, so Christianity is tailor-made for prisoners, offering them hope, and the chance of a new life. God forgives even the greatest sinners, and this is the liberating power of Christianity."

Jack Begnell's faith was the uncompromising evangelical kind, but he was also, indisputably, a man of God, and I could not argue with the legitimacy of his religious conservatism, which drew worldly comfort from the government's hard line on crime and punishment. For my part, I feared tough-on-crime policies inevitably led to the erosion of civil rights for law-abiding citizens, and too much legalism. Ordinary common sense and fair-mindedness could easily disappear, as Elliott, Blessington and Jamieson's situations had demonstrated.

I raised with Jack the possibility that the government's policy of doling out vengefulness to the victims of crime in the form of insanely harsh punishment for juvenile offenders was unchristian. What juveniles really needed was education and rehabilitation. Meanwhile, victims of crime needed reasonable compensation, and support. The assistant pastor responded by reading a passage from scripture affirming, he said, the principle of an eye for an eye. It took a moment before I realised that Jack was advocating for the death penalty. Surely the God of the Old Testament was cruel and vengeful—just like the government? Wasn't Bronson proof that rehabilitation works?

"Bronson belongs with God," Jack said. "God has forgiven him. Of all my boys, only Bronson is still in prison. Hardly a week goes by when we're not in touch with one another. He still refers to me as his pastor, even though I was just an assistant in the Cabramatta parish."

For a moment, Jack appeared to lose hope, and then his mood lightened, as if the teacher was recalling what his star pupil had already achieved during his incarceration.

"Following his baptism in the Minda swimming pool," Jack said, "Bronson studied by correspondence at the Moore Theological College, which was more than I did."

Now the assistant pastor was smiling, his steely grey eyes fully focused. "Just the other day, I was giving a talk at the local church, and I mentioned Bronson's work for the Lord in the prisons.

Afterwards, a man came up and shook my hand. He'd been an inmate at one of the prisons—traumatised by his experience—but after speaking with Bronson, his spirits lifted, and he felt he could cope." Jack lowered his voice. "I just love that boy," he said sadly.

I looked up at clear blue sky above the assistant pastor's Port Macquarie backyard. And then I informed him that Wayne Wilmot—the fourth boy originally charged with the murder of Janine Balding—had written a letter of apology to the young woman's family. Jack was puzzled by this information since the only 'other boy' he knew about was Shorty Jamieson, who was older than Bronson and Matthew Elliott, and therefore never an inmate at Minda when they were there.

"They always said that the Jamieson boy was innocent," Jack said cautiously, as if wary about passing on apocryphal information.

I'd heard it before in legal circles, when reading trial transcripts, when speaking with child welfare workers involved in the case, and in my discussions with Bronson Blessington. Matthew Elliott's lawyer, David Giddy, had no doubt that Shorty Jamieson was the wrong Shorty, describing his convictions and retrospectively legislated life sentence as the worst injustice he'd seen in 50 years of legal practice. The lawyer was with his client in the cells below Darlinghurst criminal court on the day the three convicts were sentenced. He told me that Matthew Elliott was much more upset that an innocent man, Stephen Jamieson, was convicted of abduction, rape and murder than he was about his own life sentence.

At first Jack Begnell rejected the idea that police arrested the wrong Shorty, but Bronson and Matthew both insisted that a boy named Shorty Wells had been with them when they abducted Janine Balding, not Shorty Jamieson. Questioning Bronson and Matthew separately and together about the implications of what they were saying, Jack decided that the two boys were telling the truth about Shorty Jamieson not being involved in the crimes because neither of them had anything to gain from a lie.

"Now there's a terrible thing," he said, folding his arms and shaking his head. "All those years that the Jamieson boy has been locked away—and he's innocent."

I was about to reaffirm my opposition to the death penalty because of the risk of killing innocent convicts, but the moment passed, and then it was time to say goodbye to Jack.

Later, when I played back the tape of our conversation, I was amazed to hear screeching rainbow lorikeets and the laughing voices of the assistant pastor's grandchildren in the background. At the time of our discussion, I became so engaged by the presence of the man, I was blissfully unaware of what was going on around us.

Chapter 3

MAT AND JOAN BLESSINGTON

Mat Blessington, a retired senior officer in the Salvation Army and Bronson Blessington's paternal grandfather, once supported the death penalty. But then his grandson abducted, raped and murdered a young woman, and nothing Mat believed was ever quite the same. Mat lived with his wife, Joan, in the Salvation Army retirement village on Sydney's northern beaches. The village sits on a hill above the local surf club from where the ocean appears to roll out of blue sky. A mist of sea spray drifts through stands of Norfolk Island pine and grevillea. I greeted the Blessingtons with the observation that living by the sea must be heaven on a stick.

"I never go down to the beach," Mat said dogmatically. "You've been down once or twice," said Joan, correcting him.

In the year of the murder of Janine Balding, Mat and Joan Blessington lived in the Blue Mountains at Warrimoo, and I gained the impression they would happily swap sea mist and salt spray for cool mountain air.

Mat told me that Bronson and his father, Steve Blessington, went to Goulburn in 1987—the year before the murder—where Steve had a seasonal job as a boner at the local meatworks. Steve had worked as a deep-sea fisherman until he lost his fishing trawler in a boating accident a few years before the breakdown of his marriage. He turned to boning after the insurance company went into liquidation. Mat and Joan helped out financially, but Steve wasn't able to recover his fishing business.

Steve Blessington and his son stayed in accommodation for workers at Goulburn provided by the meatworks. Bronson attended school for a few months before dropping out. The boy couldn't read or write and refused to sit in a class for children with learning difficulties. Every day for four months he wagged school, working instead for a pittance in a local upholstery shop. Then Steve's job at the meatworks ran out and the two of them headed back to Sydney, arriving on Mat and Joan's doorstep in the Blue Mountains in the New Year of 1988. Mat found them accommodation at the Salvation Army farm at Boiler Close, Prospect. Steve got a job at the Flemington meatworks, and Bronson enrolled at Blacktown High School.

The boy was also experimenting with marijuana, alcohol, cigarettes and petrol sniffing. One day he caught a train to Kings Cross after making $80 selling marijuana. The proceeds went to a prostitute. When he arrived back at Blacktown railway station the police picked him up and drove him home to the Salvation Army farm at Prospect. Bronson's father went ballistic. Conscious of his inability to look after his son, Steve headed up to the Blue Mountains, and once again appealed to his parents.

"I did everything I could," said Mat, his voice breaking up. "Steve told me, 'Dad, we'll have to do something about Bronson because I can't handle him; he's wagging school and I've got to go to work."

Mat explained that he and Steve contacted child welfare. "They're now called the Department of Community Services—DOCS or something. We were in touch with them, but they wouldn't do anything. Someone at DOCS said, 'We've got nowhere to put him'. That's all they would say."

Relating the story, Mat Blessington became increasingly angry, thrusting out his bottom jaw whenever he mentioned child welfare services.

"When DOCS couldn't help, I spent three days ringing up every institution in New South Wales—from border to border—looking for a place to put Bronson. They were either full up, he was too young, or he didn't fit the bill. Eventually we found a place for him out at Penrith, but it was basically a rehabilitation centre for adults—drug addicts and alcoholics. The fellow who ran the place said, 'Look, we're not what you want, but we'll see how he goes'."

The boy didn't go well. After a few weeks, an officer at the centre found cannabis residue and a bong in Bronson's backpack, and Mat received a phone call to come and collect his grandson. He begged the caller to give the boy another chance, but finding dope and smoking gear in a rehabilitation centre was about as popular as a bottle of scotch at an AA meeting. Someone from DOCS rang Mat and castigated him for putting the boy in an adult institution. "My personal feeling about it," Mat said, "is that what happened was the end result of his life—what happened in his life."

Did he mean that the crimes against Janine Balding were the natural consequence of the downhill road Bronson was on?

"Absolutely," Mat replied. "His mum and dad have got to accept some of the responsibility. So do the DOCS people."

The jaw tightened again at the mention of child welfare.

"That little boy was crying out for love. When they were living at Stockton—when Steve and Bronson's mother 'Rose' were living together—we went up to see them, and Bronson would bung on an act just to get attention."

Most kids bung on an act at one time or another without becoming murderers. Bronson's parents separated when he was six years old—a difficult but not uncommon problem for young children—and his mother looked after him until he turned 13 when he decided he wanted to live with his father. Mat said Bronson was a good kid until he reached puberty and then something completely bizarre happened: his grandson became a notorious killer.

Mat Blessington could not understand why the reports from the Far West Children's Home and the psychiatrist at Manly were never presented to the judge and jury in the murder trials. I explained that Bronson's not-guilty plea at trial meant the medical and psychiatric reports influenced proceedings only to the extent that they gave Bronson's lawyers some background material about their client.

"Now I don't know anything about law," he said, "but to me it's not right. I would suppose that if the boy has got an intellect of nine or ten, and a physique of 14, when it comes to sentence and cross-examination and everything like that, you don't consider him as 14, you consider him as nine or ten. Now if that happened, then I'm sure the result would have been entirely different."

The result could not have been worse so far as sentencing law was concerned.

Chapter 4

'ROSE' AND 'PHIL'

During his first year at secondary school, Bronson Blessington was unable to settle with either of his parents, and immature and bewildered, he searched desperately for his place in the world. I wondered whether he was too difficult to handle, or simply that nobody in his family had sufficient time or energy to give him the care he needed. Either way, he faced his emerging adolescence alone and without the benefit of a suitable role model. For all his troubles, until a few weeks before the crimes against Janine Balding, he had no criminal record, a fact the judge presiding over his convictions and sentence found rather surprising and unusual. Bronson's first recorded crime was the conviction in the Gosford Children's Court for stealing a pair of sunglasses from a parked car. Entry number two on his criminal record is a life sentence for the crimes against Janine Balding with the judge's recommendation that the prisoner should never be released. A closer reading of the record revealed an additional sentence condition imposed by the children's court at Gosford for the sunglasses stealing charge: *the boy must reside where directed by his mother*. Fascinated by this entry, and anxious to know what lay behind it, I contacted Bronson's mother and canvassed the possibility of an interview.

Rose Blessington agreed to see me after several telephone calls and lengthy discussions, provided I did not disclose her name, the name of the new man in her life, the place of her work or where she lived. Although the woman's love for her son was palpable—even down the telephone line—she wished to protect her identity. Rose suggested we meet at the regional office of a charitable organisation providing child welfare and family support services, where she had worked since shortly after Bronson's arrest.

A few hours out of Sydney, and I found myself on a guided tour of a federation era commercial building bustling with activity. Rose proudly explained her work for a charitable community organisation. She told me she had qualifications in welfare and human resources, which she achieved after resuming her education "when all this happened." I had a sense of her trying to make up in some small way for the havoc wrought by her son. She showed me a photograph of Bronson from his first year at secondary school on the central coast. It was taken not long before he moved out of home to be with his father. The boy was a mere child, and I could scarcely believe he committed murder in the year after the photograph was taken.

"Bronson always had lots of friends," she said, lingering over the photograph. "He was charismatic and people liked him."

Do you remember the circumstances in which he was convicted for stealing a pair of sunglasses from a parked car at Gosford?

"I can't remember."

The magistrate ordered that Bronson's mother was to decide where the boy should live.

"I really can't remember."

"Do you remember the first time you tried to get help for him?"

"It was just after he started high school. Every fortnight we visited a counsellor at Gosford Hospital. I've got all the reports. I'll have a look for them. One is dated about the time he got into trouble."

In the year before his arrest, when the boy decided to leave his mother and move into a caravan with his father, he received a prophetic letter from the counsellor.

> *Bronson, most of the consultants are still very concerned about your future... Already there have been problems at your new school as you find it very difficult to accept being in the class you are in. It seems that you have given up trying at school completely, and this can only cause you further problems. These consultants are worried that these school problems will start to affect things at home between you and your Dad and will start to cause arguments. If things do go this way, Dad may get fed up with you, and you will then be unable to live with him. You might even end up in a home of some sort, as Mum fears.*

Bronson's progression from primary to high school coincided with a new man in his mother's life, 'Phil', who moved the family into a new home near the sea. Six years had passed since Steve Blessington had left home, and unfortunately for Rose, the passage of time hadn't dimmed Bronson's fantasy that his parents would eventually be reunited. The new man was his mother's first serious relationship since her marriage had ended, but it proved to be a disaster for Bronson, who began playing up and refusing to participate in the new family.

In response to my questions about her son's misbehaviour, Rose told me a story about the boy killing a rainbow lorikeet after it flew onto the balcony of the new house. I gained the impression from the story that Bronson captured and then deliberately killed the lorikeet, although it could have been an accident if he was trying to capture the bird.

Bronson's mother could remember only that the bird lay dead on the cold cement balcony. Was she sure Bronson actually killed it? She said the boy denied killing the lorikeet and then flew into a rage when she pressed her smoking gun evidence. He must have been responsible based on his reaction to her claim.

I killed a white ibis when I was a boy. And the Ancient Mariner killed an albatross.

"But the lorikeet was left inside where it would be noticed. Bronson became angry. And then he was standing in the garage sniffing petrol." After that, his mother took him to a youth refuge on the central coast.

Bronson had told me his side of the story. He'd rescued the injured bird from the side of the road outside the house and was trying to look after it. Whatever the reasons for the dead lorikeet, he never killed it.

He remembered being placed in a room at the youth refuge with a television set and watching *Days of our Lives*. When the program ended, he realised his mother and the new man in her life had left him there.

"No, because they spoke to me, and then they spoke to Phil, and then they spoke to us as a couple. Then they spoke to us with Bronson in there as well."

"You were all in the room together? You didn't go off and leave him?"

"No, I wouldn't do that."

"What were the arrangements? That he would just stay there for a while—like respite care?"

"To be assessed."

So, was he going to stay there for a couple of days? Do you know how long?

"I can't remember."

I found myself replaying the tape, trying to get a handle on the kind of misbehaviour that warranted putting a 13-year-old kid into a youth refuge. I knew the benchmarks with which to judge his mother's response to a difficult adolescent—having been one myself. The solution in my case was boarding school, which I thrived on from the day I arrived in the second year of high school. A youth refuge for a dilettante was a different solution altogether, and one the boy remonstrated against by running away so persistently that Rose was soon asked to remove her troublesome son. It was then that the boy chose to live with his father in the caravan park—a move that included another change of school.

Rose told me that Steve Blessington was always working, or looking for work, and he didn't have a consistent relationship with the boy. Steve often planned to pick up Bronson and then cancelled at the last minute, or failed to appear altogether because of work commitments, leaving the boy feeling rejected and angry.

"These days," she said, "Bronson calls at least once a week on the prison telephone, usually on the weekend. Sometimes he will sneak in a call during the week, on Tuesday or Wednesday morning, so there's always communication."

He also spoke to his father each week.

"He's always been there for both of us."

It seemed to me the boy had achieved a remarkable balancing act from inside prison, maintaining lines of communication with his family, while at the same time holding nobody responsible for what had happened—other than himself. I expressed my surprise that he avoided the easy option of blaming his parents.

"I think he's way past that."

Bronson's mother knew few details of the crimes against Janine Balding and I asked about this gap in her knowledge.

"I think Bronson was concerned how I would react, so in a way he sheltered me."

I explained that the cement law meant her son would be treated the same as adult prisoners who were recommended Never to be Released and he may be in jail until he dies.

Rose caught her breath and changed tack.

"By the time the case went to court, Bronson was beginning to look like a man. He wasn't that little boy anymore."

Did she attend court during Bronson's trials?

"I couldn't bring myself to attend the court hearings, but I did visit him at Minda during the two trials."

I realised that Rose watched her son grow from boy to man in the relative safety of the juvenile detention centre, far removed from the environment that brought on his problems of adolescence. He was still at Minda and just 16 when Judge Newman recommended the boy serve the rest of his life in prison. He remained at Minda until he turned 18.

Rose said she visited him on his 18th birthday—the last day at Minda before he was transferred to the adult prison at Long Bay.

"It broke my heart when he went into the adult jail."

Bronson consoled his mother with the observation that prison had been his salvation, not just in the spiritual sense, but the chances of his physical survival had greatly improved now that he was an adult.

The tape ended with Bronson's mother thanking me for visiting her. She lamented a system that locked up her son and threw away the key.

"I thought prison was supposed to be about rehabilitation and correction," she said wistfully.

I attempted to console Rose with the news that Bronson was a model prisoner who seemed to have found God where others found only despair. The words rattled in my head and were meaningless on some level in the light of the unenlightened Never to be Released recommendation—especially in the case of juveniles. I explained that the State's legislators had unjustly seized upon the trial judge's inappropriate attempt to influence future consideration by parole officers of early release for her son. His exemplary good behaviour in prison was no longer a consideration following the cement law. It was just a matter of appealing to voters for the politicians, who had no idea of the differences between adult and juvenile crime, and no regard for the sentencing principle of proportionality in punishment, or the unfairness of retrospectively legislated criminal laws where politicians effectively override judges. Prisoners were supposed to be punished according to the law in place at the time of their crimes, not as bargaining chips for politicians in later elections.

"You're a politician," said the mother of the convict. "Why can't *you* do something?"

Chapter 5

SCOTT AGIUS

Less than three weeks after his conviction in Gosford Children's Court for stealing a pair of sunglasses from a parked car, Bronson Blessington made the fateful decision to run away from Minali Juvenile Remand Centre at Lidcombe. He had made a call to his mother at a number in Queensland where she was staying with the new man in her life. He begged her to let him come home. She said wait six more months 'to prove yourself'.

The opportunity to run away presented itself unexpectedly when another boy at Minali, Scott Agius, invited Bronson on an excursion in the company of a youth worker to celebrate Scott's 16th birthday. Bronson described Scott as a bigger kid than him.

"I felt sorry for him," he said, leaning back on his plastic chair, pressing it hard against the brick wall of the legals cell. "Having your birthday alone in juvenile detention is no fun."

It was just my second visit to Goulburn jail to interview the prisoner and I was finding the cell depressingly cold—even for autumn. The prisoner was wearing two green prison pullovers, green tracksuit pants, white joggers and two pair of football socks. I asked whether he and Scott planned to run away, and he said they did, putting on two sets of clothes so they could change once they escaped from the custody of the youth worker.

Freedom morning, Sunday 4 September 1988, turned out to be a perfect spring day as the two boys left the detention centre by car with the youth worker driving and Scott Agius in the front passenger seat. Bronson was roasting in his double layer of clothes as he sat on the back seat. The unlikely trio was headed for a bush walk in the Blue Mountains west of Sydney. For the trivia record, 1988 marked 200 years since the British Government established a convict settlement at Sydney Cove.

A good-hearted young man, the youth worker was anxious to give the two boys as much leeway as his training and experience would permit, and as they alighted from the car at the beginning of a walking track near Mount Victoria, he allowed his charges to go on ahead—so long as he could see them. The boys obeyed the instruction for a few hundred metres, but then the walking track turned sharply.

Once out of sight, the young detainees glanced at each other, and then headed off into the bush, running along a ridgeline and gradually working their way back towards the road. Crossing the road, they pushed through another stretch of bush before arriving at a train line. Strolling along the wooden sleepers between the tracks, they reached a railway station where they sat and waited for the next train to Sydney.

The train came along soon enough, and the boys jumped aboard, congratulating each other on their escape, and making plans for the next stage of their adventure. They arrived at Central railway station with no money and no rail ticket, so they jumped over the ticket barrier, and disappeared into the crowd on the country trains concourse.

That night, the two boys met another 16-year-old boy, Matthew Elliott, an acquaintance of Scott Agius. Elliott introduced Bronson and Scott to two of his friends: Wayne Wilmot, aged 15, who had run away from his family home in the western suburbs, and Elizabeth Lopez, aged 16. The girl was tall and of Spanish heritage, informing the boys that she was homeless because of trouble at home, and she wanted no nonsense. At Matthew Elliott's suggestion, the group walked from George Street to Belmore Park near Central railway station. Bronson Blessington and Scott Agius followed the others into the public lavatory.

"I was surprised the girl went into the men's toilet," Blessington said, shrugging his shoulders. "But it didn't seem to worry her. Then Matthew sat on the toilet seat with the lid down and the cubicle door open. I asked what he was doing, and someone said he was injecting speed into his arm. Suddenly he jumped up and started acting tough, waving the syringe around, and kicking the toilet door. I'd never seen anyone inject drugs before or carry on like that—it freaked me out."

Blessington said he was much smaller than the other boys and felt intimidated by them. Nevertheless, he found other ways to measure up by stealing food and giving cheek to a bunch of skinheads on the railway concourse. The homeless teenagers jumped a train to Flemington where Matthew Elliott and Wayne Wilmot had taken over a squat. When they arrived at Flemington, Blessington discovered another harsh reality about life on the streets—the sleeping quarters were putrid.

Lit only by candles, the squat was a two-storey terrace with two habitable rooms downstairs. One room had two filthy mattresses on the floor, and the other was littered with dirty clothes, plastic bunting and empty Coke bottles. Scraps of food and food wrappings wriggled with crawling cockroaches. A lightweight sledgehammer with a pipe handle lay on the floor. One of the mattresses had blood on it. Other than the squalid mattresses, there was no furniture in the place.

Elizabeth Lopez—or 'Lizzy' as she was known—lay on the best of the mattresses while the four boys sat around a candle recounting the adventures of the day. Wayne Wilmot heated a screwdriver in the candle flame and ran it across the bare skin of Blessington's thigh.

"The burn left a scar on me leg about an inch long," the prisoner said, measuring an inch between his thumb and forefinger. "Then Wilmot said, 'We're the most feared gang in Sydney', but he never told me the name of the gang."

At just over 150 centimetres tall, and weighing in at about 45 kilos, Blessington said he was not about to "take on" Wilmot.

I made a note to visit Wayne Wilmot at Lithgow jail where he was serving another long sentence for attempted abduction and sexual assault—crimes committed less than a year after his release on parole for the abduction and rape of Janine Balding. Wilmot made a charge-bargain deal with the prosecution in the Janine Balding case, agreeing he committed abduction and rape on condition that the Crown drop the murder charge. He served eight years for the crimes against Janine Balding and was still on parole when he committed the attempted abduction and sexual assault crimes for which he was presently incarcerated.

Blessington leaned forward and said that Wilmot was the muscle man and Elliott the ringleader of the so-called gang.

"I told them I trained at boxing and was into crime. Matthew asked what crime, and I said stealing cars and the like. We talked about women, and they said they had sex with a girl the night before."

The thought crossed my mind that Bronson's one sexual experience with a prostitute and his single conviction for stealing sunglasses from a parked car placed him in a very different category of misbehaving juvenile than the two older boys—despite his bravado.

What did Scott Agius have to say?

"Scott wasn't boasting, and like me, seemed to be quite scared."

Around nine the next day, Monday 5 September 1988, Bronson woke up hungry and asked about the arrangements for breakfast. Elliott and Wilmot decided it was Bronson's turn to 'cook' and suggested he visit the corner store in the next block. He was instructed to steal their breakfast.

"The shopkeeper was a nice man, and very politely, I ordered five hamburgers, five hot chips, three packets of cigarettes, some lollies and soft drink. He put the things I ordered in two plastic bags on the counter. I then said, 'Oh, and I'll have another packet of smokes', and as the man turned around to get them, I grabbed the plastic bags and did a runner."

There was no emotion in the detached way the young man related the story—as if he was talking about somebody else. For this I was grateful since the cold of the cell was seeping into my bones, rendering me incapable of any human response to the unfolding events. Not for the first time, I wondered about the numerous other things I might be doing to represent the people of New South Wales.

After breakfast, Matthew Elliott, Wayne Wilmot, Scott Agius,

Lizzy Lopez and Bronson jumped on a train from Flemington to Central railway station. When they reached Central, Elliott wanted batteries for his Walkman radio and sent Bronson to the newsagent on the railway concourse to steal them. Then Wilmot and Elliott directed him to steal Mars bars from another shop.

"I stole the batteries and the Mars bars the same way I stole the food from the corner store."

Once again, I observed his detachment, which was not to say he lacked remorse for his petty thievery. Perhaps the offences were simply dwarfed by the scale of the other crimes he was about to relate.

The cell was so cold my teeth began to rattle.

Leaving the railway concourse, the group headed up George Street in the general direction of The Station drop-in centre near Wynyard railway station in the city business district. Along the way, Wilmot went into a supermarket to steal a candle for the squat, but he soon discovered he was much less adept at shoplifting than the new conscript to the gang. A store detective grabbed Wilmot and took him into custody. Within minutes, undercover police were questioning Bronson, Scott, Lizzy and Matthew as they stood on the footpath outside the supermarket.

"We gave them bodgie names and addresses," Bronson volunteered, "and then we decided to go back to the squat and wait for Wilmot."

What happened then?

"Just after lunch, I seen a bunch of coppers in flak jackets through the open door of the squat. They were comin' in with guns drawn. Matthew screamed at me to pick up the sledgehammer. I grabbed it just as the coppers came through the door and one of them said, 'Put it down or I'll shoot you'. I weren't about to argue with the bloke and did as I was told. The coppers started searching the place, and through the front window of the squat, I could see Wilmot sitting in the back seat of the police car."

What were the coppers looking for?

"They found two speed pills under Matthew's mattress, and I was surprised when they just looked at them and then put them back. Checking our arms for track marks, they pointed to the bruise and needle mark on Matthew's arm, and said, 'How did you get that?' He told them he had an AIDS test. The copper who had spoken to me said, 'What were you goin' to do with the sledgehammer'? I said, 'I thought you were someone off the street'. Then he said, 'Get out of the squat. We'll be back tomorrow, and you'd better be gone'. As they drove off, I seen Wilmot again through the back window of the police car."

Late in the afternoon, the group minus Wilmot headed back into the city. I asked if anyone complained about Wilmot giving them up to the police and Bronson said nobody said anything he could remember. At Central they met another group of homeless youths including Dianne Adams who was a friend of Lizzy Lopez, a boy named Warren Purchase, and a tough no-nonsense young woman Bronson called 'Big Jude'.

Bronson, Scott, Matthew and Lizzy left the others and headed for the movie theatres in George Street after a meal at a Chinese restaurant in the Haymarket area. Along the way, Bronson stole a bottle of Southern Comfort from a liquor shop. They drank half the booze walking along the street and the rest they drank in the movie. He could not remember what was playing at the George Street movie theatre.

"Sometime after midnight, we met up with Warren Purchase again, and he came back to the squat with us. There was nowhere for him to sleep so he went next door with a bloke named Ron who worked at Flemington markets with Wayne Wilmot."

The next morning, Tuesday 6 September 1988, Warren Purchase joined Matthew, Bronson, Scott and Lizzy on an excursion by train to Parramatta where the group visited a disposal store. Matthew was looking for a knife and selected one with a yellow handle from a glass cabinet. They also bought a billycan, cutlery, plates and fluorescent tubes called 'glow sticks' for lighting. Then they returned by train to the squat.

What happened next?

Bronson sat back in the moulded plastic chair with his arms folded. "My mother put me through boxing at the Gosford Athletics Club and I decided to teach Warren and Scott how to box."

I could feel the cold in my fingers as I wrote.

"I had them sparring with each other, ducking and weaving, and throwing imaginary punches. Scott had no coordination, so I thought I'd show him how to throw a punch. I hit Warren above the eye, breaking his skin, and he began to bleed. Matthew was watching and said, 'Take him into that room', pointing to the room where we'd slept. I did as he said, and then Matthew and Lizzy tied Warren up with plastic streamers that are used on shopfronts."

Where were Warren's hands tied?

"In front of him."

According to the indictment against Blessington and Elliott, they *maliciously did inflict grievous bodily harm upon Warren Purchase.* Elliott was sentenced by Justice Peter Newman to a fixed term of penal servitude for two years for his part in the assault and Blessington received a sentence of one year and six months. Elliott struck the victim on the back of the head at least six times with the sledgehammer and Blessington struck him at least once. The most serious of the victim's injuries was *a lineal fracture to the right occipital region of his skull.* Blessington was described in the judge's sentencing remarks as the lesser assailant.

No mention was made of Scott Agius in Bronson's account of the assault on Warren Purchase and his name did not appear in any of the court papers. I asked Bronson about this, and he said Scott stayed in the other room after the boxing lesson.

"Before we left he came into Matthew's room and was freaked out by the blood all over the place. I told him we killed Warren Purchase, because I thought we had. We jumped a train back to Central railway station and Scott left us. He said he wanted to go and look at some vinyl records. He wanted me to come with him. I said no. He asked me again and I still said no. I made a big mistake. I didn't understand he wanted to get me away from the others. Scott went off on his own and I never seen him again."

Finally, hell froze over, and I was too cold to write another word. Blessington was anxious to finish his story, but I assured him it would need to wait until another day when a warmer room was available in the prison's education wing. I packed up my papers and the prisoner followed me out of the legals cell and along the narrow corridor between the box cells.

Standing with the three correctional officers on duty at the visiting area, I asked about the moon-faced officer who spoke to me on my first visit—the one who hoped I could do something for the young prisoner. Nobody seemed to know the bloke and so I asked Blessington about him.

"I know the bloke, Brother, but I never seen him before that day, and I haven't seen him since."

Chapter 6

ABDUCTION AND RAPE

By a stroke of good luck and the generosity of Goulburn jail's deputy governor, my next visit to Bronson Blessington took place in a large room in the prison's education wing with the winter sun streaming through a wide security window that separated the room from a walkway and the prison yard outside the building. As I waited for the prisoner, I looked out the barred window. Inmates were huddled together in blobs of green on the grey dust, preferring to brave the elements in company than suffer the solitude of their cells. I could see correctional officers patrolling the wire perimeter of the yard, and although they were not as cruel as the jailers of past eras, institutional cruelty was a fact of life in jail. Prisoners were increasingly isolated due to frequent lockdowns and segregation.

The lack of education in jail was another problem with classes and teachers diminishing by the day. In 2002, fewer than 200 prisoners out of a total prison population of more than 8,000 inmates were involved in fulltime education. In my visits to the prison, I hadn't seen one education class in progress or made the acquaintance of a single teacher. Prisoners who were trying to improve themselves received little support since education was regarded as special treatment doled out to the privileged, rather than an essential resource prisoners needed for rehabilitation.

Soon enough, a correctional officer arrived with the prisoner Blessington, and he was all smiles and gratitude. The officer was unimpressed, closing the door without a word. As I shook the prisoner's hand, the thought crossed my mind that he could be engaged in a clever and deceitful exercise of trying to fool everyone with his magnanimous goodwill. After my first visit, I obtained a copy of his medical history and found a note from a prison psychiatrist describing him as a *charming psychopath*. I opened the medical record—a document an inch thick—as we sat in the plastic chairs. He was neither surprised nor angry when I showed him the medical assessment.

"I can't tell you the trouble that's caused me," he said, shaking his head. "The psychiatrist lady sees me for ten minutes, writes that rubbish on my record, and I've been paying for it ever since." Studies have repeatedly found that health professionals are no better than the rest of us at predicting who might be at risk of becoming a serial violent offender. Psychiatrists will generally err on the side of caution, warning of the potential dangers of a prisoner rather than risk contributing to the harm done by those who go on to be repeat offenders with no apparent regard for the life or property of other people.

After the Warren Purchase assault, Bronson Blessington, Matthew Elliott and Elizabeth Lopez "caught a ferry to somewhere" and sat on a pier with a cask of wine. Possibly they went to Manly, a popular beachside destination in Sydney.

"We stayed there until it got dark and then we caught the ferry back to the city. We jumped a train at Circular Quay and got off at Central."

The words were flowing freely and I made a note that the psych's observation hadn't thrown the prisoner into a spin.

"At Central we met this older bloke about 30 who befriended

us. He seemed alright but then started asking questions about Warren Purchase. Suddenly, he banged me and Matthew's heads together and nearly knocked us out. Matthew broke off a piece of drainpipe sticking out of the wall. The bloke took off with Matthew and me chasing him. A couple of transit cops grabbed us as we were running along the country trains concourse and they took us to the railway detectives' office. They also grabbed Elizabeth. We explained that a bloke was trying to kill us and were just defending ourselves. We gave them bodgie names and they let us go."

For a moment, I speculated on what might have been had the railway police taken the three street kids—Elliott, Blessington and Elizabeth Lopez—into custody. Somehow the two boys wanted to see how far they could push their juvenile boundaries. I asked if they were drunk from the cask of wine, and of course they were. After leaving Central railway station, the three joined a group of Aboriginals drinking from a wine flagon at Belmore Park. From there the three wandered the streets of Sydney.

I asked where they spent the night. Maybe they spent another night at the Flemington squat after their police eviction on Monday. They had already returned to the squat on Tuesday and carried out the sledgehammer assault on Warren Purchase. The prisoner was not sure.

"Maybe we just stayed up for the night?"

The next day was Wednesday 7 September, the day before the murder, and Bronson said it was "a bit of a blur". He remembered being "tired all day" and sleeping intermittently when he had the chance. I guessed he had a hangover. That night the three of them climbed the fence at the back of Central railway station, crossed the maze of steel railway tracks and walked towards the repair yards where they found an unlocked carriage.

"Matthew and me climbed into the train and we hauled up Elizabeth. Matthew broke the glow sticks to find our way inside and then we fell asleep as soon as we put our heads on the train seats."

They rose with the morning sun on the day of the murder, Thursday 8 September, and jumped out of the railway carriage ahead of the fettlers and fitters arriving for work. Scurrying between the early morning trains, they scaled the barrier fence before sauntering up onto one of the Central railway platforms and mingling with commuters. Matthew directed Bronson to steal chips and a chocolate bar from a news stand on the platform. Bronson said he was unhappy doing it but made no excuses. He waited for Matthew and Lizzy to disappear into the tunnel under Broadway and then he did "a grab and dash," sprinting towards the tunnel entrance. He caught up with the other two as they emerged onto Broadway.

Making their way down George Street, the three crossed Belmore Park at Eddy Avenue, where they spotted Wayne Wilmot and Carol Arrow on the edge of the park. Matthew asked him how the coppers found out about the squat at Flemington. According to Bronson, Wilmot told Elliott that 'the police must have followed you there', an explanation that seemed to satisfy Elliott, even though Wilmot had been clearly visible in the back seat of the police car. His girlfriend, Carol Arrow, who also lived on the streets, was there in the park with Wilmot. She had shoulder length dark hair and dark eyes, and Bronson said that she was "small like me." The five of them walked to The Station drop-in centre behind Wynyard for breakfast.

"Matthew and me had a shower, washed our clothes and then went into the television room where we had a big conversation with about eight people, including street kids I hadn't met before: Shorty Wells, Shorty Jamieson and Bill Rowland. Rowland said he was going to Coogee to score some sticks and Lizzy said she was going too."

Go on.

"Lizzy went off with Shorty Jamieson and Bill Rowland. Matthew and me stayed there until lunchtime. We had bread rolls for lunch. After lunch we walked back to Central. Wayne Wilmot, Carol Arrow and Shorty Wells came with us. Shorty Wells wore a black duffel coat and he was pretending to flash at people in the street."

What else was Shorty Wells wearing?

"He had black jeans and a black tee shirt under the coat and he wore black boots—army boots or motorcycle boots. He also had a black bandana, tied around his neck at first, and then he tied it around his head."

What happened when you got back to Central?

"We jumped off the end of the platform, walked across the tracks and went back to the train carriage where we had slept. It was an old red rattler with studded seats. We were hungry again and Matthew said, 'Go and get some food, Bronson'. The others chimed in and said, 'Yeah Bronson, go and get some food'. I was sick of getting the food, but Matthew said there was a shop along the road beside the railway tracks. So, I walked over the tracks and crawled under the fence up the road from the shop."

Then what happened?

"I did what I done at Flemington—ordered hamburgers, chips, cigarettes and drinks. The bloke behind the counter put everything in two plastic bags. Then I said to him, 'Oh, and I'll have another packet of smokes'. As he turned around to get the smokes, I ran off with the two plastic bags. He chased me for about 30 metres but gave up." Bronson leaned back in his plastic chair. "It would've been better if he caught me."

On the way back to the railway carriage, he found a bottle shop, and slipped inside, placing a bottle of Bundaberg rum down the front of his pants, and walked out again—bold as brass.

"When I got outside, I ran without looking back, so I don't know if anyone seen me stealing the rum. I went under the fence again and back across the railway tracks to the train carriage. Everyone was really happy that the 'shopping trip' had been so successful. We drank about half the rum, ate the food and smoked some cigarettes. Then we left the train carriage and Matthew carried the remaining half bottle of rum in his jacket."

Did anyone see you in the train carriage?

"There were people about in the railway yard but nobody took any notice of us."

Looking across from any of the country train platforms, Central is a myriad of railway tracks to the suburbs and the bush intersecting with the city network. Off to the left are the tracks leading to the rolling stock storage depot and maintenance yards. It was difficult to imagine a bunch of kids negotiating this spaghetti bowl of steel in the middle of the afternoon, trains coming and going, without attracting the attention of someone in authority.

Somebody must have seen you?

"We went back under the fence and walked around to the front of the railway station. I was tired and pissed and didn't care what people thought. I knocked off a *Penthouse* magazine from the news stand in front of the station. We walked up to the electric trains platform and boarded a train. I don't think any of us knew where the train was going."

Whose idea was it to catch a train?

"Matthew's I suppose. Sometimes street kids ride round all day on the trains."

What happened on the train?

"We had four seats on the train—two seats opposite each other—and we took turns at one of us standing up or walking about."

You mean four of you had a seat and the fifth person had to stand?

"Yeah, we took turns. Just before we left the train, I was standing in the passageway, and the others were sitting down."

Who were the others?

"Wayne Wilmot, Carol Arrow, Matthew Elliott and Shorty Wells."

Do you remember anything from the train?

"We were looking at the pictures in the magazine and showing them to people on the train to shock them. It was about four in the afternoon and there were lots of school kids on the train. We were swearing and drinking the rum and flashing the magazine pictures at the school kids. Matthew said, 'Let's go and steal a car', and then we got off the train. At the time, I had no idea where we were."

Until this point, the five street kids might have been living out their version of an Enid Blighton novel, but the horror story began the moment they alighted from the train at Sutherland. They ran to the end of the platform where they crossed the train tracks and scaled a cyclone wire fence adjoining the railway carpark. The time had advanced to about 20 to five as the group entered the carpark. Matthew noticed a takeaway shop, several hundred metres up the road, and he told Bronson to do his thing.

"I didn't want to go to the shop," he said, leaning on the laminate table, "But the others said, 'Go on; we're hungry'. They said it about eight times. Then Matthew said, 'Go and do it if you want to be with us. If you don't do it, you can go'. What could I do?" the prisoner asked forlornly.

You could've walked away, as Scott Agius did.

"Yeah, I guess so."

He sat back from the table with a blank look on his face, shaking his head. There was little to look forward to in the young man's story but he pressed on, relating his usual routine: ordering food, drinks and cigarettes, and then asking for an additional packet of smokes when the provisions were put on the counter in a plastic bag.

"The bloke in the shop turned around to get the smokes and then I bolted with the plastic bag. I ran like mad, without even turning around to see if the bloke was chasing me. The others were on the side of the road where I left them near a park, and as I approached, we all turned and ran through the park into the railway station carpark where we hid behind a shed. After we finished eating, drinking and smoking, Matthew broke into a HQ

Holden, and stuck a screwdriver into the ignition, but it wouldn't turn. We found another car that was unlocked, but again, we couldn't start it."

Who tried to start the cars?

"Matthew."

Had you stolen a car before, or tried to break into one?

"Never. I couldn't drive. Couldn't even reach the pedals."

You stole a pair of sunglasses from a parked car.

"Yes, but somebody else broke into the car—it was already open."

I was scrawling words that looked like a stenographer's shorthand, trying to keep up with the prisoner, and asking questions to slow him down as he recounted the story. As he drew breath, I asked what happened next.

"Then we went back and sat beside the shed. Matthew said, 'I've got a plan. We'll get someone and push them into their car and steal it that way'. Matthew said to me, 'We'll wait for a woman to come down from the station. You use the knife to push her in the car, and we'll come up straight away'. Shortly afterwards, a woman came down the path from the station and walked across the carpark. As she walked past us, she looked over and then looked away. Matthew said, 'Ask her for a cigarette'. We were sitting on the ground, just outside the shed, and I stood up and followed the woman to her car. She was parked about ten metres away."

This was Kristine Mobberley?

"Yeah, Kristine Mobberley."

Go on.

"As she was unlocking the car, I came up behind her and said, 'Have you got a cigarette?' She turned around and said, 'No', and then jumped in the car. She wound down the driver's side window of the car and I said, 'What's the time?' She started the car and gave me the time with a cranky tone in her voice. As she drove off, I showed her the yellow handled knife. I think she seen it. I showed it to her because she was being rude."

Maybe you were trying to show the others how tough you were.

"Yeah, maybe. Anyway, I went back to the shed, and the others were standing outside on the edge of the carpark. They hadn't followed me to Kristine Mobberley's car. They laughed at me and said I should have pushed her into the car. We sat down again and Matthew said, 'We'll get someone else'. Mark Wells had got up and untied the black bandana he had round his neck. He tied it across his forehead and at the back of his head. He found a stick near the shed and went out into the carpark where he started walking up and down and calling himself a Ninja fighter."

What happened next?

"Then Janine Balding came down the railway steps and walked towards her car which was parked about four metres from the shed. She looked towards us and then looked away. As she walked past, Matthew said again, 'Ask her for a cigarette, Bronson'. I stood up and followed her to her car. It was a greenish blue Holden Gemini. This time the others followed me. As she began unlocking the car, I walked up behind her and said, 'Have you got a cigarette?' She turned around and said 'No'. I pulled out the knife and said, 'Jump in the car'. Then the car alarm went off and Matthew said, 'Turn it off or I'll kill you'. She refused, and so Matthew grabbed her keys, and he turned it off with the keys. Matthew told her to get in the car and she climbed in the back seat. I was holding the knife up against her. I sat beside her in the back seat. Matthew sat in the driver's seat."

Can a story of random and senseless murder be worse in the telling or the listening? Somehow, I was under the impression that the young man, although led, played a less active role in the abduction of Janine Balding, but I was wrong. Hearing the details of the crimes against the young woman—more than I'd read in the legal papers or court documents—made me cold with grief at the depravity and obscenity of it. Bronson was talking again and I struggled to give his story my undivided attention.

"Wilmot climbed in the front passenger seat and Carol Arrow got in the back and sat on the other side of Janine. Mark Wells got in the back and sat next to Carol Arrow—behind Matthew Elliott. Mark Wells and me closed the back doors and Matthew started driving. Janine began to cry. I gave her the cigarettes out of her bag and said, 'It's alright, we only want your car'. I also found her purse in the bag and took out her credit cards. I don't remember if Matthew or Wayne asked for her PIN number. One of them also asked for her rings and watch and she took them off and gave them to Matthew. She started calming down and said, 'My husband's a police officer'. Matthew said, 'It doesn't matter who he is. If you scream out or anything, I'm goin' to ram this car into a telegraph pole'. Wilmot told her we were a feared gang and had nothing to lose."

Then what happened?

"After about half an hour, Matthew pulled over to the side of the road and stopped the car. We were going on a highway somewhere in the western suburbs. Carol Arrow got in the front passenger seat and Wilmot took over the driving. Janine Balding was saying, 'I want to get out'. I was saying, 'You'll be alright. Nothing will happen to you'. Then Matthew got in the back seat and sat next to Janine—in the middle where Carol Arrow had been sitting. As Wayne Wilmot drove off, Matthew started fondling Janine, and as we drove along, he had sex with her."

I think you mean he raped her.

Chapter 7

MURDER

After a short break in the interview at Goulburn jail's education wing, the prisoner Blessington continued his story, telling me that Wayne Wilmot slowed Janine Balding's Holden Gemini and steered it off the Great Western Highway—as instructed by Matthew Elliott from the back seat. They were just past the Archbold Road overpass at Minchinbury. Wilmot drove across a narrow culvert on the verge of the highway and onto a grassy embankment, stopping the car just a few metres from a barbed wire fence. Beyond the fence, the outlines of scrubby paperbarks and ghostly eucalypts were illuminated by the car's headlights.

What happened when Wilmot stopped the car?

"It was pretty much dark outside. Mark Wells and me got out of the car. Wayne Wilmot and Carol Arrow stayed in the front seats. Matthew was raping Janine Balding on the back seat. We were about 30 metres off the highway. Then Matthew jumped out of the car and said, 'Have a go Bronson'. I got in the back seat and raped her. When I got out of the car, Carol Arrow and Wayne Wilmot were kissing and cuddling each other in the front seats. Mark Wells and Matthew Elliott were standing at the back of the car. They were having a conversation, but I couldn't hear what they were saying. Mark Wells gave Matthew the black bandana from around his head, and Matthew took some rope from the boot of the car. Then Matthew got Janine Balding out of the back of the car. He said, 'Come with me and Bronson', and we walked her over to the barbed wire fence. She said to Matthew, 'What are you doing?' Matthew said, 'We're going to tie you up and gag you and leave you here'."

What about the others?

"They stayed at the car."

When did Wayne Wilmot and Mark Wells rape her?

"They never."

What do you mean, 'They never'?

"They never raped her."

But Wilmot was convicted of rape. He confessed.

"The coppers did a deal with Wilmot. He pleaded guilty to rape, and in return, the coppers dropped the murder charge. But he never raped her. He had his own girl."

What about Wells?

"Matthew asked him on the train when we were going back to Sydney why he didn't have sex with Janine, and Wells said he was homosexual. I guess that's it."

That's it? I think you're ahead of me.

I showed him a copy of the front page of the *Daily Mirror* published three days after his arrest. Quoting a police 'facts' sheet, the newspaper reported that *Ms Balding was thrown over a fence and dragged screaming approximately 100 metres to a dam, where she was held under until she drowned.* I asked how Janine got over a barbed wire fence when there was no evidence of a struggle. Her body had no scratches and two children could hardly have *thrown [her] over a fence.*

"I held the wire down and she climbed over."

And what happened then?

"We walked through some tall trees for about 15 or 20 metres until we reached a paddock, and Matthew said, 'Sit down there and I'll tie you up'. She sat down on the grass and he began tying the rope around her arms and legs. Then he tied Shorty Wells' bandana around her head and placed the knot in her mouth. Matthew was kneeling down while he tied and gagged her, and I was standing there watching. Then he said, 'Let's pick her up,' and he took hold of her legs. I picked her up from the back, under her arm pits. Matthew started walking forward and I walked backwards.

"Next thing, I felt me foot go into mud. I kept walking, following Matthew's direction. The mud became water up to just under me knees, and after about four or five metres, Matthew stopped. He said, 'Push her under the water', and then he started pushing down on her legs."

I was still trying to downplay the prisoner's responsibility for his part in the crimes, telling myself he was just a child at the time, hoping to discount in some small way the horror of what the man in front of me had done as a child. His active and direct involvement in the murder tended to overshadow his extreme youth. On the other hand, if he was too young to form the intention to commit serious crime, his legal culpability must be weighed against his youth and mental age, regardless of the extent to which he participated in the crimes.

I wanted to ask him about a statement given to police. The author was Dianne Adams, the friend of Elizabeth Lopez. Another homeless young woman, Adams had stayed with Lopez and Elliott at the Flemington squat. The two young women encountered Elliott and Blessington at Hyde Park early on the morning after the murder, and Adams recounted to police what Elliott had told them.

> *Matthew then said, 'We pointed the knife to her [Janine Balding's] neck and threatened to kill her and she did as she was told and came with us. We then got into her Gemini and went through her bag and found some credit cards. We then drove her car to Minchinbury where we tied her hands and feet together, gagged her and raped her. Then we thought that she was going to talk so we held her head down in the water and tried to drown her, but she kept on kicking and I couldn't do it by myself so I asked Todd [Bronson] to give me a hand to hold her head under the water'.*

I showed the Dianne Adams statement to the prisoner, taking care not to suggest he embrace it. He read the words and I watched his focused eyes. The statement indicated Matthew Elliott as the main perpetrator with much more precision than anything the prisoner had told me. I invited a response to the young woman's statement.

"Typical Matthew."

Who pushed her under the water?

"We both did."

I asked if he was frightened and he said Wayne Wilmot and Matthew Elliott both scared him at the time.

"But that's no excuse," he added without prompting. "I'm just as guilty as Matthew. Just talking about it brings back the feeling I had—a real flat, empty feeling. It was like I was trapped by my feelings."

So, what happened after the murder?

"We walked out of the water and headed back to the car. I don't remember any conversation between Matthew and me. When we reached the car Wilmot said, 'Where is she'? Matthew said, 'We've killed her'. Wilmot and Carol Arrow were still sitting in the car and Mark Wells was still standing near the boot. Matthew and me took off our shoes because they were wet and full of mud. We got back in the car and Matthew drove off. He turned off the highway and headed towards Mt Druitt. After about ten kilometres the car engine blew up and we began walking towards Mt Druitt shopping centre. Matthew met a bloke at the shopping centre he knew from the Cross called 'Goldfinger' and sold him one of the rings. Then we went to the ATM at the shopping centre and withdrew $400 from Janine Balding's account. We shared the money and Matthew and me took the credit cards. Carol Arrow got Janine's watch."

The prisoner was beginning to fade and I urged him to continue.

"We went into the shopping centre at Mt Druitt. Wilmot bought a Walkman radio and Matthew bought thongs. From there we went to the railway station and caught a train to Central. That's when Matthew asked Mark Wells why he didn't have sex with Janine Balding and he said he was homosexual. The five of us split up at Central and Matthew and I walked around the city. We played video games in George Street near the movie theatres and then we walked up to Hyde Park where we met Lizzy Lopez and Dianne Adams. We sat on a seat in the park and started talking with the two girls and that's when Matthew told them we killed someone. Then we walked to St James station and caught a train to Wynyard."

All four of you went to Wynyard—you two and the two girls?

The prisoner confirmed that Matthew, Lizzy Lopez, Dianne

Adams and himself caught a train to the Wynyard underground station. They sat on a seat under the indicator board at Wynyard and fell asleep. After a couple of hours, Matthew and Bronson woke up. Dianne Adams had already gone. The two boys left Elizabeth Lopez sleeping on the seat and caught another train to Gosford where Bronson said he knew someone who would give them money. At Gosford, Bronson stole fish and chips and placed Janine Balding's credit cards in a bush near where they were sitting in a park. Then they went to East Gosford and stole an HQ Holden from a laneway at the back of some shops. Matthew cut his hand on the gear stick, which snapped off while he was driving. He stopped the car outside a chemist shop and the pharmacist gave him bandages for the wound.

I was fading like the prisoner though happy enough to be getting everything written down. My mood had changed since learning that Bronson's part in the murder was no less active than that of Matthew Elliott. I wanted to hastily conclude the interview. But I also wanted to hear the end of the story. They were two desperate children—desperate to avoid the authorities and yet desperate to tell somebody in authority what they had done. Matthew had been on the phone to his welfare officer, Ceily Richards, asking if he could see her at Cobham about something he and Bronson had done to Warren Purchase with a sledgehammer. They might have killed him. He rang again a couple of hours later and learned that Purchase had staggered out of the squat and was taken to hospital by ambulance.

"Matthew drove onto the highway after we left Gosford and we headed for Sydney. When we reached the Harbour Bridge the tollgate alarm went off because we didn't stop to pay. Matthew drove through the city and onto Parramatta Road, where we almost hit a telegraph pole. We did a 'fill and run' at a service station and then headed for the youth detention centre at Cobham where Matthew knew the regional director for child welfare, who lived in a house next to the detention centre. We walked down to the house after Matthew parked the Holden in the detention centre car park. The director invited us into his house, sat us down in the living room and gave us a beer. There was another man there I didn't know. Matthew told them about the sledgehammer attack on Warren Purchase."

What about the police? I already knew that somebody at the detention centre had spotted the two boys get out of the stolen car and rang police.

"I think the regional director rang the police. Anyway, they turned up after a while and took Matthew and me to Penrith Police Station. We sat in the back seat of the police car. The policeman in the front passenger seat was the Penrith footballer, Craig Izzard. I asked Matthew what I should do with the yellow-handle knife and he pointed to Craig Izzard and said, 'Give it to him'. I reached into the front seat with the knife in my hand and said, 'Do you want this?' The two policemen were startled at first, and then Craig took the knife from me. I told him I didn't think Penrith would make the football finals and we had a bet about it. A few years later, I seen him in court, and he reminded me I lost the bet."

There was something surreal about children committing murder, as if the whole tragic exercise was a game, and I was hardly surprised to hear Bronson Blessington conclude his terrible story with a bet on the football. I knew from reading the two boys' statements that Matthew trusted the regional director of the detention centre, Dick Smith, and his case worker, Ceily Richards—he often sought their assistance. Matthew confessed to the Warren Purchase attack and Bronson confirmed it. Once in custody at Penrith police station, the boys told police they knew some people who'd drowned a woman. Matthew told police he didn't know who the people were, 'But I can show you where it happened'. Two police cars made the lonely trip down the highway from Penrith to Minchinbury, Matthew in the lead car with a team of detectives, and Bronson in the second car with another team.

Matthew struggled to find the spot where Wayne Wilmot had steered the car off the highway. It was the night after the murder and he found it difficult to orient himself from inside the police car. After a couple of false stops, one of the detectives said, 'You're playing games'. Eventually he found the shallow culvert just past the Archbold Street overpass and police car headlights illuminated the barbed wire fence. The occupants of both cars climbed over the fence and searched in the dark in two separate groups. Soon enough, Matthew heard Bronson call out, 'Over here'. The dam at Minchinbury had yielded up its dark secret in the glare of police torchlights.

Chapter 8

FIRST TRIAL

In the aftermath of the crimes against Janine Balding, Wayne Wilmot entered a plea of guilty before Justice James Wood to the abduction and rape of the young woman and was sentenced to ten years in prison. Wilmot's girlfriend in 1988, Carol Arrow, received a suspended sentence from the judge as she was not considered a voluntary participant in the crimes. Wilmot and Arrow both gave evidence that the Shorty at the crime scenes was not Shorty Jamieson. Wilmot's plea before Wood was self-serving in many ways, but he did insist that police had arrested the wrong Shorty. When the Crown prosecutor questioned his motives for helping Jamieson, Wilmot said, 'Why should he go away for something he never done?' From the moment he was arrested and interviewed, Wilmot told police that the boy called 'Shorty' who was with them was named 'Mark'.

Matthew Elliott gave the same evidence—Mark 'Shorty' Wells was the right Shorty. Because Elliott, Blessington and Jamieson all pleaded not guilty to the crimes against Ms Balding, they went to trial together before Justice Wood and a jury of 12 citizens. Wood defended the decision to prosecute the three together, telling the legal representatives that the accused had given police a host of false and misleading accusations that needed to be sorted out. For example, Scott Agius was falsely named as one of the offenders, and Elizabeth Lopez had made a false confession. Lawyers for the accused objected, saying a joint trial prejudiced their clients.

Wood said police were faced with a difficult situation in that *they had a whole lot of people either deliberately or otherwise* leading them astray. As to Wayne Wilmot giving police a description of Shorty Wells as well as the name 'Mark', the judge said. *Wayne Wilmot was a person also charged and they [police] had no reason to suspect that he may not also be putting them on a false track.* But in the end Wood decided that there was a problem as to whether the right Shorty had been arrested and charged, telling the jury that the issue was important enough to abandon the trial.

> *Now, members of the jury, I have to tell you this: that the man referred to as Mark Wells during the evidence over the last week or so has been located. As a consequence of that, it is perfectly plain that a number of further investigations need to be made, both by the Crown and by the accused... The course we have all decided which is the fairest both to the accused and to the community is that you be discharged as jurors, that there be time devoted to making further investigations, and that the matter then come back for a re-trial at some time in the future.*

The last day of the first trial was 23 October 1989 and the following day was a media firestorm over the other Shorty allegation. An article in *The Australian* by Joe Morris began with the headline, 'Balding murder trial aborted as another Shorty surfaces'.

> *A Sydney judge yesterday aborted the trial of two youths and a man for the abduction, rape and drowning murder of building society clerk Janine Balding in Sydney's west last year. Justice Wood dismissed the jury in the six-week-old*

trial after police located a man who fitted the description of a person who was allegedly at the murder scene. Police launched their search for the man after evidence last week by the two youths. The youths said their co-accused Stephen Wayne Jamieson, 23, known as Shorty, had been wrongly charged and described another man, also known as Shorty, who they say was responsible...Justice Wood described the abortion of the trial as regrettable and the circumstances as "extraordinary if not unique." The judge denied bail for Jamieson after an application by his counsel, Ted O'Loughlin, but said it might be appropriate to reapply at some time in the future.

By a cruel twist of fate for Jamieson, Justice Wood did not adjudicate on the second trial despite all the parties requesting that he do so, and the judge indicating his desire to continue in the case. This is the same Justice Wood who was appointed to conduct the royal commission into the Police Service in 1994, and the received wisdom was that the Crown had some distance to travel before satisfying Wood that Jamieson was the right Shorty. I wondered what happened in the Supreme Court's list office to cause Justice Wood to be replaced by Justice Peter Newman. In the old days, judge shopping was almost a blood sport amongst well-connected lawyers, although I'd not heard of such an allegation in 20 years. I suspected some bureaucratic mix-up, or perhaps Wood himself decided the case needed a fresh mind to sort out all the conflicting stories. My attempts to contact Wood and find out what happened were unsuccessful.

Witness accounts of the events leading up to the murder

of Janine Balding left me with many questions, the most obvious one being why Shorty Jamieson was arrested for crimes in which all four co-accused insisted he was not involved. On my first visit to Goulburn jail, a long affidavit had caught my attention among Bronson Blessington's papers. It stood out crisp and white in the yellowing and worn pages. I borrowed it to copy. Joanne Harris, who'd been representing Jamieson with Legal Aid, prepared the document. Bronson swore to the truth of the affidavit and signed each page. An item on page two read: *Stephen Jamieson had no part in the events that followed. He was not present at the kidnapping, rape and murder of Janine Balding. I know this because I was there and took part in those crimes… With me at that time were Matthew Elliott, Wayne Wilmot, Carol Arrow and Mark 'Shorty' Wells. The only 'Shorty' who came with us was Shorty Wells.*

The last page of the affidavit included reference to an incident in the cells below Glebe Coroner's Court two months after the murder when the police brought in Shorty Jamieson. Blessington swore that he told his solicitor, Ken Gilson, that police had arrested the wrong Shorty. Attached to the affidavit was a transcript of Gilson's evidence given in 1990 at the second trial of Blessington, Jamieson and Elliott. Gilson confirmed that Blessington and Elliott both informed their lawyers that Shorty Wells was present at the crimes against Janine Balding, not Shorty Jamieson.

The day after Ken Gilson gave his evidence to the coroner, detectives turned up at the cells below the Glebe Coroner's Court with 12 numbered photographs, and separated the five prisoners—Blessington, Elliott, Wilmot, Carol Arrow and Elizabeth Lopez. According to both Elliott and Blessington, each prisoner was asked individually and separately to identify which of the head and shoulders photographs of the 12 young men in the photographs depicted the boy named Shorty who was with them on the evening Janine Balding was abducted, raped and murdered. Blessington and Elliott said that each of the juveniles pointed to photograph number seven, which was a photograph of Mark 'Shorty' Wells.

Chapter 9

SECOND TRIAL

The second trial began on 24 May 1990 under the experienced eye of Justice Peter Newman. Ted O'Loughlin for Jamieson called Shorty Wells to give evidence on 15 June 1990 after the Crown decided he was an unreliable witness. Wells informed the court he was currently living on the streets in Queensland, and in September 1988 he was *living on the streets around Kings Cross.* He said he remembered seeing Bronson Blessington and Matthew Elliott at The Station drop-in centre on the morning of the murder and he saw them *only once.* O'Loughlin asked Wells if he went somewhere with the two boys and he said *No.* The lawyer asked the witness whether he had ever been to Sutherland, and after a long pause, he said *No.*

Then Wells was asked if he'd been for a drive in a Holden Gemini in September 1988 and again, he answered *No.* That was the last information counsel extracted from the witness before the prosecutor produced an indemnity from prosecution from the Attorney General to protect Mark Wells from any incriminating evidence he might give as a witness in Jamieson's trial. O'Loughlin was furious at this unexpected development.

> O'Loughlin: *This is a document, which has never been brought to our attention, your Honour. I want to have...*
> Crown Prosecutor: *I do not want Mr O'Loughlin making speeches at this time.*

O'Loughlin: *To produce this document when I have this witness in the box...*
His Honour: *Mr O'Loughlin!*
O'Loughlin: *May I say something your Honour?*
His Honour: *Not while I am reading this document. Do you have an application to make?*

Ted O'Loughlin had good reason for his fury. Mark Wells had made an inconsistent prior statement to a Queensland policeman, Detective Sergeant Boyter, at the Brisbane Criminal Investigation Branch on 18 October 1989. Detective Senior Constable Taylor typed the statement and a justice of the peace, Graham Vickers, witnessed it. Wells signed the record of interview as required by Queensland law. Detective John McElroy of the Queensland police was also present during the interview. Detective Boyter asked Wells a number of questions about the crimes against Janine Balding. Wells told Boyter he was present when the young woman was abducted and he travelled in her car to the murder scene. He was asked about the car and described it as *A small one, a Gemini I think*. Wells told Boyter he knew a woman named Janine Balding on 8 September 1988. *I'm trying to remember what she looked like. It was near a barbed wire fence.*

Under cross-examination at trial, Wells' evidence became more and more bizarre as he told the court he was a devil worshipper and he had a vision about what happened to Janine Balding. Sydney's *Daily Telegraph* reported the evidence under the headline 'Janine witness devotee of Satan'.

> *A witness at the murder trial of Janine Balding said yesterday he worshipped the devil and claimed he had murdered a priest by nailing him to a wall. Mark 'Shorty' Wells, 28, was called to give evidence at the trial after two of the youths accused of Miss Balding's murder said he was present on the night she died...Under questioning yesterday Wells was asked how he had come to know details of the abduction of Miss Balding. He replied: "I dreamt it".Cross-examined by Crown Prosecutor, Bill Job QC, Wells agreed he had a history of psychiatric illness and often had trouble differentiating "dreams from reality." Wells has denied any involvement in Ms Balding's murder and has not been charged in connection with her death. In later evidence, two youths who admitted to being present on the night Miss Balding was drowned in a dam at Minchinbury, identified Wells as the 'Shorty' who was with them.*

Shorty Jamieson gave evidence at his second trial (with Blessington and Elliott) that he spent the day of the murder at the Sydney beach suburb of Coogee with Lizzy Lopez and another street kid named Bill Rowland. They caught a taxi at The Station drop-in centre at Wynyard just before lunch, bought a few beers and some marijuana from a bloke at the Coogee Bay Hotel, sat for a while on the beach promenade drinking and smoking, and then caught another taxi back to Kings Cross where they bought more beers and a stem and cone before catching a train back to Wynyard. Bronson Blessington had told me he met Shorty Jamieson for the first time upstairs at The Station drop-in centre on the morning of the murder.

"I remember him talking with Lizzy Lopez and Bill Rowland about undercover detectives and what kind of cars they drove. He'd point to cars out the window and say, 'There's one'. We spoke about being on the street and he told me about the Salvation Army refuge where he said he stayed the night before. Matthew and me found a bucket of condoms and we filled some of them with water and began chucking them at people on the street from the upstairs window. Jamieson thought that was pretty funny, but someone working in the place came up the stairs and said if we didn't cut it out the police would be called."

Blessington gave evidence at his second trial that Shorty Jamieson left The Station on the morning of the murder with Lizzy Lopez and Bill Rowland, and he, Blessington, and Matthew Elliott stayed at the drop-in centre until lunchtime. Then he and Matthew walked back to Central with Wayne Wilmot, Carol Arrow and Shorty Wells, and the five of them boarded the Cronulla line train. Blessington insisted that Shorty Jamieson left The Station with Lizzy Lopez and Bill Rowland.

On the morning after the murder, Jamieson was taken into custody by police at The Station, not for the crimes against Janine Balding, but for the assault on Warren Purchase. Lizzy Lopez was already inside the police paddy wagon. Although not present at the Purchase assault and released after questioning and being placed in a police line-up, Jamieson was a suspect in the sledgehammer assault purely on the basis of his association with Lopez. He and Lizzy were an item for the purposes of any criminal activity involving either of them. Their relationship was not sexual, but they were good friends. They must have been the oddest of couples on the street: she, a beauty queen in another life; and he, the archetypal axe murderer according to the press of the day, feared and loathed for his appearance.

Lizzy Lopez was charged as an accessory to the assault on Warren Purchase and remanded to the Cobham Juvenile Detention Centre. Five days after the murder, she gave a statement to Detective Sergeant Graham Rosetta at Mount Druitt Police Station 'confessing' to being one of the street kids who had travelled by train to Sutherland and murdered Janine Balding. It was a lie, of course, but nobody could know how much of the 'confession' was to be attributed to her vivid imagination, and how much was information provided by others. Unfortunately for Shorty Jamieson, Lizzy's bizarre 'confession' immediately put him in the homicide frame because of their friendship. When police started looking for a boy named Shorty for the Janine Balding murder, picking up Shorty Jamieson again after having him in custody a couple of days earlier for the Warren Purchase assault was just a formality.

In sentencing Jamieson, Elliott and Jamieson to life imprisonment with the recommendation they should never be released, Justice Newman said he was unconvinced about the wrong Shorty story: *I find that the jury concluded that the other 'Shorty' allegation made by all [three] prisoners, and indeed by Wilmot and Arrow, was nothing but a tissue of lies designed to hide their respective roles in this matter.* According to Jamieson's defence team, the tissue of lies was Jamieson's fabricated police record of interview. His Honour noted the involvement of Elliott, Blessington and Elizabeth Lopez in the assault on Warren Purchase two days before the crimes against Janine Balding, but the judge failed to mention that Stephen

Jamieson was also taken into custody for those crimes because of his friendship with Lopez.

Newman's sentencing remarks emphasised the importance of the gang's activities at the Mt Druitt shopping centre after the murder, and the *identification there made by persons who saw them, in particular identification of Jamieson was made by one Andrew Lonergan. This identification, and that made by Elva Matyas must have been strongly persuasive to the jury in determining whether Jamieson was in fact present that evening.* What the judge might have noted was the evidence of other identification witnesses who encountered the four juvenile accused in the company of an older boy at the Mt Druitt shopping centre on the evening of the murder. Within two days of the crime, police had eight witnesses (including the four juvenile accused) providing a description of the older boy accompanying the gang that fitted Shorty Wells, not Jamieson. Lonergan and Matyas did not come forward until the second trial—almost 18 months after the crimes.

One identification witness, Kristine Mobberley, observed the four juveniles and an older boy at the Sutherland railway station car park—shortly before they abducted Janine Balding. Fortunately for Ms Mobberley, the gang tried unsuccessfully to hijack her car. As they approached, she climbed in the car and locked it from the inside. She told police that the older boy had a long face badly pock marked. At the end of her statement, which she made at Sutherland police station on the day after the murder, Ms Mobberley made a final observation. *One thing I forgot to mention to you was that the second guy with the pock marked face was wearing a black cloth head band which was about an inch to an inch and a half in width.*

Chapter 10

STEVE BLESSINGTON

Bronson's father, Steve Blessington, was happy to talk with me, and as I made my way up the Old Pacific Highway to the coastal fishing village where he lived, I wondered whether the adopted son of strict Salvation Army parents could provide any answers to my questions. I turned into a concealed dusty driveway that runs off a tricky bend in the highway and Steve was standing under the shade of a lilly pilly tree at the front of his house. He had the appearance of a man slightly stooped, even weighed down, although he welcomed me with a friendly handshake.

As I followed him into the house, I was aware that he seemed to be physically smaller and much more self-effacing than Bronson. Steve apologised that his house was so small, and I explained that it seemed many times larger than Bronson's cell at Goulburn. The comparison was not a good one, but I was rescued when Steve's partner, Marie, offered me coffee and a biscuit. I introduced myself, and Steve and I sat at a wooden table under the window in the living room, bathed in the afternoon autumn sunlight that filtered through the lilly pilly.

Steve was back on the fishing trawlers. The latest coastal real estate boom had given him just enough equity in his modest fibro house to contemplate going into hock for another boat. While he was deciding, he skippered a boat for a man with two boats and no mortgage.

In the warmth and comfort of the sun—amplified somehow by

the extra sparkle it generates on the coast—Steve appeared at first to be unconcerned about being identified in his local community as the father of a notorious murderer. But then he was angry at the *Daily Telegraph* for publishing Bronson's name in 2001 when the cement law was passed.

"What I'd like to know is why they had in the newspaper about all these people who were never to be released, and they had photos of them, except for Bronson, but they had his name there and just a silhouette."

I remembered well the front page of the newspaper.

"I thought when you were 14 that your name and everything wasn't allowed to be divulged."

I thought so too, until I discovered that the privacy laws in force at the time meant a child's name could be published once he or she turned 18 years of age.

"I felt a bit upset because I didn't do the crime, but it's my name."

I asked how often he was questioned about his connection to the Blessington kid who's a killer?

"A fair bit," he said resignedly. "It's a small community and people talk. When that thing come out with them all splashed over the front page, well, I'm not goin' to deny he's my son."

Marie interposed from the kitchen that she also had two boys. "So, when it come out in the paper, we sort of told them rather than someone else tell them."

I asked whether anyone in the family had been verbally abused or attacked over Bronson's crimes and the answer was an emphatic no. People were generally supportive.

Steve said Bronson was seven or eight years old when he, Steve, left Bronson's mother, Rose, but the boy was doing alright until his mother started a relationship a boyfriend. Without resentment, Steve told me that Bronson and the boyfriend didn't get along. He also admitted he didn't spend much time with the boy in the first couple of years after he left, working on the boats at Tweed Heads for the first year, and then landing a job in the Northern Territory as a boner.

Why did he split with Rose?

"I was drinking a fair bit then and only working four hours a day. I'd spend another four hours at the club or pub and then come home. I was making good money though and still supporting the family."

After a few more questions about the breakdown of the family, he pressed on.

"She said, 'Well, if you're going to get pissed every night, I'm going to go out on Friday night'. I said, 'Well, that's not the same'. She said, 'Yes it is'. I said, 'No it's not'. I said, 'You go out on Friday night and I'm leavin'. Then she went out, and so I left."

I asked Steve about the months leading up to the murder. How was Bronson while they were at the Salvation Army farm at Prospect?

"He seemed alright at first," Steve said, "but then he just went downhill, sort of thing."

I pressed for more information, and he said he put the boy on a bus for his first day at Blacktown High School because he had to go to work at the Homebush Abattoirs.

"He wouldn't go to school, and I'd get home from work, and he wouldn't be home until ten o'clock at night. It was no good him living in Sydney and being able to run his own race. I didn't want him on drugs or anything, so I sort of said, 'Oh well, I'll just have to warn him'."

What was the warning?

"I said, 'Look, if you don't go to school when I've got to work, I'm going to have to put you on a farm and see how it's like for three months. After that, you can come back out and see how it's going'." Steve learned about the farm, when, exasperated by Bronson's refusal to attend school, he took the boy to the local court and tried unsuccessfully to have him declared a ward of the State.

"Before I put him in as unruly, they said they'd take him away to this farm." Steve liked the idea of the farm. "He'll get an education, jump on a tractor and everything will be sweet."

So far as Steve could recall, Bronson did finish up on the farm. He said he knew nothing of the boy's court appearance for stealing a pair of sunglasses, and his subsequent incarceration at Minda Juvenile Remand Centre in Lidcombe.

"It was a shock the coppers comin' round and sayin, 'Your son's up here and we're questioning him on the murder thing. Do you want to get dressed and come up to the station?' I said, 'He's on a farm'."

Our conversation ended with Steve lamenting his son's sentence.

"Nowhere in the world would they say you're goin' to be locked up never to be released at 14."

Nowhere other than the United States of America and Somalia. And now in Australia. I told Steve that his son is the youngest person in Australia sentenced to life in prison since transportation ended in 1840.

"It's shockin," he said, "but you know, I think he was more led than anything."

Chapter 11

ELIZABETH LOPEZ

After my second visit to Bronson Blessington, I contacted various hospitals in Sydney, inquiring about street kids who might have known someone connected to those accused of the crimes against Janine Balding. I left my phone number in case anyone could help, and to my surprise, one hospital staffer called back. The hospital had heard from Lizzy Lopez after the medical records' officer passed on my request for information about the murder. I telephoned the officer and she reminded me that the privacy laws did not allow her to disclose patient information. Nevertheless, she did expect Lizzy Lopez would be in touch. A few days later, Lizzy contacted me by phone and agreed to talk about the question of Shorty Jamieson's innocence. I drove out to see her straight away and arrived at a modest fibro house in the western suburbs less than an hour after she called.

"Geez ya keen," she called out as I opened the front gate and walked down the path to where she was sitting on the front verandah with a man who was obviously devoted to her. She introduced him as her partner and said they'd been together nine years. I'll call him 'Will'. They had two kids in primary school and a toddler running about.

After the formalities, Will and the toddler disappeared, leaving Lizzy and me to discuss her former life on the street. She was 16 when Janine Balding was killed, which made her 32. Tall and dark, she still exhibited the classical beauty of her Spanish heritage, despite her hard life, and few secrets were concealed in her earthy brown eyes. Born in Madrid, she came to Australia with her parents when she was ten years old.

I told her what I knew about the assault on Warren Purchase, describing in detail the appalling facts, and she confirmed most of them. Her face was quite mobile, black eyebrows arching and dipping as the memories rose and fell. I wanted to know if Warren Purchase was left for dead and she was almost indignant.

"He was crawling out the door and the neighbours seen him so we took off."

She told me that Matthew Elliott rang the police after the assault. "After he hung up, I said what did ya tell 'em, and he said he told 'em about the crime [against Warren Purchase] and who was there."

We moved on to the morning after the murder. Lizzy and her friend Dianne Adams had met Matthew Elliott and Bronson Blessington at Hyde Park in the city at around 3.00am. The boys were still covered in mud after drowning Janine Balding in the dam at Minchinbury. Elliott introduced Blessington to Dianne Adams and said his name was 'Todd'. Lizzy told me what happened after the four of them sat on a bench in the park.

"I said to the boys, 'Where were youse all day? I couldn't find youse'. And I asked 'em how they got so filthy. Matthew said, 'We were in Sutherland and we killed this lady'. I said, 'Bullshit, yer didn't kill nobody'. Matthew then showed me the jewellery he took from the lady and I knew straight away there was something wrong. But I wasn't sure if he killed her or just robbed her. Then Matthew said, 'We killed her and drowned her in a dam'. I stopped listenin' then because I knew they were in a lot of trouble. Matthew was not ashamed about what he did and I couldn't understand that he was talkin' about it."

I asked Lizzy about Bronson Blessington's appearance.

"He had red cheeks and a very mean look—like he really did kill somebody. I do believe Matthew Elliott wanted to get somebody and Blessington just followed. I think Blessington was scared—if he doesn't do what he's told he'll get killed. But he did look different after the murder. His eyes were evil and I was frightened. I remember Matthew sayin' that if we tell anyone about this he'll kill us."

She told me the four of them then caught a train from St James station in Hyde Park to Wynyard where they fell asleep on the seats under the indicator board. When the police woke Lizzy at Wynyard station she was alone. It was then that she was taken into custody, charged as an accessory to the assault on Warren Purchase, refused bail and remanded to the Cobham Juvenile Detention Centre.

I asked if she remembered going to Coogee with Shorty Jamieson and Bill Rowland on the day of the murder.

"I don't know if I went with Bill Rowland because I can't remember what he looks like. We used to meet down at Coogee where Jamieson used to hang around. I think I seen him in the morning at Coogee."

At that point I became totally bamboozled. I asked how she got to Coogee. She said she walked, and I suggested it was too far to walk.

"No, not Coogee, but that place like an old shop where he used to hang out. Where the bridge is and the cars go through and a set of lights. That street that takes ya straight to the railway station at Central."

The description sounded like Eddy Avenue at Central railway.

"Anyway, that's where I seen him."

Surely she was talking about Jamieson, not Bill Rowland?

I produced a copy of Dianne Adams' statement to the police given five days after the murder in which Adams said she was the first to wake up at Wynyard on the seats *where the train timetable boards are* and tried unsuccessfully to wake Lizzy.

Lizzy picked up Dianne Adams' statement, as if to refresh her memory, and again I found myself staring at the increased activity reflected in her eyebrows. She read out the names of the street kids mentioned in the statement and identified the names she recalled.

"I remember Matthew sayin' he asked Janine for her PIN number, and she refused, and so he said, 'If you don't give it to me I'll kill you'. Before this happened with this person, me and the boys stole quite a few cars, and Matthew always drove."

I asked if these were the same boys she accompanied to Sutherland, referring to her false confession. To my surprise, she rose like a phoenix from the ashes of her testimony.

"I didn't go with them because I was looking for Shorty."

My initial concern that police may have 'signed up' Lizzy for the murder of Janine Balding was put to rest when I realised she 'confessed' her involvement to youth workers at Cobham Juvenile Detention Centre on at least two separate occasions. She said in her police record of interview that her part in the murder was to hold Janine Balding's legs. Detective Rosetta asked who was with her at the time and she said, *Matthew, Wayne and the other one who was fourteen but I don't know his name.* The policeman asked if anyone else was there other than the three boys. *No, only the three of them and me*, she replied. Rosetta then asked, *Did you see 'Shorty' on the day Ms Balding was killed?* Her answer was *No.*

Eventually Lizzy resiled from the 'confession' when her story was no longer plausible, but by then Shorty Jamieson was well and truly in the breech. A year after the murder, she gave another statement to the police in which she corroborated Jamieson's alibi that they went to Coogee on the day of the murder. Then, as now, her memory was unreliable, although I remained curious about why the lawyers for Jamieson didn't call her to prop up the defence. No doubt the prosecution would have done so if she had something negative to say about the accused. In the end, nobody got to hear what Lizzy had to say.

The police took Lizzy to Flemington police station in a paddy wagon after they arrested her on Wynyard railway station. She denied nothing when they asked her about the Warren Purchase assault. I asked if she remembered Jamieson being taken into custody over the Warren Purchase assault. Did she remember the police stopping at The Station drop-in centre on the way to Flemington police station and Jamieson getting in the paddy wagon? Again, she had no memory of the event. Her patchy recollection was driving me crazy, and I'd a sense of why the Jamieson lawyers refused to call her as a witness.

Lizzy Lopez was fiercely loyal to Shorty Jamieson and spoke about him with great affection. She related an incident when she tied him to a parking meter for "goin' off" and agreed to release him only when he promised to behave himself. She asked me to help her write a note to Shorty at the Goulburn jail. I listened to her words and wrote: *Best of luck getting out of jail because I know you're innocent. I wish I could turn back the clock for you. I will always think of you as a good friend and I will never forget you.*

I decided to call it a day when Will reappeared on the verandah. We chatted about motor cars—he had a couple of Fords under repair down the side of the house. He worked on them whenever he had the chance. I asked Lizzy whether her past life ever visited her and she told me a story I found disturbing if unsurprising. Police in the day were known on the odd occasion to fill in gaps in a brief of evidence.

"About two years ago the coppers came to see me and asked if I could identify a woman from some photographs. They told me that Elliott, Blessington and Jamieson had killed another woman and they wanted to know if I knew her. I said I didn't know any of them women and that Shorty Jamieson was innocent. I told 'em he wouldn't hurt a fly. They kept sayin' I should identify one of the women in the photographs and they wouldn't let me go. Eventually I did identify a woman—the one the coppers said had been killed—but I didn't know her even though I said I did."

Will said that if he'd been home he would have told the coppers to piss off. "Some coppers are good and do their job, but others are just lazy and drive you mad to save themselves doing any homework. They just pick the first person they grab and stitch up the poor bugger."

As I left, I thanked Will and Lizzy for letting me talk to them, and I asked Lizzy if she would sign an affidavit for Shorty. First she wanted me to give her note to him at Goulburn jail and then she'd let me know.

"I've moved on since them days, but I loved Shorty as a brother. Maybe I'll get to see him again sometime."

Chapter 12

STEPHEN 'SHORTY' JAMIESON

It troubled me no end that Stephen 'Shorty' Jamieson signed a police record of interview admitting to the crimes against Janine Balding when he'd claimed his innocence at every opportunity since. I wrote to Corrective Services NSW seeking permission to visit the prisoner and a favourable reply turned up in a few days. On a sweltering hot day in late summer 2002, the air as dry as dust and the Goulburn Plains in the grip of the worst drought for 100 years, I headed south on the Hume Highway. Two hours later, I veered left at the turnoff to Goulburn and then turned right at the bridge that spans Mulwaree Ponds, a series of grey waterholes that might pass for a moat on the northern boundary of the prison. At reception, I asked to see Stephen Jamieson for a legal visit. This time I was escorted directly into the prison, avoiding the delay of the main visitors centre, although the usual security checks still applied, including the thumbprint recognition machine that never seemed to work.

A taciturn, red-faced correctional officer squinted in the hot sun as he led me through a metal gate in the prison wall, and then across a paved quadrangle to an iron fence. Beyond the fence, I could see lawn and flowerbeds outside the deputy governor's office. Prisoners were tending the blooming garden, which somehow resisted heat, the tangle of razor wire, iron bars and endless red bricks. We followed a concrete path to a clock tower which stood like a sentinel above an arched brick entrance to the

Circle or command point for the main prison. From the Circle, correctional officers had a clear line of sight to all the yards and a direct view of the red-brick walls of the prisoner accommodation, which consisted of four blocks in a radial design: A wing and D wing were two-storey buildings to the right and left of the Circle; B wing and C wing were longer three-storey buildings set on a radial alignment to the other two. In fact, the Circle is half a circle, with the offices and a common yard at its axis point.

The officer informed me that the interview with Jamieson was to take place in the Circle offices because the education rooms where I would normally be taken were fully occupied. A crowd in the education rooms was a subject worthy of further discussion, but the officer was unwilling to expand upon the subject. My attempt to engage the man in conversation was a complete failure. He abandoned me at the main gate to the Circle, saying that the deputy governor would be along shortly.

I waited in the hot sun for the deputy governor, my forehead now burning from the lack of shade. Still, I counted my blessings—the opportunity to get inside the Circle was not to be missed. Built in 1883, the semi-circle layout of the double and triple-storey red-brick accommodation blocks are outdated by modern standards of prison design. Steel stairways and narrow galleries provide access to the cells, each one accommodating two prisoners in a cramped space of just a few square metres. B wing was the most interesting of the cell blocks as it included two larger condemned cells for death-row prisoners with a gallows trap on the first floor, just above the security and administrative offices. The death penalty was abolished in New South Wales in 1985.

As I stood there and wondered whether I would rather hang by a rope than spend my remaining life cooped up in a steel cell, Deputy Governor Wayne King wandered over to the fence and unlocked the gate. He was a laconic and amiable sort of bloke, shaking my hand as he invited me inside. We walked to the Circle offices where he introduced me to the office staff and placed me in a room with a wooden table and two vinyl covered chairs—upmarket by the standards of the usual plastic furniture prison décor. I could see across the Circle yard to the fan of inmate buildings and their adjoining yards, each yard separated by brick fences topped with bars and razor wire. Fragments of clothing and strips of paper clung precariously to the razor wire, blown on a breath of wind long gone in the limp heat of summer. Prisoners sat in dust and concrete, some seeking shade under corrugated iron awnings, others toughing it out in the sun's full glare, bare-chested and bound up by their rippling muscles.

In such a bleak place where death and life took on such poignancy, I found it difficult to avoid thoughts of Jamieson as the monster emerging from his cage to greet the curious visitor. I was shamefully influenced by the tabloid newspaper clippings in my file, especially an article published in the *Daily Telegraph* after the convict was sentenced to life—as in no parole and Never to be Released—in September 1990. It was a small inset piece published with the convicted killer's photograph to emphasise the horror of violent crime. The accompanying headline read: 'Ape-like street kid's crime path'.

> *Stephen "Shorty" Jamieson was not born to greatness. At 149 cm tall and with ape-like features, Jamieson would*

> *tag along with others, a servile acquaintance...[who] duly went along with the gang that was to commit one of the "most barbaric" crimes in the state's history... His Counsel said Shorty Jamieson suffered from the "overwhelming physical disadvantage of an unattractive appearance and almost dwarfish stature." Yesterday the court heard how Jamieson had an "extensive criminal record" involving sexual assault, theft, malicious wounding and robbery. He maintains his innocence despite being convicted by a jury. He is a singularly unattractive man "whose appearance would not endear him to people" said Justice Newman.*

I returned the press clipping to my file along with the convict's criminal record which ran to six pages. Soon Stephen Jamieson strolled out of B wing and ambled across the Circle yard at the heels of a correctional officer. Jamieson wore a prison-green tee shirt, green tracksuit pants and blue and white joggers. I could hardly believe he was so short—barely reaching the middle of the officer's back. I recognised the long brown hair, pursed lips and disproportionate limbs from newspaper photographs. Then he stood at the door with the officer, who pushed the door wide open before leaving. Shorty Jamieson wandered up to the nearest vinyl covered chair on his side of the wooden table, dropped one foot on the seat from the back of the chair, and then swung the other foot over the back, sliding into the chair in one exquisitely effortless movement.

Was that a party trick?

"You could say that" he said, grinning mischievously.

He placed a sheaf of papers on the table, and as I reached

across the table to introduce myself and shake his hand, I noticed he had unusually long fingernails that folded and then curved downwards—identical to my mother's nails when she let them grow. He reeked of tobacco and his papers ponged like the last shelf at the back of a condemned bookshop, which was hardly surprising given they'd probably seen neither natural light nor fresh air in his then 15 years imprisonment. He should have been out of prison by now but for the cement law. Up close, he had an orange goatee beard and moustache that might have altered the line of his simian facial features. Monsters are a matter of taste, I suppose, but Shorty Jamieson looked much more like an animated garden gnome than an ape in my humble opinion.

At the top of his papers was a child welfare file going back to his birth. A nursing sister reported that his birth deformities included a left eye turned inwards; neck muscles on his left side noticeably shorter than those on the right side; right leg shorter than the left leg; right foot turned at a right angle to his right leg; hip joints rotating at an obtuse angle; and distorted facial features thought to be those of a mongoloid child. After several weeks in hospital and corrective surgery, his mother took Stephen home, where she lived alone with the grog. She was so drunk the next day she almost suffocated him, and child welfare returned him to the hospital. The nursing sister reported that his mother was *too drunk to be aware of his presence* and the decision was made to declare him a ward of the State.

Also included in his papers was a chapter of a true-crime book *Never to be Released* by author Paul Kidd (1993), in which some of the material from the prisoner's controversial record of interview with the police was woven into the narrative. The chapter was titled 'Kids Who Kill' after the UK case of Robert Thompson and Jon Venables, ten-year-olds who killed three-year-old James Bulger and left him on a railway track.

"Do you know the bloke who writ this bastard?" Stephen asked in a threatening tone.

I remained silent.

"That book has caused me quite a bit of therapy in prison," he added apologetically.

I informed him that I knew of the book, which included on the front cover a cruel airbrush representation of his face. On the back cover, his enlarged and darkened eyes appeared with the publisher's blurb that the author had *compiled the inside stories of Australia's most horrendous crimes to help ensure that their perpetrators remain behind bars.*

The prisoner also had a copy of *Juice* magazine from May 1993, which included an article by journalist Rob Johnson pointing out that Jamieson's looks were the result of foetal alcohol spectrum disorder. *Imagine the uproar,* Johnson said, *if someone with Down Syndrome murdered somebody, and the headlines screamed 'Mongoloid Killer'.* Referring to the prisoner's long history of street crime, the author of the article concluded that *Jamieson may not be guilty of the murder of Janine Balding, but he is by no means an innocent.*

It was true that Shorty Jamieson had a long record for petty street crime plus a conviction for sexual assault which worried me. Even so, I reckoned utilitarian punishment was alive and well in the villages represented by the State's justice system.

Stephen Jamieson's most neglected papers were the yellowing

press clippings about the Janine Balding case. The first one I picked up reported a psychiatrist giving evidence at trial that Jamieson was a classic example of *negative charisma*, a condition that *repels other people*. From my immediate experience, this was a harsh judgement—unless the shrink was testifying about the musty paper and stale tobacco smells.

I showed the prisoner his criminal record. He elaborated on the first three pages—petty street offences committed while he was still a child. At age 18 he was charged with sexual assault and sentenced to six months hard labour. What was that about?

"Some kids pushed me in front of a pregnant woman. The coppers charged me with sexual assault."

In the same year, 1984, he was charged and convicted at Parramatta Local Court with malicious wounding and robbery, given a three-year good behaviour bond and told not to leave the Werrington area. He could not remember the details. In 1985 when he was 19, he was sentenced to six months hard labour for *take and use conveyance*. What's that?

"I was a passenger in a stolen car."

Other petty crime followed over the next two years, and in 1987 there were two more stolen vehicle charges, and a conviction for trespass for which he was fined *50 cents or the rising of the court*. The last two pages of the criminal record were taken up with a list of driving offences at Campbelltown Local Court in March 1988 which consisted of convictions and fines of $50 for each offence. And finally the 1988 crimes against Janine Balding for which he was convicted by a judge and jury and sentenced by the parliament to life without parole.

"I think that's a mistake. I don't remember going to Campbelltown Court. They've got the wrong bloke."

We can check that. What about the crimes against Janine Balding? Bronson Blessington says you're innocent.

"He's right about that."

You had nothing to do with the crimes against Janine Balding?

"Not a thing."

What about all the evidence that went to the jury?

"It's a load o'bull. I weren't there."

So, what happened?

He asked if he could borrow a pen and a page of my notepad. Slowly and meticulously, he began drawing a plan of The Station drop-in centre near Wynyard railway station. He said he was sitting on the steps, waiting for the place to open, when Matthew and Bronson arrived. He had never seen Bronson before—a young boy not much taller than himself. Matthew he knew from the streets.

When the drawing of the building was completed, he wrote across the steps: *This where I meet they others on the 8th of September 1988*. The drawing was elementary, but it helped him tell the story—or rather, answer my questions. He did not communicate easily.

The prisoner answered questions in one or two sentences and then sat stone-faced, or grinned impishly, depending on what he'd said. His short responses meant I could write down his answers without disrupting our dialogue—a small victory over the prison rules which did not permit the use of tape recorders. I asked what time he met Matthew and Bronson at The Station and he said some time before nine.

How could he be sure of the time?

He replied that he spent the previous night at the Matthew Talbot, a hostel for homeless men, and you had to be out of the place by seven in the morning. The Station didn't open until nine. While they were waiting, Matthew and Bronson walked over to a red Commodore parked on the other side of the street and tried to break in. Then they came back and sat on the steps of the drop-in centre.

Wayne Wilmot and Carol Arrow arrived—he could not remember whether it was before or after the other two. More kids turned up, and when the place opened, they all walked upstairs, made coffee and watched television. The prisoner pointed to the TV room in his drawing. I asked about the lounge room, which he'd also drawn, and he agreed that some of the kids sat in the lounge room. The other kids he recalled being there included Mark 'Shorty' Wells, Bill Rowland, Lizzy Lopez, and her sister, whose name he'd forgotten.

What happened then?

"Bill Rowland told me and Lizzy to stay away from them two."

Stay away from Blessington and Elliott?

"Yeah."

And then what happened?

"The three of us went to Coogee, about ten thirty."

You, Bill Rowland and Lizzy Lopez?

"Yeah. We were comin' back to The Station for lunch, but the plan backfired."

How did the plan backfire?

"Because when we went to Coogee we got some drugs."

And?

"We got out of it on the drugs."

What kind of drugs?

"Marijuana."

What about other drugs?

"No, just marijuana."

I wanted to know if he remembered anything else about the day at Coogee apart from the marijuana. He said an off-duty detective told him where to buy more drugs after threatening to arrest him. And then he spoke with an elderly lady who had two scrawny chihuahuas. The dogs were yapping at him so he yapped back at them. He apologised to the lady when she said, 'Don't go off at my babies'.

Around lunchtime, Stephen, Lizzy and Bill Rowland headed back to The Station and arrived about one thirty or two in the afternoon. They hung around at the drop-in centre "to find out what Lizzy was gonna do," and then they left when Lizzy said she would stay and do some washing.

Rowland lived in a squat at The Rocks where he took Jamieson and the two continued drinking with another boy. Jamieson said he stayed at the squat for a couple of hours and then went back to Central railway station where he caught a bus to the Gold Coast in Queensland. I asked when he bought the ticket and he said in the morning—before The Station opened. He said he travelled to Manly and back by ferry after he left the Matthew Talbot hostel. It sounded like he was conflating different events.

I found myself working out how long it might take to get from Kings Cross to Manly, buy a bus ticket and then return to the city in time to meet Elliott and Blessington on the steps of The Station before nine in the morning. It seemed like a quick and unlikely trip to make in the peak-hour traffic—including ferry rides to and from Manly. I asked if he was talking about the morning of the murder or some other morning? He wasn't sure, but I could check his St George Bank account if I had time, because he'd withdrawn the money for the bus trip on the same day he bought the ticket.

Why did you go to the Gold Coast?

"I used to go there every coupla months lookin' for work. I knew some people."

What happened when you got there?

"I got off the bus at about 6.30 in the morning. We was a bit late cause the bus broke down and we had to change buses."

What happened then?

"I caught a taxi to Southport. Normally I do fishin' at Southport cause I know people in the caravan park."

Where did you stay?

"Stayed at the Salvation Army place near the hospital at Southport."

How long were you there?

"Stayed there for two weeks then the coppers turned up."

What happened with the coppers?

"What happened was me and this other bloke went out and got pissed. We came back and kicked up a ruckus and got kicked out of the Salvo's after we had breakfast."

What about the coppers?

"Me and me mate met these old fellas in the park, and we were sittin' around, drinkin' and carryin' on."

When did the coppers turn up?

"Yeah, I looked over at me mate, and I thought he had a nice shirt on—little red dots all over it."

Was that the coppers?

"Yeah, laser scopes from the TRG (Tactical Response Group) police. I looked around, and I thought, I've got red dots on me too. I looked up and alls the last words I heard were, 'If you move you're dead'. That's when detectives arrested me."

According to other evidence, Jamieson left the Salvation Army hostel and walked down to the park at Southport beside the beach where he joined a group of older men drinking. Between them they had a bottle of bourbon, several cans of beer, a bottle of scotch, some marijuana and a bicycle. Next minute, Tactical Response Group police arrived with guns drawn and rifles at the ready. Two detectives drove into the park in a white Commodore and stopped in the middle of the police. The detectives jumped out of the car and interrogated him.

After a short discussion, the detectives put him in the police car with the bottle of scotch, threw the bicycle in the car boot and drove to Southport police station where Stephen said he sat from seven in the morning until 10.30 at night "spewin' me guts up." I questioned him further and concluded he vomited only once in the police station and the police cleaned up the mess with paper towels, throwing them in a bin in the corner of the interview room. I asked if he could recall anything about the room. Apart from the stink of the place, he remembered bright blue carpet.

"I got a good look at it when I was spewin'."

The story of his arrest was more or less consistent with a report in Brisbane's *Courier Mail* on 23 September 1988 under the headline 'Sixth arrest in Balding murder case'.

> *A Sydney man, 22, was charged last night with the murder of Sydney woman Janine Balding. The man, Stephen Wayne Jamieson, of no fixed address, was arrested on the Gold Coast yesterday. Jamieson was picked up by Broadbeach detectives and uniformed officers on the beach at Southport at 8.15am. He had earlier been evicted from the Southport Salvation Army Hostel for drunk and disorderly behaviour. A Salvation Army welfare officer, Mr Dave Hatchman, alerted police after hearing a radio news broadcast about the hunt for Ms Balding's killer. Sydney detectives last night executed a warrant for Jamieson's arrest...Five teenage members of a Sydney graffiti gang have already been charged with having abducted, sexually assaulted and murdered Ms Balding.*

I asked the prisoner to read a copy of the newspaper report, and he struggled, so I read it to him. He agreed it was a fair report of his arrest. The six suspects now in custody were Bronson Blessington, Matthew Elliott, Wayne Wilmot, Carrol Arrow, Shorty Jamieson and Lizzy Lopez.

"But I didn't know nothin' about the murder," he insisted. "The coppers showed me photographs of a dead woman and freaked me out."

I questioned him about Lizzy's involvement. He sat back in the vinyl-covered chair and smiled ambiguously.

"Lizzy said she was there, but she weren't."

Further questioning confirmed what I'd already read in Bronson

Blessington's papers: Lizzy Lopez and Stephen Jamieson were taken to Flemington police station on the morning after the murder of Janine Balding for the Warren Purchase assault. The police picked up Jamieson from The Station soon after it opened and put him in the back of the paddy wagon with Lizzy, who they'd collected from Wynyard railway station.

"The coppers thought me and Lizzy were in the bashin' of that fella in the squat."

I told him the fella's name was Warren Purchase, and Lizzy was in fact involved in the assault—she was present when it happened. So far as I could recall, Lizzy was charged with common purpose assault.

"But I weren't there," he reminded me. He was referring to the Warren Purchase assault. "The coppers interviewed me and put me in a police line-up."

I waited expectantly for more information, and when there was none, I asked if the police charged him.

"No way. They cleared me straight away and let me go."

Did they take you back to the city?

"The bastards left me at Flemington railway station with no money."

Did the coppers in the Janine Balding case put you in a police line-up?

"Not that I recall," he said in a soft voice, as if surprised by the question.

Surely, I was not the first person to ask him about a police line-up during the Janine Balding murder inquiry. He was so short and his facial features so distinctive that anybody who laid eyes on him would remember him. At the first trial, in answer to a question from Jamieson's barrister, Detective Raue told Justice Wood and the jury that it would be difficult to arrange a fair line-up of persons of similar size, age and appearance to the accused Jamieson because of his unusual physical appearance.

I asked if he had copies of the police statements tendered at his trial, particularly his police record of interview in Queensland. I held my breath as he began rifling through his papers. Eventually he emerged with copies of two police statements. One was a copy of the statement he was alleged to have made to the Sydney detectives at Southport police station; the other was a statement by a Queensland policeman, Detective Sergeant Roy Wall, who happened to be on duty when Stephen was taken into custody. Wall's statement was an important record of what the prisoner had to say to the Queensland police immediately before New South Wales police interviewed him. Jamieson denied that he was involved in any murder and said: *Is this the one with the sledgehammer 'cos they've already questioned me about that'.* Wall replied: *Look, we don't know much about it. It'll be best if you wait for the Sydney detectives to tell you what it's about.* Wall's statement ended with the arrival of the New South Wales police and Jamieson's arrest for the crimes against Janine Balding.

As I considered the statement, I did my best to ignore the details of the bus trip to the Gold Coast. According to Wall, Jamieson said he arrived *last Wednesday*. As he was arrested on Thursday 22 September 1988, last Wednesday would have been 14 September—six days after the murder on 8 September. I was also curious that there was no reference in the statement to his sobriety if he vomited in the police station. Detective Senior Constable Markey was asked during the second trial in cross-examination whether the prisoner was drunk and the policeman answered *No*. The question was almost incidental and I wondered why the defence team did not pursue the issue of alcohol consumption more vigorously. Even in the days of typewritten interviews, police were required to wait for a drunk person to sober up before taking a statement.

After reading Detective Wall's statement, I asked to read the record of interview the prisoner gave to the Sydney detectives at Southport. Up to that point, Stephen had been giving credible answers to my questions, but when I began questioning him directly about the contents of the record of interview, he became evasive, and his answers made no sense. The seven-page document was the critical piece of evidence against him in the prosecution case, and he readily handed it to me, but not before making an impossible claim. He pointed to the handwriting at the foot of each page of the document and told me he'd "finally worked out how the coppers forged me signatures." He then embarked upon an elaborate explanation about the indent left by signatures, and how the indent can be lifted using a lead pencil and white paper. The process sounded entirely feasible, except that the most cursory examination of the document suggested the signatures were authentic.

Apart from his own distinctive signature, each of the seven pages included the signatures of two police officers. One of the Sydney detectives signed as did one from Queensland—as well as a Justice of the Peace. The JP attested that he read the record of interview to Stephen before he signed it. Whatever the flaws in the document, the signatures on it were genuine. On the other hand, Stephen was quite incapable of giving the narrative answers set down in answer to the police questions. At best he answered my questions in two or three sentences, whereas I counted 25 sentences in one answer he was supposed to have given to police, and 21 sentences in another.

I remained doubtful that the prisoner had sufficient time on the morning of the murder to get from the Matthew Talbot hostel to Manly by ferry, buy his bus ticket to the Gold Coast, and then return to the city in time to be waiting on the steps of The Station when the doors opened at 9.00am. The whole story about how he got to the Gold Coast—not just the purchase of the ticket but the discrepancy in the number of days between the murder and the bus trip—gave me pause for thought. Why was he making things more complicated than they already were? Add to that the needless speculation about the signatures on his police record of interview, and I was inclined to give up on the case at the end of our first meeting. I told him I would decide over the weekend whether I could help, and he thanked me for looking at his case.

Back in Sydney, I re-read a transcript of evidence given in the second trial of Blessington, Elliott and Jamieson before Justice Newman. All three accused were resolute that Jamieson had nothing to do with the abduction, rape and murder of Ms Balding. One way or another, the court transcript answered all my questions about his alibi, where he stayed on the night of the murder and the bus trip to Queensland.

His signatures on the police record of interview remained a

moving feast. At the first trial he said they were forged, but by the time of the second trial, he agreed with the Crown Prosecutor that he'd changed his mind—the signatures were his after all. Police had forced him to sign, he said, and I found that to be a much more credible explanation than forged signatures. But I was still baffled that he would tell me his signatures on the record of interview were forged when he'd resiled from that idea on his own evidence in the second trial.

Chapter 13

YVONNE AND ARTHUR YATES

Yvonne and Arthur Yates—the nearest thing Stephen Jamieson had to a family—were happy to talk with me, so I boarded an early morning flight from the Gold Coast to Townsville and checked into the 'Sugar Shaker' hotel—named after the shape of the building and not its location on the edge of the Queensland sugarcane fields. Even in late winter, the Sunshine State heat was stifling, carried to the east coast by a prevailing westerly from the Great Sandy Dessert. A few country miles north of Townsville, I found the Yates family in a timber and corrugated iron Queenslander where we walked onto the verandah and chatted about their time with Stephen. Just beyond the verandah, a Mexican wave of sugarcane bent and yielded in the hot wind.

Stephen had joined Yvonne and Arthur as a young boy aged seven years when they were State ward carers operating Clairvaux House at Katoomba in the Blue Mountains, a State institution for boys and girls who'd been abandoned by or removed from their birth families. Shorty was part of the family until age 16 when the State ward rules required older children to move out of the Yates care accommodation and engage with less supervised juvenile housing at Werrington Park in western Sydney. From then on Stephen began living intermittently on the streets in preference to the new juvenile housing arrangements.

"It was devastating to see him go," said Arthur as he seated himself in a cane armchair on the verandah. "But those were the rules. All the children had to leave us when they turned 16. Child Welfare organised to move him. They just turned up in a white van and took him away. We tried to put a positive spin on the move for Stephen, but really, it was devastating for all the children when they had to leave."

I sat opposite Arthur.

Yvonne Yates brought us tea and scones, which she placed on a small circular coffee table with a glass top, and then she sat on a three-seater cane lounge beside us. I guessed the two carers were both in their mid-to-late sixties given they'd recently retired to the coast. Yvonne showed me an album of photographs and press clippings, much of which was replicated in Stephen's records. One faded article from page 3 of the *Daily Mirror* on 13 June 1975 was news to me. The headline read: 'Abandoned as a baby, Yvonne is now mum to a dozen waifs'.

> *Yvonne Yates was dumped on the doorstep of a children's home when she was two—unloved, unwanted, a tiny, abandoned waif. The tragic event led Yvonne to choose a life looking after children who would otherwise miss out on the most precious gift of all—a mother's love. Today Yvonne is "mother" to 12 State wards and a son of her own.*

Yvonne went on to tell the *Daily Mirror* journalist that the love she and Arthur gave 'their' kids was a way of giving back the love she received as a child. It turned out that the doorstep where Yvonne was abandoned was in France where she was born. For some inexplicable reason, she ended up on the beach at Dunkirk as a three-year-old in 1940 and then transported to a London children's home from where she was adopted by a loving family. She fell in love with Arthur when she was 15 and *now he's not only a wonderful husband but my mother, father, brother, sister and lover all in one.* When her adoptive parents died in England, Yvonne and Arthur decided to emigrate to Australia. For this, Shorty Jamieson's 'Mum' and 'Dad' won the newspaper's love story of the month award which included a P&O cruise on the Arcadia.

Arthur remembered Stephen as "a happy little bugger," a boy who "always had a smile and was always laughing." As he matured he grew strong, and his unusual physical features earned him the nickname 'caveman'. He had a presence about him that marked him out from the eleven or twelve other children in the group home. Arthur remembered him as grateful and content with his place in the Yates family.

"Stephen was never a problem," Arthur said. "I don't remember one fight that I saw him in. He never caused any trouble, even though we had some kids who were very big problems. We had some real bad ones, but Stephen never got into trouble. He never stole, he was always kind and good mannered. And he looked after the females."

Yvonne said that Stephen was always protective of the girls and she could never understand how he was involved in the abduction, rape and murder of a young woman. She showed me copies of photographs of Stephen with the family that I hadn't seen before.

I expressed my surprise that Stephen had showed me some photographs but not others. Yvonne said that she "read the riot act" to Stephen about giving out information that might put the family in danger. I explained that the family had little to fear—

without legal access to Stephen's records, I would not have known of his life with the Yates family.

Twenty years later, after Yvonne and Arthur Yates had passed away, I made the acquaintance of their son Garth, and traveled north to the Queensland sugarcane fields to meet his family. Garth had fond memories of Stephen in his formative years at Clairvaux House in the Blue Mountains. The two 'brothers' were in touch from time to time afterwards. Garth confirmed his late mother's opinion that Stephen harming a woman was unimaginable.

Chapter 14

JOANNE HARRIS

The government's cement law appeared to have ended all appeal rights for Blessington, Elliott and Jamieson. On the face of it, the three were condemned to prison for the rest of their lives now that the Never to be Released recommendation of the trial judge, Justice Peter Newman, had received statutory endorsement. Other countries had judicial review bodies in place to test unsafe convictions and unfair sentences, including Britain's Criminal Cases Review Commission and various innocence projects in the United States of America. In New South Wales, an Innocence Panel was being set up in a back room of police headquarters, but I was sceptical about the police assisting prisoners to prove their innocence.

The Supreme Court has a procedure for the Chief Justice to order a judicial inquiry into a conviction where there is a doubt or question as to a convicted person's guilt. But the court may refuse to consider the application for an inquiry if the court is not satisfied *that there are special facts or special circumstances that justify the taking of further action.* In other words, a judge had to be satisfied about fresh and compelling evidence before a judicial inquiry could be held—rather like putting the cart before the horse. While evidence that police arrested the wrong Shorty was compelling, it was evidence available to Jamieson's jury in one form or another, and so the Supreme Court's judicial inquiry procedure made no allowance for the fact that juries like judges make mistakes. Ultimately, nothing was likely to change the catch

22 of a judge having to approve a judicial inquiry before one could be held. In the absence of a dedicated and independent criminal cases review commission, I doubted I could help Shorty Jamieson.

Meanwhile, on a quiet afternoon in State parliament, I took a stroll across Hyde Park from Macquarie Street and introduced myself to Joanne Harris, Shorty's latest pro bono solicitor. His previous solicitor during both trials was Joan Baptie who'd recently been appointed to the bench as a Local Court Magistrate. Joanne Harris was an affable woman in a long black dress with straight brown hair down to the middle of her back. She told me she had the smallest criminal law practice in Australia as she leaned over her desk and swept a fistful of hair away from her face. The size of her single room in the Mirvac Trust Building confirmed she sailed in a small legal ship. She volunteered that Shorty Jamieson's case was the most appalling injustice she'd ever seen.

"If we think we're anything other than a penal colony we're kidding ourselves," said Joanne angrily, drawing back another fistful of hair.

Joanne Harris had unsuccessfully argued in the Supreme Court for Jamieson's convictions to be reviewed. She tried to establish to the court's satisfaction that the new science of stylometric analysis demonstrated that the prisoner could not have answered the police questions in the way suggested by the record of interview. A stylometrics expert, Andrew Lohrey, gave evidence that the police record of interview had composite authorship—it did not represent Jamieson's words during the interview. Justice Bruce James decided on 15 June 2001 that the stylometric analysis of Jamieson's record of interview with the police *does not raise a doubt and does not give rise to a sense of uneasiness about the convictions of the applicant for the offences committed against Ms Balding.*

In rejecting Jamieson's application for a review of his convictions, Justice James said that the so-called science of stylometrics was not a recognised field of scientific expertise in Australian courts. His Honour also cited the High Court's Chief Justice Sir Gerard Brennan AC who spoke for the majority of High Court judges when leave to appeal the convictions was rejected. Brennan went to the heart of the problem:

> *It appeared in argument before us that the convictions of the applicant [Stephen Jamieson] depend chiefly upon the reliability of his confessional statements. For that reason, the respondent [the Crown] correctly acknowledges that, if further evidence comes to hand with respect to the authorship of the answers to the record of interview, it may well be necessary for further consideration to be given to this case under section 475 of the Crimes Act [now Part 7 of the Crimes (Appeal And Review) Act 2001]. But on the material before this Court there is no question of law raised which justifies the grant of special leave to appeal. Accordingly special leave to appeal is refused.*

I asked Joanne whether she was aware of any medical evidence about Jamieson's ability to give comprehensive answers to the police questions given his foetal alcohol spectrum condition. She showed me a copy of part of the transcript of the second trial which included the testimony of psychologist William Taylor. Taylor said

Jamieson had an IQ of about 75, which meant he had the mental capacity of a child. *He would be very limited in his ability to perceive the meaning behind questions being put to him and I expect him to be fairly immature as you might expect a child to respond to this situation... I defy a lot of people, including the people in this courtroom, to respond [to police questions] in that sort of detail.*

Joanne and I discussed the role of police minister Paul Whelan in setting up the Innocence Panel. He seemed to be the right man for the job, famously telling a class of journalism students in June 2001 that police fabricated evidence to obtain convictions in 'countless cases' prior to the appointment of Judge James Wood to head the Royal Commission into the Police Service. To avoid any doubt about what he'd said, the minister added, 'People would be shocked to find out how many people have been wrongly convicted'. That was Paul Whelan the defence lawyer talking.

The police minister was also a publican with interests in at least three hotels in the State, convincing Labor premier Bob Carr that the viability of the hotel industry depended upon pubs getting access to poker machines. For every poker machine they acquired, the capital value of Whelan's hotels increased by $350,000. Acquiring ten poker machines, for example, meant the capital value of a hotel increased by a whopping $3.5 million. Today, the hotel industry has boomed exponentially to the point where New South Welshmen (and women) are losing about $3.67 billion dollars every year on the 22,000 poker machines acquired by hotels since Whelan's windfall according to the last quarterly report published by Liquor & Gaming NSW.

Meanwhile the State's prisons were acquiring people who were once accommodated in mental institutions on a scale comparable to increases in the capital value of hotels. According to figures published by Corrections Health Service, about 85 per cent of female prisoners and 70 per cent of male prisoners were treated for mental illness in the twelve months before their incarceration. But Joanne and I agreed that Stephen would not be classified as a mentally ill prisoner, and we were sceptical about his supposedly low IQ. The intelligence rating had limited value when applied to people who lived in institutions for most of their lives. Many simply lacked the experience to understand the questions posed in the IQ test. Stephen was intuitive and intelligent in areas not measured by the psychologists.

Joanne repeated her observation that New South Wales was still a penal colony so far as she was concerned. Few crimes went unpunished when the Rum Corp ran Sydney—suspects were routinely rounded up by the constabulary and flogged until someone confessed. Officers of the Rum Corp simply jailed anyone who spoke out against their corrupt practices, including Governor William Bligh, who knew a bit about insurrection from his experience as ship's captain on 'The Bounty'. Twenty years after the British founded the colony of New South Wales, the Rum Corp arrested Bligh and overthrew the government.

Joanne wanted to know if I thought Bob Carr was ratcheting up police powers in the State. The jury was still out on the former journalist turned politician who did much for national parks and education but little for civil liberties and human rights in the State. He came to government in 1995 in the early days of the Wood Royal Commission into police corruption—without knowing terribly much about what police were doing wrong. I worried that Carr wanted a Forensic Research Investigation and Science Centre as part of the police portfolio, competing with the Australian Federal Police who were already underway with their state-of-the-art forensic laboratory in Sydney for investigating federal crime. Plans were in hand to change the corporate identity of the New South Wales police from 'Police Service' to 'Police Force'.

When I was first elected to the upper house crossbench in 1999, Carr invited me to his parliamentary office for a chat. I told him about my work in the aftermath of Queensland's Fitzgerald inquiry into political and police corruption when I was responsible for drafting a human rights bill for the Sunshine State. Although an aficionado of American history, the premier was no fan of a bill of rights whether constitutional or statutory. He thought it gave too much power to unelected judges.

One of the first things I did in the upper house was ask Attorney General Jeff Shaw QC for a reference to the Law and Justice Committee (of which I was a member) to investigate the possibility of a bill of rights for New South Wales. Carr was furious and never invited me back to his office. The bill of rights inquiry went ahead, and although the government refused to recommend a bill of rights for New South Wales, the people of the State secured instead a Legislation Review Committee—thanks largely to the hard work of Labor committee chair Ron Dyer OAM.

Back in my office in Macquarie Street, I contacted the office of the police minister and picked up some application forms for Stephen Jamieson and a couple of other prisoners who wanted to question the DNA evidence used to convict them. The forms ran to just two pages and were to the point—if crime scene material could be found, it would be re-tested using new and more sophisticated DNA enhancing technology.

A recent case in Queensland had highlighted the potential problems of flawed DNA testing. Frank Button was convicted in 1999 of raping a 13-year-old girl in her home and sentenced to a lengthy jail term. In 2001, the Queensland Court of Appeal overturned the conviction when further DNA testing identified the real offender. Button had always maintained his innocence even though there was no statutory right to a review of the DNA evidence against him. It seemed never to have occurred to the authorities that the DNA laboratory doing the testing was capable of making a mistake. Only when comparing DNA from the victim's bedsheets to the national DNA database did the laboratory identify the right perpetrator.

While the case of Jamieson, Blessington and Elliott was the first case in Australian legal history where DNA evidence had helped convict the accused, Button's case was the first in which DNA evidence was used to acquit an innocent convict. Button's defence team relied on the common law to secure his conviction review. Jamieson would need to go down the same track via the Innocence Panel as there was still no statutory right to a review of DNA evidence in New South Wales.

In a review of the State's forensic DNA laws published in February 2002 by the parliament's Standing Committee on Law and Justice, consideration was given to a submission by the Privacy Commissioner, Chris Puplick AM, which included the following: *The issue which is being addressed at the moment is part of a continuing debate within New South Wales seeking to balance the need for community protection...against the need for there to be some limitation on the powers of police and law enforcement authorities.* Puplick was a former member of the Australian Senate nominated by the Liberal Party, a member of the Innocence Panel and an acquaintance since the 1970s when he was federal president of the Young Liberals. At the time, I fancied myself as a prospective federal MP.

One recommendation of the 2002 Standing Committee's review of forensic DNA laws asked the Attorney General to *consider examining the access of defendants to crime scene samples and the availability of funding to enable independent DNA analysis by the defence.* Professor Mark Findlay of the University of Sydney's Institute of Criminology prepared a response to the review on behalf of the Attorney, expressing *budgetary concerns if, as the Committee recommends, Government funding should be made available to facilitate independent analysis [of DNA] for defence purposes.* Like Frank Button in Queensland, innocent convicts in New South Wales still had some distance to travel if they hoped to question the DNA evidence that helped convict them.

Chapter 15

MATTHEW ELLIOTT

In 1983 a teenage girl, Lynda Mann, was raped and murdered in a small village in Leicestershire in the UK. Three years later in the same village, Dawn Ashworth, another teenager, suffered the same fate. The crimes were almost identical and Leicestershire police charged Richard Buckland with the second killing when he revealed, after long and intensive questioning lasting 15 hours, certain previously unreleased information about the body of Dawn Ashworth and 'confessed' to her rape and murder. But Buckland denied any knowledge of the earlier crimes against Lynda Mann. Because of similarities in the two crime scenes, police sent semen samples from vaginal swabs of the two victims to Alec Jeffries of Leicester University who had discovered a method of identifying individuals from their DNA.

Professor Jeffries completed his analysis of the semen samples and confirmed that the same person was indeed the culprit in both cases. But that person was not Richard Buckland, who later said he confessed to the rape and murder of Dawn Ashworth only to put an end to the police questioning. A mass screening of the male population of the village then followed with no match to the killer's DNA profile. Afterwards, one of the locals was overheard boasting about standing in for his friend, Colin Pitchfork, the local baker, during the screening. In 1988, police secured a sample of the baker's DNA. Pitchfork was tried and sentenced to two life terms for the crimes committed against the young women.

At the beginning of 2003—when the Innocence Panel began its work—the genetic 'fingerprint' evidence was routine, and DNA profiling technology so sophisticated that a person could be identified from just a few cells left at a crime scene. Further DNA analysis of the bandana used to gag Janine Balding might help resolve the question whether Shorty Jamieson or Shorty Wells was involved in the crimes against the young woman. But finding the physical evidence from the trial after a dozen years would be the first challenge, not to mention the problem of access since police held all physical evidence from crime scenes in New South Wales. Following conviction of an offender, the head of police investigations decided whether the evidence would be destroyed, and the decision usually turned on whether the offender had appealed.

While I was keen to get access to the evidence in the Balding case, I was also painfully aware that the young woman's parents would be mortified by any attempt to diminish the culpability of those already convicted of degrading and then extinguishing the life of their daughter. Part of me wanted to contact the Balding family and alert them to my efforts on behalf of Jamieson, explaining my motivation as the need to protect the justice system from corruption. Another part of me understood that anything done to help convicted prisoners was often condemned as an act of treachery against the victims of crime and their families.

Victims play a significant role in the investigation and prosecution of crime, although problems can arise for prisoners and their advocates because of the natural alliance between victims and police. Lawyers are taught that it's better for ten guilty people to go free than to allow one innocent person to be convicted—the Blackstone ratio. Police and the families of victims would first like to know the criminal records of the ten and whether they represent a threat to the community. The tension between the two positions was the 'Laura Norder' (law 'n order) debate, which frequently lead to a widespread belief that the justice system was failing everybody. A greater understanding between victims and their supporters and those representing perpetrators would be a useful contribution.

In the face of Justice Newman's unambiguous Never to be Released legal assessment of Shorty Jamieson's involvement in the crimes against Janine Balding—plus the horror stories in the newspapers based on the convict's physical appearance—I knew on some level that the only response I could anticipate from Janine Balding's family was hostile indignation. How would I feel about a complete stranger opening old wounds on account of some fanciful idea that an injustice had been done?

My worst fears exploded into the real world on 14 June 2002 when a five-column article with photographs of myself and Janine Balding appeared in *The Australian* newspaper under the headline 'They've got the wrong Shorty, says MP', and quoting Janine Balding's mother, Beverley Balding, to the effect that she was devastated by my support for Jamieson. On the following day, a further article on the front page of the same masthead implied I was romantically in love with Jamieson.

For two days, I went to ground while the media services peppered the message bank service on my mobile phone. By the time I rang back, the story was no longer news, and almost nobody wanted to talk with me. One good outcome prompted by the newspaper story was a telephone call from John Curtinsmith who was head of the Young Offenders Board when Janine Balding was murdered. Now retired, Curtinsmith said his staff also believed Shorty Jamieson was innocent, and he related a story one of his staff told him about Matthew Elliott's reaction to the life sentences. According to the staff member, Elliott turned to Jamieson following the judge's sentencing diktat and said, 'What's it like to be sentenced to life for a murder you never committed?' The retired head of the Young Offenders Board also informed me that Shorty Jamieson was an 'old boy' from Werrington Park, a home for State wards located behind Cobham Court. Psychologist Peter Irons and juvenile justice manager Lee Mansfield may be able to provide more information about the *Jamieson case.*

I wrote to Carmel Tebbutt, the amiable Minister for Juvenile Justice, and one of my colleagues in the Legislative Council, seeking permission to approach Lee Mansfield and Peter Irons for an interview. The minister had no objection to me contacting Lee Mansfield, but Peter Irons no longer worked for the juvenile justice department. I called Lee Mansfield who filled me with hope that I could secure another independent opinion about Shorty Jamieson's convictions. I made a note in my fast-growing file.

> *Spoke to Lee Mansfield, manager of the Juvenile Justice Community Services office at Blacktown. She was the Juvenile Justice Officer for Matthew Elliott and did a report and gave evidence for him at his trial...Matthew told her right from the beginning that police had the wrong Shorty...After the boys were sentenced, she went downstairs*

at Darlinghurst court to the cells. The boys were in three separate glass cages. Matthew and Bronson had white shirts on and their faces were as white as their shirts. She spoke with Matthew while Peter Irons spoke with Bronson. Nobody was there for Stephen 'because of the way he is'. Bronson was curled up in the foetal position in his cell. Peter Irons asked how he felt and Bronson said, 'I can only think about how Jamieson must feel...' About a year after the three were sentenced, Lee spoke to Matthew at Minda and said, 'Please tell me Jamieson was there that night'. Matthew said, 'I wish I could say something else, but he wasn't there'.

Another response I received to the newspaper story was a call from Judge Peter Moss KC, head of the Serious Offenders Review Council (SORC). Moss expressed his concern about life sentences for juveniles. During Joanne Harris' application for a judicial inquiry into Shorty Jamieson's convictions, Judge Moss spoke with Matthew Elliott at Long Bay jail. Elliott offered to provide an affidavit confirming that Shorty Jamieson was not involved in the crimes against Janine Balding. The judge described Elliott as 'an impressive young man'. I asked whether Elliott had provided the affidavit and the judge said that Shorty Jamieson's lawyers hadn't followed it up.

Judge Moss informed me that SORC made a submission to the Attorney General about the illegality of the cement law and he, Moss, was concerned that the submission failed to surface in parliamentary debate on the bill. One of the unfair aspects of the law, he said, was that it prevented a reduction in the security classification of the affected prisoners, which meant they received no incentives or rewards for good behaviour. A copy of the SORC submission appeared on my fax machine soon afterwards and it emphasised the injustice of the ten Never to be Released prisoners being treated as a job lot.

> *Most importantly, no account has been taken of the prisoners' history since the commencement of their respective sentences, nor of evidence pointing, in some cases, to considerable attempts having been made towards rehabilitation. The legitimate expectation each prisoner [had] of eventually becoming eligible to apply for parole under the currently applicable principles of law has not been recognised.*

Chapter 16

LAURA NORDER

A few days after Easter in 2003, I arrived late one morning at Goulburn jail to interview Jamieson and Blessington together, an arrangement the correctional officers called a 'combined visit'. The visit caused no grief to the authorities as the two prisoners were classified as co-offenders and both were housed in B wing, the cell block for inmates who were not a threat to themselves or others, but who had been targeted by other prisoners. As before, my visit was designated for the education wing which adjoined the Circle, where the fan of four cell blocks meet at their axis point. Due to staff shortages, the education wing was closed, so the usual gaggle of professional visitors to the jail crowded into the Circle offices.

Social workers, lawyers, prison chaplains, police and psychologists jostled each other for space and privacy in what seemed to be a morning of chaos in the prison. Squad officers—the prison equivalent of a tactical response group—mingled with the crowd and everyone seemed uneasy. I realised the squad were there to access the yards for the usual lunchtime muster, a menacing sight in their black military boots, thick black belts drawn tightly around blue overalls, and blue baseball caps.

I shared the corner of a desk with a Legal Aid solicitor until his client arrived, and then I discreetly moved my chair to a quiet spot in the foyer, on the fringe of the hullabaloo caused by too many people in the Circle offices. A man introduced himself as the senior correctional officer. He asked if I was alright and I assured him the midday muster was no big deal—I was happy to share my time in prison with Laura Norder.

By the time Blessington and Jamieson arrived, a measure of calm had been restored to the Circle offices, even while the number of squad officers was steadily increasing. I conducted the interview in the foyer for perhaps ten minutes, traversing the weather, prospects for our favourite teams in the rugby league competition and the latest news from the people at Legal Aid who were considering the prisoners' appeal rights. Our respective papers languished on the floor in three separate piles.

Then another half dozen squad officers burst into the Circle offices and announced a security problem. Prison staff could not conduct the midday muster in the Circle yard with so many visitors in the offices and we were ordered to leave. I gathered up my papers and began making my farewells when the senior correctional officer asked whether I would like to continue the interview with Blessington and Jamieson in B wing. I would indeed and I followed the officer and the two prisoners through the melee and out into the Circle yard.

I stopped for a moment and gazed out over the accommodation buildings and their adjoining yards, overcrowded with bored and restless men whose living conditions were similar to a zoo. A prisoner called out at the top of his voice from one of the yards.

"Fuckin' 'orrible, ain't it!"

Another yelled out, "Piss off, civvy cunt!"

I seemed to be stuck in my stride despite the exhortations from all directions to move on. The squad officers were clustered around an open gate that lead to D wing where the Aboriginal inmates came forward in response to their names being called. One of the squad officers turned in my direction and called out.

"What the fuck are you doin' in here?" He began walking towards me, striding along with a menacing gait.

I took off like a summer blowfly and hurried towards the B wing gate where the two prisoners and the senior officer were waiting, their faces devoid of any reassurance.

"It's alright," the senior officer called out, waving away the squad officer bearing down on me.

Jamieson grinned broadly while Blessington rolled his eyes as I attempted to make light of the situation by praising the value of free speech. Animals in the zoo will sometimes throw shit at visitors. No doubt I would do the same if I were a prisoner. The senior officer opened the steel gate and suddenly we were inside B wing—seriously in jail.

Prisoners were housed on three levels in cement cells with cream coloured steel-plate doors in the style of nineteenth century prisons. You could see the prisoners inside their cells only by pressing your face against the narrow slit in the cell door. I'd no stomach for such an intrusion. Two steel-mesh nets were strung overhead between the upper levels like a double safety net at the circus, presumably to stop inmates jumping off the steel landings. B wing was designated for 'protection' inmates, the senior officer told me, prisoner movement was highly regulated. My own observation suggested that inmates were wandering around like Brown's cows.

Prisoners criss-crossed in front and behind us as we hurried along at a quickening pace, and although I could see prison officers walking the landings upstairs, none of them were within barking distance. By the time we reached the offices at the other end of the building, I was almost walking on the heels of the senior prison officer, and it was a great relief when he opened the door of the main office and locked it behind us. The two prisoners and I followed him into an adjoining office. He offered us seats at a wooden desk where we placed our papers and then he gave us instructions to knock him up when we were ready to leave.

I wanted to know about Stephen's biological family and he informed me his mother visited him once, just before she "joined the bloke upstairs" in 1985. He had a sister who lived in the country and two brothers in the Blue Mountains. His father lived in Sydney. I asked for their addresses, which he knew "off by hand," but he told me not to bother writing to them because they won't write back. Nobody visited him except for lawyers and welfare workers—perhaps the worst of his many punishments.

"You could be right about that."

His earliest memory as a child was being moved around between foster families until he was seven or eight years old when the State placed him in Clairvaux House at Katoomba in the Blue Mountains. There he came under the fortuitous care of Yvonne and Arthur Yates, who raised him as if he were their own child—a younger 'brother' to their boy Garth.

The discussion led to Mark 'Shorty' Wells, a subject the prisoners found highly amusing. During their trial, they came under relentless attack from the media for fooling around and joking in the dock, but they could not help themselves—Shorty Wells always sent them into fits of laughter. A diagnosed schizophrenic, Wells adopted the dress and mannerisms of his multiple personalities. On one occasion he turned up to court in army fatigues and green beret, announcing he was in the SAS and to please get on with the case because he had to leave early and make a parachute jump. On the day of the murder of Janine Balding he was a Ninja fighter replete with fighting stick and black bandana around his head.

Jamieson produced from his papers Mark Wells' statement to Queensland police. Once again, I was astounded by the extent of his records, and his ability to produce on demand almost any document in the case. Blessington had very few papers by comparison. I noticed Jamieson had a different bundle to the collection he had at our first interview. They were rank like the last lot, but neatly folded and stacked chronologically. I asked again about his meticulous files and he said he intended opening a corruption museum when he got out of jail. His papers would be "exhibit number one." When I laughed, he wanted to know what was so funny, and I apologised profusely.

Wells' statement to Queensland police gave a chillingly accurate description of Janine Balding's abduction, nominating himself as one of her kidnappers. He said he was in the back seat of her stolen car as it travelled from Sutherland railway station to Minchinbury and he described the place of her murder. He also named Shorty Jamieson as the main offender and Elliott and Blessington as co-offenders.

How did Wells get away with that?

"The Crown Prosecutor got Wells in the witness box and asked him how he knew about the murder," Blessington said. "Wells then told the Crown Prosecutor he was a devil worshipper and he had a vision about what happened. Then Jamo's barrister said to Wells, 'You know about the crimes because you were there, isn't that right, Mr Wells'? Wells then broke down and cried in the witness box and that's when the Crown Prosecutor produced the indemnity from prosecution. After that, Shorty Wells said he's not answerin' no more questions, and the judge told him to stand down. So, nobody got to hear what else he had to say."

I speculated that Jamieson's legal advisers would probably have been reluctant to call for production of Shorty Wells' statement to police as it was given more than a year after the murder. And in view of Wells' mental state, one year down the track was probably a sufficient passage of time for Wells to have no idea whether he or Jamieson made the fateful trip on the train from Central to Sutherland. Wells naming Jamieson as the main offender was also a free kick for the Crown Prosecutor who had no convincing evidence against Jamieson other than his police record of interview.

"What about Ian Glover," said Blessington, "the bloke in prison who said Jamo told him he was there?"

Glover was the convicted paedophile who told a jury of the first trial that Jamieson 'confessed' in prison to his involvement in the crimes against Janine Balding. Glover died before the second trial—his evidence was read to the new jury. Notoriously unreliable, prison 'confessions' were generally at the bottom of the evidentiary pile in criminal trials. On the day Jamieson was supposed to have told Glover that he, Jamieson, was involved in the Janine Balding crimes, Glover was actually attending court and housed in another prison. Nobody could take him seriously, but unlike Shorty Wells, there was nothing funny about the prison witness.

"He was a lyin' dog," Jamieson volunteered.

Perhaps the most damaging part of Glover's evidence was that it caused Stephen Jamieson to seriously misbehave in court. He swung onto a handrail surrounding the dock and launched himself in the general direction of the public gallery where a group of police officers had incurred his wrath with sotto voce comments to the effect that Glover's evidence was the last nail in the prisoner's coffin and he was about to go down.

"I overshot the mark and had to come back for the copper given' me the lip," he said with gusto and bravado.

The police officers wrestled the crowd-surfing prisoner to the floor of the court—even as he was punching and thrashing at them—handcuffed him and dragged him downstairs to the cells. A short time later he was back in court and resumed his place in the dock as if nothing had happened.

"That was just me goin' off," said Stephen Jamieson to nobody in particular.

With that profound and unexpected insight, the two prisoners collapsed in gales of infectious laughter. I looked out from the office into the cavernous prison, hardly knowing whether to laugh or cry. The prison resembled the inside of a giant sea monster. Overhead, the wire safety nets fanned out like sagging sinews between the creature's steel ribs.

From a legal perspective, Stephen Jamieson's prosecution was a terrible thing—the word sickening came to mind. To put a man on trial for crimes that anyone who looked objectively at the evidence would know was a police stitch up beggared belief. I confirmed that his application with the Innocence Panel was being processed and I promised to stay on the case until it was resolved. I explained that the panel was supposed to give innocent convicts the chance to get the evidence that convicted them tested for DNA if there was any possibility that developments in forensic science might help them.

"What about getting that Innocence Panel to test the bandana for DNA?" said Blessington, now recovered from the hilarity.

What good would that do?

"Well, Shorty Wells' bandana was used to gag Janine Balding, and maybe his DNA is still on it," Blessington said, flicking through his papers and locating the affidavit he'd prepared and signed with Joanne Harris. It was a long affidavit. He spent several minutes reading the last few pages, then checking what he'd read previously, before going over the earlier pages.

"I thought it was in there."

You thought what was in there?

He handed me the affidavit. "I thought I said how Matthew Elliott gagged Janine Balding with Shorty's bandana."

I glanced absent-mindedly at Stephen Jamieson as I looked through the affidavit. Matthew gagged Janine Balding with your bandana?

"I weren't there," he said resignedly, repeating his mantra. The penny dropped. Sorry mate!

Wells would need to explain how his bandana turned up at the murder scene, but any evidence linking Wells to the crimes against Janine Balding was just one more piece in the evidentiary jigsaw puzzle. Even if the bandana belonged to Shorty Wells, how did that prove Shorty Jamieson wasn't there? I was still looking at Jamieson without expecting him to answer my rhetorical question.

"I'd hardly be wearin' the bastard's bandana," he said, an expression of indignation on his face. But then he looked at Blessington, and it was all too much—the three of us fell about laughing. The prisoners were effusive in their unnecessary apologies for dragging me into their convict humour. To the contrary, humour was an important part of our mutual defence mechanisms—probably embedded in our DNA.

When the laughter subsided, I asked Jamieson about his police record of interview. Had he given any more thought to it since we last spoke? Did he still say his signatures on the document were a forgery?

"I've been thinkin' about that," he said, leaning casually across the desk. "It's a bit weird me admittin' to a crime and givin' the coppers all the information about it when I weren't there." He sat back on his chair. "I would'na signed the confession if I was sober."

I gave thanks for his improved memory, and at the same time I hoped he was not simply picking up on an idea I'd put in his head. Anything was possible. Still, it was comforting to know he'd returned to the evidence given at his trial. Depending on the outcome of the new DNA testing, I would then consider handing him over to the Prisoners Legal Service at Legal Aid for another crack at a judicial inquiry. Failing that, it was back to the common law.

As for Blessington, I realised that the decision to help with his case was made the first time I met him because I was so moved by the work he did in prison teaching scripture to other prisoners and offering them hope. I was also fascinated by his willingness to take up Shorty Jamieson's cause. The second trial judge, Justice Newman, gave no credibility in his sentencing remarks to the claim that police had arrested the wrong Shorty. If Jamieson's claim of innocence proved to be *a tissue of lies* as the judge had decided, Blessington would do immense damage to his own efforts to appeal his sentence by perpetuating the lies. He appeared to me to be a truthful witness and I observed that Jamieson respected him.

Following the combined visit, I left the prison thinking that Shorty Jamieson had the bones of a case to demonstrate his innocence of the crimes against Janine Balding, and Bronson Blessington was an unlikely candidate for a life sentence—even though he was certainly guilty of his crimes. Given his age and mental capacity at the time, Blessington's life sentence with no opportunity for parole was disproportionate punishment on a grand scale. But many people would still say that liars and sociopaths were leading me up the garden path. There was also the print and verbal abuse I received when I argued the case for the prisoners during parliamentary debate on the cement law, abuse I could expect to be repeated with a vengeance if Jamieson's proposed application to the Innocence Panel caused undue anxiety to the victims of crime.

At the end of the street outside the prison, I took the wrong turn and found myself driving along the avenue of churches that winds its way through the city of Goulburn. The greenstone Catholic Cathedral of Saints Peter and Paul is a modest building by comparison with the Gothic sandstone grandeur of the Anglican

Cathedral of Saint Saviour, just down the road. Settling myself into the back pew of the lesser cathedral, it occurred to me that if God exists, he/she/they must celebrate our differences. Abandoning prayer after the usual disconsolate invocations, I searched about for something to read before seizing upon a folded church bulletin wedged into the back of the pew in front of me—a relic from the recent Easter services. Under the heading 'Prayers of the Faithful', the bulletin read: *Pray for those unjustly deprived of their freedom; may they draw hope and comfort from the risen Lord.*

Chapter 17

STEVE PEARSON

The Director of Public Prosecutions for New South Wales, Nicholas Cowdery AO, KC, was a giant amongst lawyers in my opinion, and one of the few public figures in the law who was genuinely free to say exactly what he thought on account of the independence of his office. When I wrote and asked him one too many questions about the prosecution of Shorty Jamieson, Cowdery sent an instant reply, effectively telling me to jump in the lake, and enclosing a copy of a protocol from the Attorney General's Department informing bureaucrats how they should deal with troublesome politicians. For good measure, Cowdery suggested I direct future correspondence about Shorty Jamieson through the office of the Attorney General.

A few weeks earlier, a more amenable Nick Cowdery had kindly written to me with information in the public arena about Jamieson's joggers, which were taken from the convict for forensic analysis following his arrest. Jamieson had alerted me to the missing joggers when he asked if I could arrange to get them back from police. Prior to that, I knew nothing about his footwear—other than what appeared in the trial transcripts. Cowdery informed me in a letter that the joggers were delivered to Senior Constable Steve Pearson who was in charge of the physical evidence in the Janine Balding case. Pearson observed shoe impressions in the edge of the dam where the young woman was drowned and he photographed them soon after her body was found. Jamieson said nobody was about to find his shoe impressions near the dam "because I weren't there." He could see no reason for police not to return his joggers.

I was anxious to confirm what was glaringly obvious from the credible evidence: Blessington and Elliott were the only offenders involved in drowning Janine Balding. Several witnesses saw the boys at the Mt Druitt Shopping Centre within two hours of the murder, and all who gave evidence at the first trial said Elliott and Blessington had mud up to their knees. Some witnesses said the two youths bought thongs at the shopping centre and discarded their muddy shoes. There were no outstanding issues concerning Shorty Jamieson's joggers or Shorty Wells' motorcycle boots. If anything incriminating had turned up about either Shorty's footwear, a reference to it would have appeared in transcripts of evidence at one of the two trials.

I telephoned Steve Pearson at the Dubbo police station where he was part of the Orana Local Area Command. On the phone he sounded like a nice bloke, good for a chat, professional at his work and anxious to help in whatever way he could. He was reading *The Blooding* by Joseph Wambaugh at the time of Janine Balding's murder, a book about Colin Pitchfork and the Leicester murders, and he told me the book gave him the idea to send forensic samples from the Janine Balding crime scenes to Professor Jeffries at Leicester University for DNA testing. Meanwhile, Jeffries had licensed Cellmark Diagnostics at Abingdon near Oxford to undertake the testing procedure. Cellmark did the DNA profiling and provided expert witnesses for the trial of Jamieson, Elliott and Blessington. I asked Pearson about tracking down other exhibits in the case—apart from the forensic samples—and he gave me several names and telephone numbers to begin my search. The physical evidence was stored in sealed plastic bags at Penrith police station, he recalled.

Mention of sealed plastic bags was bad news so far as preserving DNA was concerned since any moisture in the bags would create a hothouse environment—ideal for fungal growth that damages or destroys DNA material. Steve Pearson said the principal investigating officer would usually decide to destroy the physical evidence once the appeals process was exhausted. This was seriously bad news and I wondered why police had total control over the exhibits in a murder trial other than to bolster their law enforcement powers. Then Pearson cheered me up no end—he had a copy of the court brief together with photographic negatives of the exhibits including the black bandana. I asked if I could travel to Dubbo and visit him. No problem, since we were both fans of the radio shock jocks who dominated country airwaves, especially John Laws. I particularly liked Lawsy even though he'd torn strips off me a few times over my involvement in the *Jamieson case*.

I called Detective Sergeant Andrew Brady of the Crime Scene Section at the Sydney Police Centre. Brady agreed that the physical evidence from the trial would most likely have been destroyed after all this time. I quoted some reference numbers, which I'd obtained from Penrith police, and the policeman said he would check them out and contact me. A few minutes later Brady called back and explained that the numbers I'd given him were crime scene reference numbers. He needed the numbers on the exhibits receipt. If I could get those numbers he would know where to look for the exhibits. At that point I was contemplating my weekly lotto numbers as the best bet for getting access to the crime scene evidence, and then I remembered that Steve Pearson had a copy of the court brief, which was likely to include the correct numbers.

My plans to visit Steve Pearson included preparing a list of the things I wanted to follow up. I had the benefit of his statement of evidence from the trial, which I borrowed from Joanne Harris. I wanted to know about the fingerprints found in Janine Balding's Holden Gemini; the photographs of the shoe impressions around the dam; the position of the body in the dam; and the photographs of the black bandana. The statement of evidence also revealed that Steve Pearson attended the Westmead mortuary and took photographs of the body before and after it was cleaned. He was present when an autopsy examination was conducted by the government medical officer, Dr Peter Ellis, who handed over a sexual assault information kit, which included body cavity swabs to be tested against blood samples from the accused for matching DNA profiles.

The trip to Dubbo to discuss the Janine Balding case with Steve Pearson was a drama from beginning to end. I woke late in the morning after a night of bad dreams. Falling out of my hole-in-the-wall flat in Sydney, I stumbled along College Street with my overnight bag. A taxi rolled along in the prickly heat. The driver mercifully ignored me on the trip to the airport while I stared down the last of the night demons. Somewhere between the taxi and the aircraft, I managed to lose my keys and mobile phone, and so I recalled my overnight bag which I'd checked in at the departure terminal. After what seemed an eternity, my overnight bag appeared at the baggage counter in the hands of a young man dressed in engineer's overalls. Rifling through the bag, I could not locate the keys or the mobile phone, and then I found them in a plastic tray near the hand luggage X-Ray machine—exactly where I'd placed them after checking in.

On the way to the departure lounge, I gulped down a cup of coffee that was too hot to drink quickly, and it gave me an instant headache. I reached the half-empty plane just before the stairs were withdrawn and flopped into my allocated seat, which smelled like vomit. Several times I changed seats until it dawned on me that the stink was in the air conditioning. I buried my head in Chris Geraghty's *Cassocks in the Wilderness*, a book about the junior seminary at Springwood where I spent a couple of curious years in my youth studying philosophy and theology. Chris taught liturgical studies at the senior seminary at Manly. Years later, our paths crossed in the law—he became a District Court judge—and in the business of writing books. I liked his progressive writing about an anachronistic Christian church.

Air turbulence jolted me out of my reverie as the plane lurched and bounced through the opposing forces of rising heat and the cold jet stream. The harbour city was shrouded in brown smog and heat haze, with just the tops of the tallest buildings visible from the aircraft window. Soon the aircraft was crossing the Blue Mountains. I peered down at the rocky grey ledges, towering treetops, deep ravines and gorges of the World Heritage national park. Beyond the mountains the western slopes and plains stretched out like a scalloped baker's tray, scattered mud-pie dams and water holes struggling to survive the latest drought. Fifty minutes after leaving Sydney, the aircraft dropped into the hot air and tracked a bumpy course to the Dubbo airstrip.

My mother was a Parkes girl who left home as a teenager to work in the Dubbo branch of the Commercial Banking Company of Sydney, a brick and stone building in a main street lined with fleshy hackberry trees and golden Robinia. She married my father during post-war celebrations and had a child every two years for the next 16 years. My primary school years consisted of serial dusty schoolyards and changing curricula, traipsing along with my siblings from one country town to the next, while our parents searched for the right job, the cheapest house and the best Catholic school education they could afford for their children. I attended a different school each year of my primary education, and by the time I arrived in Sydney in the late 1950s, I was a restless, rebellious youth.

Around the corner from my mother's old bank, I found the Dubbo police station, a modern three-storey brick and steel building that included regional police headquarters. Senior Constable Steve Pearson turned out to be the consummate professional policeman, a beanpole bushy with silver grey hair and searching blue eyes to match his blue serge uniform. I handed the policeman a copy of the letter from Nick Cowdery nominating him as the person in charge of physical evidence in the Janine Balding murder investigation.

The policeman said he still held the negatives of all the photographs in the police brief of evidence. I wanted to confirm that only two sets of footprints led into and out of the dam—those of Blessington and Elliott—consistent with those two offenders being the only ones to have mud up to their knees and to have sexually assaulted and murdered Ms Balding. Pearson told the jury of the first trial that he photographed two sets of footprints running parallel to each other. The impressions leading into the dam were slightly deeper than those leading out. I was also interested in the results of the physical examination of Jamieson's joggers. The policeman did not recall receiving the joggers but promised to check his records. Other details of the case he recalled "as if it happened yesterday" and the thought occurred to me that police investigating serious crime were never far from the trauma they shared with the victims' families.

We chatted about life in the country and the policeman informed me that he'd travelled to Wagga Wagga a few days earlier and looked up Janine Balding's parents, Kerry and Beverley, who owned a joinery business in town. The policeman handed me their business card, urging me to pay them a visit and "see what crime does to families." I agonised over Beverley and Kerry Balding, who still suffered inconsolably from the death of their daughter. Beverley's book about Janine's murder, *The Janine Balding Story*, was a cry from the heart, and she remained a fierce advocate of the death penalty for those responsible for the crime. How do you tell a mother that the two children who sexually assaulted and murdered her daughter appeared to have grown into men who led reformed lives, while their convicted co-accused seemed to be innocent?

Steve Pearson would not have a bar of Stephen Jamieson being the wrong Shorty. As evidence, he pointed to the way the prisoner "went off" in court. I explained Jamieson's version of what happened—police in the courtroom had provoked him—and perhaps his reaction was consistent with his claim of innocence.

The investigator in Steve Pearson said it was a possibility, but his words were unconvincing. For all that, the policeman was affable and open, and I had the feeling he would consider any credible information on offer. The longer we spoke, the more talkative he became, and I made a note to ask him if the black bandana was tested for DNA.

One myth I wanted to explode with Steve Pearson's help was the suggestion that any of the accused had anal intercourse with Janine Balding. I reminded the policeman that Blessington, Elliott and Wilmot were all convicted of rape, but only Jamieson was convicted on the anal intercourse charge for which he was sentenced to eight years. I remained baffled as to how the judge arrived at this discrete conviction and sentence when the prosecution appeared to have offered no evidence for the allegation—other than the questionable police record of interview. Pearson said he had spoken to Michele Franco, the crime laboratory biologist who examined the forensic material taken by Dr Peter Ellis during the autopsy, and Michele may be able to assist with my inquiries. He gave me her contact details.

I asked the policeman if he wondered why just one of the police witnesses, Andrew Lonergan, could identify Shorty Jamieson in the dock while three of the four co-accused identified Shorty Wells as the culprit. The senior constable screwed up his face and perhaps he was recalling the haunting television and newspaper images following Jamieson's arrest.

"Jamieson looked almost normal during his trial. His hair was cut short, he was clean-shaven and he wore clean clothes," said the policeman. "His only recognisable feature was those

Neanderthal jowls," he added disconcertingly, rolling clenched fists around his cheeks.

Andrew Lonergan said that one of the young people he observed at the Mt Druitt Shopping Centre on the night of the murder looked *a bit like an ape* according to a statement he made to Detective Sergeant Dayment in 1990 after the first trial was abandoned. Lonergan picked out a photograph of Jamieson as *the one I would describe as an ape...I did see him on the news when he was arrested and I recognised him immediately.* The evidence was too cute by half—a rabbit hole for another day—but highly damaging to Jamieson. I conveyed my thoughts to Pearson about the Lonergan evidence.

"What about Mrs Matyas?" said Pearson. "She identified Jamieson."

Like Andrew Lonergan, Elva Matyas did not come forward until the end of the first trial when a sketch of Shorty Jamieson appeared in a Sydney newspaper. In fact, the witness presented herself to police on the basis that none of the boys she had seen that day looked like the boy depicted in the newspaper sketch. Matyas gave evidence that she was on the train to Sutherland on the afternoon of the murder and at one stage during the trip, two of the boys sat in the seat opposite her in the railway carriage. Ultimately, she could only say that a photograph (not the newspaper sketch) of Jamieson "looked like" the person she saw on the train. She was unable to positively identify him in court. And the witness could not recall whether the newspaper publishing the sketch of Shorty Jamieson that concerned her in the first place also included an accompanying story that said Jamieson was the last of the Balding killers to be arrested.

The only other evidence to implicate Shorty Jamieson in the crimes against Janine Balding—apart from the contested police record of interview—was the testimony of prison inmate Ian Glover. I handed the Glover statement to Senior Constable Pearson, pointing to the words that Jamieson was supposed to have used in his 'confession' to the prisoner.

Glover was interviewed by Detective Sergeant Kevin Raue at North Sydney police cells on 2 November 1988. According to the statement, Jamieson had a discussion with Glover in the protection yard at Long Bay jail on 11 October 1988 when they were both on remand and Jamieson was supposed to have admitted his part in the abduction, rape and murder of Janine Balding. It turned out that Glover appeared at North Sydney Court on the day of Jamieson's 'confession'—miles from the Long Bay prison complex at Malabar in Sydney's east.

When I suggested to the policeman that Glover's evidence was designed to help him, Glover, as much as the investigating police, Pearson reminded me that questions to that effect were put to Glover at the first trial. Even though evidence volunteered by prison inmates about each other was notoriously unreliable, Glover told the court he was infected with the AIDS virus and would receive no benefit from lying to the jury. Indeed, Glover died of the disease between the first and second trials, and whatever advantage he obtained from his testimony, he took it to the grave.

At some point, I realised that Steve Pearson and I had an abyss between us. He was never going to assist in deconstructing the case against Stephen Jamieson. Looking at new evidence was one thing, but tampering with the existing case put together by police and prosecutors was not on the policeman's agenda. I asked again about photographs of the footprints at the dam and he said it was impossible to distinguish between the various impregnations in the mud. He promised to have another look at the photographs and to make inquiries about Stephen's joggers. I asked about the fingerprints in Janine Balding's car and the policeman gave me the telephone number of Senior Constable Geoff Smith who was in charge of the latent print section of police forensics.

Leaving Dubbo airport just on dusk, the aircraft banked to the right before heading east, and I enjoyed a splendid view of the sun setting behind pink and gold ribbons of rainless cloud. I found myself running my fingers along the edge of the Baldings' business card as I gazed out the passenger window. Was meeting the Balding family the right thing to do? Steve Pearson had given me some good leads and his invitation to contact Kerry and Beverley Balding seemed important to him.

Even so, I worried about the possibility of any perceived treachery against the Balding family. More importantly, I had no wish to add to their grief. I glanced once more at their business card before placing it in my shirt pocket, and then I made a list of the things I needed to follow up. It was then I realised I'd forgotten to ask Steve Pearson what forensic material had been sent to Cellmark Laboratories in the UK for DNA testing and whether it included Shorty Wells' bandana.

Chapter 18

RAY HALL

Steve Pearson caused me to worry about Shorty Jamieson's alibi for the afternoon and evening of the crimes against Janine Balding, so I set about looking for Bill Rowland, who was supposed to have left The Station drop-in centre with Jamieson and Lizzy Lopez between ten and 10:30am on the morning of 8 September 1988. Tracking down Rowland proved to be a challenge. I checked out the usual places in Surry Hills, Kings Cross, Darlinghurst and Woolloomooloo where the homeless sleep and eat. Rowland was about, but nobody had seen him for a few weeks. Someone at the Talbot suggested I try Ray Hall at the Flemington Markets where Rowland worked casually off-loading trucks.

I set my alarm clock for four in the morning one Saturday and arrived at the markets at five—before the sun was up and before I was properly awake. I stood at the iron gates with a ragtag line of casual workers ready to lay siege to a corresponding line of produce trucks loaded to the gunnels with fresh agricultural produce from country New South Wales. None of the people standing about wanted to be engaged in conversation and I knew how they felt. When the gates opened, I asked a security guard if he could direct me to Ray Hall. The security guard pointed to a bloke riding an orange motor scooter and wearing a matching orange vest.

"That's Ray Hall," said the security guard.

I gave chase as best I could, but soon realised I'd failed to keep up with the motor scooter. I seemed to be walking forever and further away from the casual workers. Lawyers always follow instructions, so I ambled along in the half-light of dawn through a jumble of steel frames and wooden trestles—partly constructed market stalls. I passed an endless line of empty railway sheds, shiny steel railway tracks, signal boxes and dusty red and green lights. The place would be bustling with activity when the country produce trains arrived to be unloaded. Eventually I reached the gate on the opposite side of the market and spoke to another security guard.

Can you tell me where to find Ray Hall? Just then, another orange scooter raced past and headed in the direction from which I'd just come.

"That's Ray Hall," said the opposite-side security guard pointing to the receding motor scooter and its diminishing rider—a different person to the one I'd chased previously.

I began jogging after the second scooter and then it turned to the right between two corrugated iron sheds where early occupants were sorting fresh flowers and seafood before setting up their stalls. When I arrived breathless at the end of the sheds, Ray Hall was nowhere to be seen. I made my way through the stalls to a gated area where I found another security guard—a big Maori bloke—who eyed me suspiciously. I asked the bloke if he knew where I could find Ray Hall and he pointed to yet another orange scooter. This one was parked against a shed alongside its orange-vested rider—a woman eating a sandwich. Surely the woman could not be Ray Hall, but I was not about to argue with the guard, and I thanked him politely.

As I approached the scooter, the woman glared at me over the top of her sandwich, and I did my best to smile and not look like a creep.

The Maori bloke on the gate said you're Ray Hall.

"Who wants to know?"

For a moment I hesitated, not expecting the question, and then I gave my name and explained that I was actually looking for a bloke named Bill Rowland.

"You'll hafta go to the office," said the woman, nodding in the direction of the rising sun—the same direction from which I'd come. "The office is nexta the delivery dock." She gave me a second on-your-way nod for good measure.

After another long walk, I found myself reunited with the casual workers, some of whom were already unloading the first of the produce trucks. To the left of the loading dock was an office with a sign above the door that read, 'Sydney Markets Transport Services', and half a dozen orange scooters were parked outside. I opened the office door.

Is anyone here *not* Ray Hall?

A man came forward from the group inside—the only one not wearing an orange vest. He looked like the boss and he didn't look happy. He stepped past me and outside the door, closing it behind us, so we were both standing on the dusty ground near the orange motor scooters. We were about the same age and height and he gave me a long hard look.

"What do you want, mate?"

I asked if he knew a bloke named Bill Rowland who sometimes did casual work for Ray Hall.

"What are you, a copper or somethin?"

I handed the man a business card. I was doing some work for a bloke named Stephen Jamieson and he needed to contact Bill Rowland.

"I've been here for 20 years and never heard of Bill Rowland." He examined the business card more closely and then said, "We get people comin' along here all the time chasin' our casual workers, but you're the first politician."

You've never heard of Bill Rowland?

"Never heard of him."

I turned to leave and then checked myself. What's the story with Ray Hall?

"Ray Hall used to own the business, but now he's retired—lives on the south coast." He pointed to the sign above the office door. "It's now called 'Sydney Markets Transport Services'." He was about to go back inside and then turned on the spot and gave me a more sympathetic look.

"What's this bloke Rowland look like?"

I opened my mouth to speak, but it took a moment for the words to come out. I'd no idea what Bill Rowland looked like.

"He might look like Ray Hall," the bloke said with a broad grin as he opened the office door and walked back inside.

Chapter 19

JOHN BRACEY

Heading back to my parliamentary office in the city, I decided to call John Bracey, the private investigator who worked with Ted O'Loughlin and located Shorty Wells in Queensland. I rang directory assistance on my mobile phone to get Bracey's office number. As the number rang and then the answer service clicked in, I realised it was Saturday, so left my name and phone number and the message I was trying to find Bill Rowland.

Indulging a bad habit—working on the weekend—I parked out the back of Parliament House and told myself I'd stay just a couple of hours. The State Library coffee shop was open and I took my usual detour. Thinking about my prospective discussion with John Bracey, I read again Wells' police record of interview and the transcript of his evidence in the second trial. To refresh my memory about the evidence that caused the first trial to be abandoned, I also re-read the dialogue between Justice James Wood and Ted O'Loughlin on the last day of proceedings.

It appeared that the police visited the Matthew Talbot hostel and asked hostel staff about a young man named 'Stephen' who was also known as 'Shorty'. Staff produced the hostel's card records of homeless men that used the facilities and handed over a card describing Shorty Jamieson's full name, date of birth and the nights he had stayed at the Talbot. This card became part of the police brief of evidence. Ted O'Loughlin pointed out to Justice Wood that no inquiry was made at the Talbot about a person named 'Mark' who was also known as 'Shorty'. Indeed, the lawyer had attended the Talbot the previous week and was given a card record in relation to Mark 'Shorty' Wells that recorded similar information about Wells to the one given to police a year earlier describing Jamieson.

Downing the dregs of my cold coffee, I packed up my papers and left the State Library building, which was bustling with young people preparing for their second-term exams. I switched on the mobile phone and there was a message from John Bracey. After making my way through Parliament House security and up to my office on the eleventh floor, I managed to offload my gear just as Bracey rang again. I told him he was keen—as Lizzy Lopez might have said—working on a Saturday.

"Ah, mato, there's no end to it!" said Bracey in a laughing and mischievous tone of voice—part Pommy and part strine.

Stephen Jamieson says you're the bloke who found Shorty Wells?

Bracey's tone was suddenly serious as he speculated aloud about Stephen's situation. "That poor little bastard," he declared. "What the police did to him is absolutely frightening."

I expect they thought they had the right bloke.

"That's no excuse" said the private investigator who was also head of the Australian Institute of Private Detectives. "Police are the only people empowered under the law to investigate criminal matters on behalf of the Crown. They must make all the evidence available—not just the stuff that suits their case. They're not judge, jury or executioner." He cited a case of *Penny* and said it was a benchmark in the criminal justice system. "If the police withhold evidence, and that evidence might have benefited the accused, the courts have no choice but to quash a conviction."

All I could say was yes, but I was thinking that the legal process for overturning a criminal conviction in Australia was not that straightforward. Even the Innocence Panel, for all its good intentions, still operated out of a back room in head office of the Police Service, just down the road from the old convict barracks in Macquarie Street. Once a prisoner went down for serious crime in New South Wales, it had always been near impossible to prove unjust and wrongful conviction. Few prisoners were successful in overturning their convictions even though commentators agreed that between one and two per cent of the prison population was innocent of the crimes for which they were convicted.

John Bracey chatted on and related the information in his two police statements. One of them recorded a conversation he had on 14 October 1989—just four days before Shorty Wells was apprehended. Bracey recorded the police officer as saying the search for Wells was a complete waste of time as Jamieson 'was in fact the party and that he was guilty'. I told Bracey that investigators sometimes preferred opinion over evidence.

"Mato, they do it all the time," said the private investigator. "That statement they got from Jamieson is just disgraceful, absolutely disgraceful! It's frightening! You and me should go out to Goulburn prison and go over his statement with him."

John Bracey picked me up in Macquarie Street as arranged in his grey Ford Fairmont, and we hightailed it out of town in the direction of the Hume Highway and Goulburn. He looked to be in his sixties, with a high forehead and receding hairline and thick white hair swept back like a mad professor. He had a remarkable ability to look at me sideways while he was talking and still watch the road. I assured him it was not necessary to make eye contact in order to speak and he knew immediately I worried about his driving. We were scarcely out of the city and he told me the police were "frightening;" he left England because foreigners were taking over and they were "frightening;" Muslims were "frightening;" and women drivers—especially those who overtook his Ford Fairmont—were "frightening."

For a man of the world, he was easily frightened, and he laughed so hard at the idea that he nearly ran off the road.

I explained that Stephen's case would not be re-opened unless a judge of the Supreme Court was satisfied that fresh and compelling new information raised a doubt or question about the guilty verdicts. And then he told me he'd been to see Andrew Lonergan—the only witness who said he saw Stephen at the Mt Druitt shopping centre on the night of the murder. Bracey pointed out that Lonergan's evidence was at odds with seven other identification witnesses at the shopping centre: Elliott, Blessington, Wilmot, Arrow, and three other young people who gave statements to police. The private investigator suggested I talk with Lonergan. While there was no property in a witness, my instinct told me it was not a good idea to play devil's advocate with witnesses.

"You should go and talk with him," Bracey insisted, and he looked away from the highway to see me scowl.

Watch the road!

I was beginning to wonder what I'd let myself in for. Leafing through my papers, I found a copy of Joanne Harris' application for a judicial inquiry, and I reminded Bracey of the sentencing judge's observation that *the identification made by Mr Lonergan is clear, strong and unambiguous.*

"Give me a break," the private investigator cried out in a remarkable Benny Hill impersonation. And then I was laughing too like some obscure comic foil. He told me he migrated from the United Kingdom in 1966. I floated the idea that the British people now had much better protections for their rights and freedoms than Australians since Britain joined the European legal system and enacted a UK Human Rights Act. What we needed Downunder was our own statutory rights charter.

"The problem in Australia," Bracey said, "is the police. I wouldn't trust them with a two-bob watch." His main concern with the police was the deals offered to witnesses—in return for the evidence police wanted to hear.

I thought the adversarial justice system was a bigger problem than the police.

"What about the way the police stitched up that poor little bastard? He could never have given those long-winded answers to the questions the police put to him. It's ridiculous actually—the greatest load of rubbish since sliced bread."

Another mixed metaphor? Frightening!

"Absolutely frightening!"

He was kookaburra laughing in staccato. By the time we reached Goulburn jail, I'd discovered nothing about the private investigator's client base except he seemed to know an awful lot about the police and politicians. I asked a few questions and he steadfastly refused to give me the name of one client. If I'd any interest in conspiracy theories, I might have thought he was a plant. But I didn't, and he wasn't.

As we walked past a painted sign at the entrance to the jail prohibiting recording equipment, I asked Bracey whether he'd remembered to bring his tape recorder and the letter giving us permission to record. He gave me a wink and said I shouldn't worry as the machine was concealed in his coat pocket.

You did bring the letter giving us permission to use a tape recorder?

"Don't worry," he said again, and then I realised he'd forgotten the letter from Corrective Services. In case he thought he could walk in without disclosing the tape recorder, I cut him off at the pass. The correctional officer at reception was Maynard Robinson, who I was now acquainted with after my several visits to the jail, and immediately I informed Mr Robinson that Mr Bracey would like to record our conversation with Shorty Jamieson for evidentiary purposes. After a phone call to the jail's governor, we got the green light, and were escorted into the prison.

I was particularly annoyed by the tape recorder incident, which might easily have compromised my good relations with the prison authorities, and I was still brooding when Stephen Jamieson poked his head into the empty classroom in the jail's education wing.

I discovered that Stephen knew John Bracey only as a name on the legal papers. The private investigator introduced himself and set up his tape recorder, explaining that he intended arranging for an expert in linguistics to analyse a recording of Stephen's voice. Bracey proceeded to ask a long list of leading questions that only required one or two-word answers. My bad humour continued. I'd no objection to the process for the purpose of recording Stephen's voice modulation and speech patterns, but Bracey had slipped into his Sherlock Holmes persona—as if he might be extracting useful information from the witness. I thought the witness needed to string together a few sentences about his life in prison if the recording was to provide any useful assistance to a linguistics expert.

As the discussion between the two of them proceeded, I became more interested when Stephen revealed he had a conversation with the Justice of the Peace who witnessed his signature on the police record of interview. His name was Paul Ryan, an ambulance officer, who signed each of the seven pages of the document. The other signatories were Jamieson, Detective Sergeant Raue, plus a Queensland police officer, Ken Martin. When Ryan read the document to the prisoner as required by Queensland law, Stephen was now claiming to have said to him: 'As far as I'm concerned it's not my statement.'

I didn't recall reading that in the trial evidence and I made a note to check it. I asked Stephen what the Justice of the Peace said in reply to this putative repudiation of the document.

"The bloke looked up and shrugged his shoulders."

And then you signed it?

"I signed it and the other people had signed it so..."

But you did say to the ambulance bloke, 'As far as I'm concerned that's not my statement'?

"Yeah."

So why did you sign it if it wasn't your statement?

"I don't know... at the time... I don't know. I just wanted to get it all over and done with, get out of the room and away from them."

That was the longest answer Stephen had given to any question in the presence of John Bracey.

Looking over Bracey's copy of the police record of interview, I thought it should not be too difficult to prove most of the document was not consistent with the way Stephen speaks. The record of the interview began with the usual series of questions referring to an earlier conversation in which one of the Sydney detectives, Detective Sergeant Raue, had asked the prisoner to confirm his previous admissions. That statement alone was sufficient to raise questions in my mind. Of the first 23 questions, Stephen answered 'Yes' to 19 of them, with the other four responses being a sentence or two. The next question, number 24, prompted an answer of 350 words in 20 sentences. The prisoner could never string together more than three or four sentences in my experience, let alone 20.

I produced from my papers a copy of the prisoner's application to the Supreme Court for a judicial inquiry into his conviction prepared by solicitor Joanne Harris and it included the stylometric examination of the record of interview. Andrew Lohrey, a research consultant from the Centre for Language and Literacy at Sydney's University of Technology, said that he compared the confessional statements *with known utterances of the applicant.* Lohrey concluded his report by saying the record of interview had *composite authorships* and *the utterances attributed to Stephen Jamieson cannot be accepted as such.*

I read the last few words to Stephen and he said, "The bloke's right about that." The Supreme Court, the Court of Criminal Appeal and the High Court had all rejected the science of stylometric analysis as a *recognised field of scientific expertise* in the *Jamieson case.*

I also produced the judgement of Justice Bruce James of the Supreme Court deciding that stylometrics *does not raise a doubt and does not give rise to a sense of uneasiness about the convictions of the applicant for the offences committed against Ms Balding.* James' judgement was dated 15 June 2001. Six days later, the New South Wales Parliament passed the cement law, re-sentencing Jamieson, Elliott and Blessington to spend the remaining terms of their natural lives in prison—with no serious or credible opportunity for parole. If there was some other way besides stylometric analysis to demonstrate to the satisfaction of an appeals court that police had fabricated the Jamieson record of interview, I wanted to know about it.

On the way back to Sydney, John Bracey drove more sedately when I told him the visit to Stephen was a complete waste of time. The stylometrics evidence was rejected out of hand by the courts and was unlikely to get a guernsey in any further review of the case. Stephen's assertion of the day—that he told the Justice of the Peace in Queensland that the record of interview was *not my statement*—was almost certainly another figment of his vivid imagination. Bracey asked how I could be so sure, and I explained that, subject to checking the transcript of the two trials, I thought it was the first time the assertion had been made. The case against the prisoner involved many injustices, but something he suddenly remembered 16 years down the track was unlikely to be one of them. Bracey looked at me obliquely and I reminded him again to watch the road.

Chapter 20

BILL ROWLAND

Shorty Wells and Shorty Jamieson were both regulars at the Matthew Talbot Hostel for homeless men at Woolloomooloo, a stone's throw from the streets of Kings Cross and on the opposite side of the Domain Park and playing fields to Parliament House. The Talbot is a three-storey, clinker-brick building run by the Society of Saint Vincent de Paul. During the late 1980s, it stood incongruously among fenced carparks, endless road works, rundown terraces, factories and the furtive groping of luxury apartment buildings. House guests had to be in by 6.00pm and latecomers slept on cardboard bedding in Talbot Lane. Some nights the guests in the lane outnumbered those in the hostel. At daybreak, the insiders hit the streets, and those sleeping outside got to use the hostel's showers and toilets.

In the week after the first trial of Jamieson, Elliott and Blessington was abandoned on 23 October 1989, police made inquiries about the two Shortys as directed by Justice James Wood. They visited the Talbot and interviewed security staff who were working in September 1988. Matthew Taplin told police on 28 October 1989 that he was not on duty on the night of the murder, but he knew the two Shortys. Taplin's statement was useful because it accurately recorded the usual apparel worn by the two Shortys.

I know a person by the name of Stephen Jamieson. His nickname was 'Shorty'. I know that he did spend a good

> *deal of time at the hostel and I was on speaking terms with him. He would always wear sandshoes, jeans, T-shirt or check shirt and that tan-coloured leather type jacket... I also know a boy by the name of Mark Wells. He was under psychiatric care at the hostel. He was a regular at times at the hostel. He would always wear Rambo type army gear with black lace up boots, army style with an army style belt. Sometimes he would wear a cap and sometimes a headband.*

An accounts clerk at the Talbot, Keli Cook, was working as a security gate person in September 1988, and gave a statement to police on 27 October 1989, which was similar to the Matthew Taplin information. Keli Cook's evidence was important even though it was hearsay because it corroborated Shorty Jamieson's alibi that he was with Bill Rowland and Lizzy Lopez at the time of the crimes against Janine Balding.

Keli Cook received a subpoena from Jamieson's lawyers to give evidence in his second trial. She mentioned receiving the subpoena to Bill Rowland, who worked part-time as a kitchen hand at the Talbot. Cook said to Rowland: *I got a subpoena from Stephen Jamieson's solicitors and they mentioned your name and if you can tell them anything you should contact them.* Rowland replied: *I can't tell them that much because I left the girl [Lizzy Lopez] and Stephen at Wynyard at 2.30 that day.* Cook gave Rowland the solicitors' telephone number and said: *If you can tell them anything and help your mate you should ring them up.* A short time later she observed Rowland on the telephone and the next day he said to her: *I've been up all-night thinking about it and I remember now that Stephen was with me until ten o'clock that night so he couldn't have been involved in the murder of Janine Balding.*

Jamieson's barrister, Ted O'Loughlin, decided not to call Keli Cook in the second trial. Perhaps he was concerned she would also corroborate a Crown witness, Alan Barnard, a security officer at the Talbot, who told the court that Rowland informed him that he left Shorty Jamieson at Wynyard station at around two o'clock on the day of the murder. According to his statement given to police on 25 October 1989, Barnard said to Rowland, *Well, that was enough time [for Jamieson] to get out to Sutherland.* According to Barnard's statement, Rowland then replied: *Well, I don't know. That's where I left him [Jamieson].*

Under cross-examination by the Crown Prosecutor in the second trial on 18 June 1990, Bill Rowland denied having this conversation with Alan Barnard. He also explained to the court that he didn't come forward earlier because he was afraid of being 'tied in' with the murder of Janine Balding.

> *Q. Why did you think you might be tied in with this killing of Janine Balding on 8 September 1988?*
>
> *A. Well, Stephen Jamieson has been tied in with it. I thought I might have been tied in with it too.*
>
> *Q. You thought you might have been tied in with it too. Why did you think that?*
>
> *A. Well, I would have to say that, you know, with my long criminal record, the police might have just thought that 'We will get him; we will put him in too' so I didn't come forward straight away.*

The Crown Prosecutor pressed Bill Rowland about the conversation with Barnard, but Rowland denied telling Barnard what time he left Jamieson, only that he was with him. The Crown Prosecutor then suggested to Rowland that he was claiming he hadn't mentioned a time to Barnard to give Jamieson *an out*.

> Q. *You understand what I mean by that [an out]?*
> A. *No I don't.*
> Q. *You were helping out your friend?*
> A. *No. I did help him out because I knew he was not there at the time.*
> Q. *You knew he was not there?*
> A. *Yes, he was with me so in other words you are trying to say I was there too, that is what you are trying to get at.*
> Q. *Well, were you there?*
> A. *No I was not, neither was Stephen.*

It seemed to be a possibility that Rowland had told Alan Barnard and Keli Cook that he left Shorty Jamieson at around two o'clock on the day of the murder and the prosecutor did a good job of making Rowland look and sound like a liar. It was no less obvious, however, that Rowland had every reason to fear being implicated in the murder, and he might have said he left Jamieson early in the afternoon to avoid any suggestion of being 'tied in' to the crimes against Janine Balding.

Shorty Jamieson gave evidence at the first trial that he left The Station with Elizabeth Lopez and one of her friends, adding *I am not sure what his name was.* During the second trial, the Crown Prosecutor made much of this statement, suggesting to Jamieson he would remember Bill Rowland's name, and that the Rowland alibi was a recent fabrication. Jamieson' s evidence in the second trial was given on 13 June 1990 and he denied the prosecutor's assertion.

I'd read that street kids hardly knew one day from the next, where they'd been or the company they kept. Street kids usually had no documents they might consult to check their movements. Another possibility was that Jamieson didn't want to implicate Bill Rowland by name at the first trial. It was also highly likely that Jamieson was smashed off his face on alcohol and drugs both on the day of the murder and the day he was arrested in Queensland.

In fact, by his own admission, Shorty Jamieson regularly consumed a cocktail of drugs and alcohol.

I doubted that the Bill Rowland evidence was a recent fabrication for a number of reasons. First, Keli Cook was quite specific in her statement to police that Rowland stayed at the Talbot in September 1988 and she had a conversation with him shortly after the arrest of the accused in which he said he was with Lizzy Lopez and Stephen Jamieson on the day of the murder. She had similar conversations with him over the ensuing twelve months. Secondly, Bronson Blessington gave evidence at the second trial that Jamieson, Rowland and Lizzy Lopez left The Station together. *They said to some of us that they're going out to Coogee to score some drugs.* Blessington was the first of the accused to give evidence and he gave it five days before Rowland took the stand.

In his evidence, Rowland said he arrived at The Station on the morning of the murder and he overheard a conversation between Elliott, Wilmot and Blessington about stealing a car. *I pulled*

Stephen and Elizabeth aside and asked them if they would like to go to the Coogee Bay Hotel with me. The purpose of the trip was to score drugs—a trip that Jamieson and Rowland had made before. Rowland said Jamieson and Lopez agreed to the proposal and the trio left by taxi. Rowland then said they arrived at Coogee twenty minutes later. *I left Stephen and Elizabeth on the corner and I walked into the Coogee Bay Hotel where I scored some marijuana.*

Jamieson and Blessington had separate legal representation and neither of them had any opportunity to influence Rowland's evidence. The most plausible explanation for Blessington and Rowland giving identical evidence about the trip to Coogee to score drugs is that it actually happened. Indeed, Blessington gave evidence that after the arrangements were made, he heard Lizzy say: *How much longer until we're going?* It was possible that Lizzy and Jamieson were hanging out for drugs. I suspected that drugs held far more interest for them than car stealing.

In late November 2002, I walked across the Domain Park and playing fields at the back of Parliament House and wandered into the Talbot which is close by the concrete pillars that hold up the eastern suburbs railway bridge at Woolloomooloo. I spoke to the woman who referred me to Ray Hall and asked if she had any more ideas about the whereabouts of Bill Rowland. When I told her the story about the orange scooters and their matching riders, the woman asked me to take a seat while she made a phone call.

A brochure on the reception room table told me that Vincent de Paul, the patron saint of charities, was born into privilege near Paris in 1581, and ministered as a priest to the French aristocracy until he was falsely accused of being a thief. After that, de Paul worked for the poor, building schools, hospitals, orphanages and shelters for convicts leaving prison.

Soon I was on my way back to Parliament House with the news that Bill Rowland was in Long Bay jail at Matraville. The next day I drove to the prison complex on the northern headland of Botany Bay, just 15 minutes from the city, where I presented identification and details of my visitor number. Bill Rowland was located in a low-security section of the prison. He knew I was working for Stephen Jamieson and he seemed pleased to see me. A shortish man, thickset, with a skin graft on the bridge of his nose, Rowland wore prison green shorts and tee shirt, white joggers, and a green baseball cap pulled low over his forehead. He struck me as a man who really wanted to escape his destructive cycle of crime and prison, and said he was desperately unhappy with himself for being back inside. I explained that I needed him to confirm the evidence he gave in Shorty's trial and he said nothing had changed.

"We were friends. I called him 'Sheep' because of the way he laughs. Other people called him 'Shorty'."

Bill Rowland reiterated that he and Lizzy and Stephen left The Station by taxi, arriving at Coogee at about 10.30am on the morning of 8 September 1988. He detailed their movements until they returned to The Station at about two in the afternoon, when he suggested to Lizzy and Stephen that they come back to his squat. Lizzy opted to stay at The Station to do some washing so Bill and Stephen walked back to the squat—a rundown terrace building at The Rocks—stopping at the Wynyard Railway Station bottle shop on the way.

"When Stephen and I reached the squat we went upstairs and

started drinking and smoking. Somebody else was there but I forget his name. Stephen stayed until about 10.00pm and then said he was leaving. He also said he would see me the next day. I didn't see him again until I seen him on television two weeks later when he was arrested in Queensland for the murder of Janine Balding."[7]

Then Bill Rowland told me some things that raised my eyebrows, so I wrote them down in an affidavit and asked him to sign it. About the time Stephen Jamieson was arrested, two detectives from the homicide squad went to see Rowland at the Matthew Talbot Hostel. At first he did not want to talk with them, but they said he would be subpoenaed if he did not co-operate. Reluctantly, he submitted to an interviewed in a room at the hostel and thedetectives placed several photographs on a table in front of him.

The detectives wanted to know if Rowland knew any of the people in the photographs. He picked out Jamieson, Wells, Wayne Wilmot, Matthew Elliott and Bronson Blessington. He said he knew Jamieson, Wells and Wilmot from living on the streets and he recognised Elliott and Blessington from The Station on the morning of 8 September 1988. The police did not ask him to sign the photographs and they did not take a statement from him. He did not see the two detectives again until he went to the police station in October 1989 after the first trial had been abandoned and the jury discharged.

Chapter 21

WAYNE WILMOT

Shorty Jamieson's police record of interview greatly overstated the role of Wayne Wilmot in the crimes against Janine Balding. As the police investigation proceeded, it became apparent that the principal perpetrators of the major offences were Matthew Elliott and Bronson Blessington. When Janine Balding was abducted, Matthew Elliott drove the car and Wayne Wilmot travelled in the front passenger's seat. At some point on the journey to Minchinbury, Elliott stopped the car and got into the back seat next to Janine Balding. Wayne Wilmot took over the driving while Carol Arrow sat next to him in the front passenger seat. Blessington remained in the near-side back seat behind Carol Arrow. Shorty Wells remained in the off-side back seat behind the new driver, Wilmot. Elliott sat between Wells and Janine Balding so she was between Elliott and Blessington. Just past the Archbold Road overbridge, Wilmot slowed the car and drove off to the side of the highway as directed by Elliott.

Police interviewed Wilmot at Campbelltown police station on 11 September 1988 and he told them that the Shorty who was with him and the others when they abducted Janine Balding was named 'Mark'. Police asked him whether he had sex with Janine Balding and Wilmot answered, *No, I've got me own girl.* Wilmot also said that Elliott and Blessington had sex with the woman on the back seat of her car while he and Carol Arrow remained in the front seat, consistent with Blessington's assurance that nobody had sex with Janine Balding except him and Elliott. What puzzled me was that Wilmot pleaded guilty to four counts of sexual intercourse without consent, which was longhand for rape. I needed to talk with Wayne Wilmot, and like Bill Rowland, he was not hard to find once I looked in the right place.

Lithgow Correctional Centre is 60 miles west of the Blue Mountains on the edge of the western tablelands, just over two hours from Sydney by car. The complex is a maximum-security prison, although its modern design and bush location at the base of a steep hill give it a deceptively open appearance. Weekday visits in the middle of the day were unusual and I seemed to have the place to myself as I waited in the large visiting area. The walls were festooned with Aboriginal motifs. I sat at one of five fixed metal chairs that encircled a fixed metal table. There were another 50 identical seating configurations that gave the place a surreal feeling, like being a feature in a contemporary art installation. Wilmot appeared with a correctional officer at the far end of the room in joggers, green shorts and green sloppy joe. The prisoner zigzagged his way through the tables and chairs. He was eight months older than Bronson Blessington, with thinning blonde hair, prominent cheekbones, pasty skin and greenish blue eyes.

Wayne Wilmot had been a ward of the State since he was nine years old and lived on the streets of Sydney since he was 14. He was one of those unfortunate criminals who seemed destined never to learn from their mistakes. While Bill Rowland tried to do the right thing, and was successful for many years, the same could not be said of Wayne Wilmot. He told me he was "stitched up" for his latest crimes, committed while he was on parole for the crimes against Janine Balding. When I offered to assist him, he said "It's no use, you can't beat the system." I told him the way to beat the system was to do the right thing and he scoffed at the idea. I asked if he raped Janine Balding and he repeated what he told police—he had his own girl.

I thought you were courageous to tell the prosecutor that Jamieson shouldn't go away for something he never done.

"They were wrong to put Shorty Jamieson away."

You went away for something you never done; you didn't rape Janine Balding.

"That's different," he assured me. "I did a deal with the coppers. They agreed not to charge me with murder if I pleaded guilty to abduction and rape. What could I do?"

But you didn't rape her!

"That's the system," he said triumphantly. "Like I say, you can't beat the system."

In fact, Wilmot was convicted as part of a joint criminal enterprise to commit abduction and rape of Ms Balding. He was released from custody after serving eight years in prison.

During the second trial of Stephen Jamieson in 1990, Wilmot gave evidence that Mark 'Shorty' Wells was the Shorty who was with Blessington and Elliott when they abducted Janine Balding from the carpark at Sutherland railway station. Wells happened to be in the courtroom while Wilmot gave his evidence. Counsel for Jamieson cross-examined Wilmot.

> *Q. You see down the back of the Court there is a man there in dark clothing, right in the back on the righthand side. Do you recognise him? A. Yes.*

Q. Do you know what his name is? A. Mark Wells.
Q. When did you last see him? A. On that night.
Q. That is 8 September 1988? A. Yes.
Q. Where was he? A. At Central.
Q. Where else was he? A. At the [crime scenes].

During two years of freedom from 1996 to 1998 after serving his eight-year sentence for the crimes against Janine Balding, Wayne Wilmot demonstrated that he was a serial sex offender, attacking and sexually assaulting four women. He went back inside, remaining in prison until 2024 when he was released on strict conditions of good behaviour. He was outside for just two weeks before being arrested again and returned to prison for breach of his parole conditions.

Chapter 22

THE BANDANA

More than a year after Police Minister Paul Whelan announced members of the Innocence Panel, it finally got off the ground in late 2002. Every interest group in the criminal justice system seemed to be represented including former judges, victims groups, police, the health department, the public defender, the public prosecutor and Legal Aid. The panel's problem getting started was caused by panel members' needlessly worrying about government indemnities—protecting themselves from the consequences of a botched decision. By the time the panel doors opened for business, Paul Whelan had retired and Michael Costa was the new police minister—his first ministerial job in the Carr Labor Government. Costa was a smart bloke though he ignored my concerns about the lack of prisoner representation on the Innocence Panel. His time in the top police job lasted 16 months and then schoolteacher John Watkins took over.

The government placed information about the panel in the State's 39 prisons, together with prisoner application forms. A few politicians, various justice lobby groups, a gaggle of law students and academics and a couple of private super sleuths worked hard to get application forms into the panel, which operated from a back room in police headquarters at Goulburn Street in inner Sydney. To give it a semblance of independence from police, only the panel's post box address was included on its letterhead. I anticipated a flood of applications for DNA testing of crime scene material and

I made sure Jamieson's was one of the first to be lodged. The panel received his application on 6 January 2003 along with my covering letter describing the bandana used to gag Ms Balding and what I'd done to try and find it. A few likely places were excluded but it was still missing.

With no conceivable way of proving to the satisfaction of the courts that Jamieson's police record of interview was fabricated, new DNA evidence seemed to be the only way to attempt to reopen his case. As luck would have it, I was able to contact Michele Franco, the forensic biologist who Steve Pearson had called at the health department. Franco was responsible for DNA testing of crime scene material at the Institute of Clinical Pathology and Medical Research (ICPMR) Division of Analytical Laboratories (DAL) and she'd just received a request from the Innocence Panel to conduct further tests of forensic samples in the Janine Balding case. It was the first I knew that the Innocence Panel had accepted Jamieson's application to prove his innocence. Franco informed me that she held crime scene material going back to 1986—including exhibits from the trial of Jamieson, Blessington and Elliott.

Unbelievably, the black bandana/headscarf was among the exhibits found in a cardboard box at the Mt Druitt police station where the Janine Balding murder investigation was based. Before I could get too excited, Franco informed me that the headscarf had been stored in a plastic bag, and the chances of DNA material surviving fungal growth over the years was not good. Demonstrating my ignorance on the subject of DNA testing, I told her not to worry, as I'd read somewhere that DNA samples going back thousands of years had been preserved. This was the extent of my knowledge of DNA testing so I arranged to visit her laboratory after lunch—before any new analysis of the crime scene material took place.

Looking at my UBD Gregory's map of Sydney, I realised that the health department's DNA testing laboratory was located just across the railway line at Lidcombe from Minda Juvenile Detention Centre, the place where Bronson Blessington was locked up as a juvenile. To my surprise, the entire detention centre was a dusty pile of rubble surrounded by a cyclone wire fence. I decided to fill in the time until my appointment with the forensic laboratory by sitting in my car outside the Minda remains and drafting the letters arising out of the meeting with Senior Constable Steve Pearson. I began with a letter to Senior Constable Geoff Smith—the man in charge of the latent print section of police forensics—who located fingerprints in Janine Balding's Holden Gemini. Shorty Wells admitted in his initial record of interview that he was involved in the abduction of Janine Balding and the theft of her car. Police might have his fingerprints from the car.

At the appointed time, I drove across the bridge over the Lidcombe railway line to the office building occupied by the health department's DAL. Michele Franco was waiting for me in reception and took me upstairs to an interview room. She placed an ageing manila folder labelled *Janine Balding* on the table between us. A man entered the room and sat at the head of the table. Michele introduced him as Robert Goetz, the director of the DAL, and she proceeded to open the folder. Goetz was not very talkative.

Michele could not have been more helpful as she explained the content of her forensic report dated January 1989. She confirmed that the Sexual Assault Information Kit (SAIK) delivered to her by Senior Constable Steve Pearson on 27 September 1988 included the body cavity swabs taken by Dr Ellis during the autopsy of the deceased. The DAL had decided to send the forensic material from the crime scene to Cellmark Diagnostics in the UK for DNA testing. Because the trial of Jamieson, Elliott and Blessington was the first New South Wales case in which DNA evidence was included in the prosecution brief, few rules were in place to guide the testing procedure. Michele said she made inquiries of Cellmark and was informed that only the vaginal swabs should be sent to England for DNA testing. Robert Goetz explained that any analysis of the single spermatozoon found in the rectal swabs would provide one half of the DNA profile and therefore it was useful only for exclusionary purposes.

I realised for the first time that rectal swabs had never been tested for DNA even though Jamieson alone of the accused had been charged and convicted of anal intercourse without consent—based solely on his contested police record of interview. I asked whether glass laboratory slides could be checked again and Goetz informed me that the DAL did not retain slide samples. He cautioned that the swabs themselves were tested at the time for the presence of semen and the testing was likely to have destroyed the semen. I gathered that the testing product was a dye or enzyme that broke down the semen's molecular structure.

Following his tentative foray into the conversation, I asked Robert Goetz a question about the black bandana. He confirmed Michele's advice that the chances of picking up a DNA profile on the headscarf were slim, particularly if it was placed in a plastic bag while it was still wet. People were not conscious of DNA profiling in the late 1980s and thought only about fingerprints. Clothing evidence like the bandana was frequently handled without gloves because it couldn't be used for extracting fingerprints. Nevertheless, he said it was possible that hair was lodged in the weave of the bandana. I expressed my concern that the testing procedure may destroy the bandana's silk fabric. I was assured that although small portions of the cloth material were removed for testing, the garment would not be significantly depleted, and it would remain pretty much in its original condition should additional testing be required.

Back in the city, I dispatched the letter to Senior Constable Geoff Smith asking whether any attempt was made to match fingerprints in Janine Balding's Holden Gemini with Mark 'Shorty' Wells. The letter met with no response. Steve Pearson had tried to ring Smith from the Dubbo police station and gave me the number when it failed to answer. I tried calling the number several times over a few weeks, and eventually another police officer answered the phone, saying Geoff Smith was on sick leave. The police officer confirmed that Smith was the officer in charge of the latent print section, police forensics. I rang the telephone number intermittently over the next couple of months until finally another officer told me Senior Constable Smith was on permanent sick leave.

Meanwhile the Innocence Panel was trying to work out its protocols and how it should operate. In the United States by the early 2000s, some 160 citizens had been released from prison after DNA evidence proved they were wrongly convicted. About 20 of those prisoners were on death row and some of them had been in prison for more than 20 years. In the State of Illinois, almost six per cent of convicted prisoners sentenced to death under the existing law were shown to be innocent. The outgoing governor of Illinois was so appalled he commuted the sentences of all prisoners on death row to life terms. The United Kingdom Parliament established the Criminal Cases Review Commission in March 1997 as an impartial and independent body to review convictions. As at late 2005, Commission staff had successfully referred 151 convictions which were quashed on appeal. By late 2024, the number of quashed convictions in the UK following Commission reviews had risen to about 550.

There was every reason to expect that Australian courts may have wrongly convicted a proportionate number of its citizens, and yet the Innocence Panel was the first attempt by local politicians to come to grips with the fact that judges, juries, prosecutors and defence lawyers are fallible and make mistakes. Politicians had trumpeted the promise of DNA as a break-through to exonerate the innocent as well as convict the guilty, but we were way behind the rest of the common law world in our efforts to establish a legislative framework to review doubtful convictions. According to the Innocence Project at Sydney's University of Technology, the review process needed to be independent of the health department and police; DNA and other information from crime scenes should be preserved and stored in a particular place along with evidence from the trial; and convicts should have reasonable access for the purposes of checking for a DNA match.

A prisoner lobby group, Justice Action, told me that the Innocence Panel was set up to fail and that the government had no intention of allowing more than a few token cases to be run on the basis of new DNA evidence. The government planned to demonstrate the deficiencies of the panel and then 'expand the DNA database in line with overseas trends'. I'd no idea what all that meant, particularly how an expanded DNA database would be detrimental to a person wrongly convicted. Justice Action explained that the more people on the DNA database the easier it was for police to find an offender. And how was that a problem? Police had full control of criminal investigations once they controlled the DNA database—nobody else got access to the database except through police.

I'd no way of knowing whether Shorty Wells was on the DNA database even though I knew he'd been released from prison in the year of Janine Balding's murder after a long stretch in Cooma and Long Bay jails. Mine was a cynical view, but police had their Shorty for the crimes against Ms Balding, and little incentive to check out any alternative suspect. Would police use the DNA database to match DNA profiles from crime scenes in the same way fingerprints were compared using the National Automated Fingerprint Identification System?

Chapter 23

MARK 'SHORTY' WELLS

I understood from the second trial of Jamieson, Blessington and Elliott that Mark 'Shorty' Wells was born in Queensland. Perhaps I could track down his family at the Queensland Registry of Births, Deaths and Marriages. I had his date of birth and his father's name, 'Moon', from the evidence in the trial—the name 'Wells' was apparently his mother's name—which ought to be sufficient information to get his birth certificate. After that, it was a matter of finding his relatives in Queensland, and whether they knew his whereabouts. I lived on the north coast of New South Wales and the drive to Brisbane took a bit over two hours. Along the way, I checked out the Salvation Army bloke who found Stephen Jamieson at Southport.

I'd no trouble finding the witness Dave Hatchman, whose name appeared in the *Courier Mail* as the person who alerted police to Jamieson's presence at Southport on 22 September 1988. Hatchman was still with the Salvos working for a drug and alcohol rehabilitation centre near the Gold Coast campus of Griffith University. He turned out to be a gentle and friendly bloke in his early 50s with a memory like a steel trap.

"The police picked up Jamieson around eight o'clock on the Thursday morning," Hatchman said from behind his modest veneer desk. "On the Wednesday night, I found him in the street outside the hostel. I thought it was a hessian bag in the gutter, but when I went to look it was Jamieson, reeking of alcohol and out like a light."

Hatchman rang police early on the Thursday morning when he heard on the radio they were looking for Jamieson in connection with the Janine Balding murder investigation. He went to Stephen's bed at the hostel, expecting to find him asleep after the night before, but one of the staffers said Stephen had just left for the park at the end of the street. When the police arrived, they were told where to find him.

I asked if Stephen was still drunk in the morning and Dave Hatchman didn't know. I pressed him about the night before.

"I'll tell you what happened. One of the guys said, 'Look, I'll take him upstairs', and he picked him up to put him on his back, but Jamieson went straight over the guy's shoulder and crashed on the ground on his head. I thought, 'You'll kill the poor bloke—break his neck'. But he was alright. And then the staffers picked him up between them and took him upstairs."

It appeared Stephen was comatose during the whole affair and I wondered how he could have been in a fit state the next day to be interviewed by police and charged with murder. I was hardly surprised that records of his interactions with Queensland police were punctuated with interruptions along the lines that the local police commander at Southport was checking on the prisoner and inquiring about how he was getting along.

I headed up the highway that links the Gold Coast with Brisbane, driving past Water World, Sea World, Movie World, shopping worlds galore, housing worlds and various other worlds I preferred not to visit. I was always happy to stop at the Strawberry Farm and feed the farm animals, but it was now so complicated getting on and off the highway I just keep barrelling along with the traffic until I hit Brisbane. I parked on the southern side of the river, near the concrete pillboxes that frame the State Library building and took the opportunity to check the local newspapers as to what else was happening around the country at the time of Jamieson' s arrest.

The September 1988 newspapers were on microfilm and I found what I was looking for without any problem. On the day Stephen arrived in Southport, the Northern Territory Supreme Court finally exonerated Lindy and Michael Chamberlain, finding they did not kill their daughter Azaria. The decision effectively affirmed the original finding of Coroner Denis Barritt in 1981 that a wild dog or dingo took the baby. The case is probably the most infamous example in our sorry criminal history of convictions based on opinion rather than evidence. A reputable survey of Australians immediately following the Chamberlain acquittals found 70 per cent believed Lindy was innocent while the remaining 30 per cent *knew* she was guilty and got away with murder. Police and so-called experts were blinded by preconceived ideas when they investigated the death of the child.

In his closing remarks to the Morling royal commission inquiry into the Chamberlain convictions, Jack Winneke QC for Lindy said the police were so obsessed with their belief in the Chamberlains' guilt they couldn't accept with an open mind any material suggesting innocence. The expert evidence came under close scrutiny, and in particular, supposed arterial blood spray under the dashboard of the Chamberlains' car turned out to be sound deadener overspray. Counsel assisting the inquiry, Chester Porter QC, credited a practical scientist named Les Smith from the Sanitarium Health Food Company at Cooranbong, with the initial discovery of this flaw in the Crown case. Northern Territory police and chief minister Paul Everingham might have avoided the dim view of history had they accepted with humility and grace the original finding of Coroner Denis Barritt, but instead they were determined beyond all sensibility to acquit the dingo.

One positive outcome from the unimaginable horror of the Lindy Chamberlain experience was the establishment at the Commonwealth level of government of the National Institute of Forensic Science, an independent body created by statute and reporting to the Australian Police Ministers Council. In New South Wales and the other States and Territories, forensic science remained under the control of police and health services, with mixed results for convicts attempting to review the evidence against them.

In other microfilm news from September 1988, journalist Evan Whitton reported on the Commission of Inquiry into Possible Illegal Activities and Associated Police Misconduct (the Fitzgerald royal commission). Jack Herbert, the self-confessed police bribes bagman was giving evidence to the inquiry that a former Queensland government minister, Don Lane, acted as a 'pipeline' connecting the State Cabinet to corrupt police. Allegations were flying thick and fast, including by recently suspended commissioner, Sir Terence Lewis, who alleged that certain politicians were using the inquiry to advance their careers. Lewis said that although he had information about government MPs, *I don't believe I'm ever going to fight dirty.* It was a measure of how seriously things had gone haywire in the Sunshine State that 'fighting dirty' meant telling the truth.

Leaving the library, I crossed the Brisbane River and wandered past the shameless former Treasury Building, which was then Brisbane's casino. I walked down George Street and into the foyer of the Capital Hill Building where I worked in the early 90s following publication of the Fitzgerald report. Unlike in those days, the notice board in the building had no entries for government departments undertaking inquiries into human rights and individual freedoms. I fondly recalled my time working in the building on a draft Human Rights Bill for Queensland. Premier Wayne Goss considered introducing the bill into the single chamber parliament before the *Courier Mail* effectively torpedoed it, wrongly identifying a proposal for the right to bodily integrity as changing the law on abortion. Australian citizens by and large are under the considerable misapprehension that human rights and freedoms are protected by the common law.

After this small interlude, I left the foyer of the Capital Hill Building, and I was on track again. I walked several blocks to the top of the hill, which is the central point of convergence for Brisbane's city streets. With the benefit of directions from passers-by, including a kindly woman who handed me a giveaway tourist map, I found the Queensland Registry of Births Deaths and Marriages. I filled out two application forms, one in the name of Mark Wayne Wells and the other bearing the surname 'Moon'. I answered the relevant questions about his age and date of birth and stood in a queue waiting to be served.

Handing over the forms and my money, I expected an argument about my authority to make the applications, but the young woman who served me had nothing to say about my remarks under the heading, 'Relationship to the Person Named in the Certificate'. Within five minutes or so, the young woman returned with the boss, a charming older man of Caucasian appearance and bearing a wide smile. He returned my money and application forms with the advice that even though I may be an elected representative from a State with two parliamentary chambers, I was most definitely not entitled to the birth certificate of anybody in Queensland unless I happened to be their legal representative or otherwise legally related to them. And in any event, he had checked the register, and there was no person with the name 'Wells' or 'Moon' born in the Sunshine State on the date I'd provided.

Losing nothing but a little self-esteem, I found a coffee shop in the imposing stone edifice that is Brisbane's Central Station. As I sipped coffee and worked out from the tourist map the best route back to the car, I realised I could walk through the Queen Street Mall and check out where John Bracey found Shorty Wells in 1989. Street kids in those days gathered in a paved area near Hungry Jack's and nothing much had changed when I worked in Brisbane in the 1990s.

Walking down the hill towards the city's main shopping precinct, I veered left at King George Square, from where I had a direct line of sight down to Hungry Jack's. In the middle of the square where I was standing, a preacher in a felt hat was inviting a group of Korean tourists to get to know Jesus. I gained the impression that the visitors hadn't a clue what the good man was saying as they chattered amongst themselves and jockeyed for a position on either side of him to take photographs of themselves.

"Jesus is your friend," said the preacher as the travellers shuffled off with their giggling images.

I gave him a friendly wave and he raised the stakes. "Repent of your sins; this is the day of the Lord."

Startled, if not chastised, I headed for the Queen Street Mall. The city's visitor information centre was where I recalled it—about 20 yards from Hungry Jack's. A low stepped brick wall ran down the side of the visitors centre facing the hamburger joint. A number of kids were hanging about, some of them sitting on the wall and others standing in small groups. A few were school kids, but others were scruffy looking with dishevelled and dyed hair, cutaway denim skirts, grubby jeans, tracksuit tops, bomber jackets and assorted junk jewellery hanging from the oddest places.

I waited in a short queue at Hungry Jack's, glancing over my shoulder at the group behind me who seemed to be kids from Melbourne looking for accommodation. They became aware of me listening to their conversation and stopped talking. I stepped up to the counter and ordered chips and a Coke as the kids started talking again in low whispers. I made my way outside and found a spot at the lower end of the visitors' centre brick wall where I sat down with my American fare and the tourist map. I was the last person seated on the brick wall before it dropped away to an inaccessible place on the perimeter of the public convenience. The kids from the Hungry Jack's queue wandered across the paved area with their burgers and chips and stood near where I was seated. I avoided making eye contact with them. What did I hope to achieve by this unplanned reconnoitre?

Then an older boy joined the group, unmistakeable in his long black duffle coat, black military boots, black tee shirt and black cotton pants. He was even wearing a black bandana around his head. His hair was dark brown, longish and straggly, his face was long with a prominent nose, and he was noticeably pockmarked with cauliflower ears. He bore no resemblance at all to Shorty Jamieson except that he was short—about five feet tall. A young woman with short blonde hair, long skirt and leg warmers gave him a hug, but no words passed between them. And then he wandered aimlessly around the group before settling himself on the wall beside me. Strapped diagonally across one shoulder and hanging in the middle of his back was a bedroll.

I was completely dumbstruck and had no idea what to say to the man, or whether it was appropriate to say anything. I remembered the legal principle that there's no property in a witness. Shorty Wells had a heavy cold or chest condition and was coughing like a man with consumption.

Before I could work out what to do, a police paddy wagon appeared in the mall and parked adjacent to the visitors' information centre. Two male officers emerged from the vehicle and began talking with the street kids who nodded and shook their heads and put on a good show of acting indifferently to the police. Nobody was comfortable being interrogated by police officers. One of the officers interrogated the kids near the entrance to Hungry Jack's while the other moved along those seated on the wall, eyeballing them one after the other, until he reached Shorty Wells, and stopped. For a dreadful moment, I feared the policeman was about to remove Wells from the mall, and then the other policeman called to his mate, and the officer walked away.

The police removed two kids from Hungry Jack's, put them in the paddy wagon and drove off.

I caught Shorty Wells' eye and he nodded and looked away. The group from the Hungry Jack's queue was still standing nearby and their conversation had returned to the subject of accommodation in Brisbane. One of the kids said he was told to look out for a bloke named 'Shorty' who knew all the places to stay.

Without thinking, I turned to Wells. You're Shorty, aren't you?

"Not me, mate," he replied, squinting in the late afternoon sunlight.

I told him my first name and held out my hand, hoping the chance to talk with him was not lost.

"I'm Mark," he said confidently, shaking my hand.

I explained how I was writing about street kids and I'd just been to the Registry of Births Deaths and Marriages looking for a bloke I thought was born in Queensland.

"I was born in Palestine and served in the Israeli army," said Shorty Wells with not a flicker of mischief in his eye.

I asked if he knew whether soldiers in Israel used Ml6 rifles and he assured me they did. He explained in detail how to load the rifle and I reached for the notebook in the inside pocket of my jacket, placing it on the brick wall with the tourist map. I offered him a chip from my Hungry Jack's wrapper and he declined. Then he coughed so hard it seemed his lungs would burst and he slagged on the mall pavers between us. I looked at the slimy brown and green phlegm for a terrible moment of uncertainty, and then I reached into the pocket of my jeans where I happened to have not just a clean but a brand-new handkerchief. Taking a deep breath, I deliberately dropped the chips in front of him and bent down to pick them up. I surfaced from the pavers with a handful of chips in one hand and the bloke's slag on my handkerchief in the other.

I slipped the handkerchief inside the tourist map and put the gruesome package in the back pocket of my jeans. Any appetite for the chips was well and truly gone, but I picked up the Coke and gulped it down in greedy mouthfuls.

The sun had dropped behind the buildings on the opposite side of the mall and the quiet figure in black was now gazing into the distance. Armed with my notebook and pen, I was ready to write down anything else he might want to tell me. Wells had no idea I'd taken his DNA, although glancing along the wall, I noticed that a young boy about 17 had his pimply face turned my way. I knew enough about sleight of hand to be certain the kid knew nothing of what I'd done, but I suspected his curiosity would draw him into our discussion. Unfortunately, I was right on the money, and the kid stood up and walked to a position where he was standing directly in front of Wells and me with his left gym boot neatly covering the wet spot on the pavers.

"Whad are ya talkin' to Shorty about?" said the kid, and his tone of voice was menacing.

I'm writing about street kids and maybe Shorty can tell me about the places he stays and where he can get something to eat.

The young man began telling me to fuck off and the expression was half out when one of the kids from the Melbourne group joined us, a tough-looking young woman with dyed black hair and a nose ring. She said to Mark Wells, "So, you're Shorty."

Wells looked at me as though his problems were my fault and then looked away without another word.

It was time to leave, and like the dog that caught the car and didn't know what to do next, I placed the notebook and pen back inside my jacket and stood up. Avoiding eye contact with the young man who wanted me off his turf, and the young woman who wanted to interrogate Shorty Wells, I headed back to the centre of the mall and scurried up to George Street where I walked so quickly I was almost falling over myself.

Encountering Shorty Wells had unnerved me. My heart was racing despite my head saying I'd nothing to worry about. I slowed down as I approached Victoria Bridge. Halfway across the Brisbane River I turned around to make sure a horde of murderous street kids wasn't following me. And then I felt ashamed of myself as I gazed out over the wide expanse of water. Unreasonable fear of the homeless and the mentally ill was just the kind of negative stereotyping and prejudice that landed innocent people like Stephen Jamieson in prison.

Chapter 24

MICHAEL STRUTT

For several months, I engaged in nice polite correspondence by post with the Innocence Panel. I'd no idea what information to give them, and I suspected they had the same problem as to what material they should be handing over to applicants. This was the first attempt by a government in Australia to establish a forum to allow people who claimed to be wrongly convicted to use DNA testing to help prove their innocence. Just as those of us representing prisoners were feeling our way, so were members of the panel. Unfortunately, it was more of a standoff than a collaboration—adversarial rather than inquisitorial justice.

Justice John Nader QC was originally the panel chairman, and then towards the end of the DNA testing process, Nader retired because of other commitments, and Judge Mervyn Finlay QC took over. I knew Finlay from his days as inspector general of the Police Integrity Commission and my role as a member of the parliamentary oversight committee. I complained in several letters that the panel was heavily weighted against prisoners with victims' groups, privacy interests, police and public prosecutors all looking for a place in the sun while prisoners were left in the dark on every issue from finding the forensic material to organising DNA testing.

When I grew impatient about the time taken for the testing, I was told it would be done slowly to provide the best possible chance of obtaining meaningful DNA profiles. No doubt I was partly responsible for the delay after seeking unreasonable assurances that the testing procedure would not irretrievably damage the molecular structure of any biological material in the bandana. I wanted the forensic biologists to preserve as much of the garment as possible for further testing in line with later developments in DNA profiling technology—a piece of fabric that resembled a cheesecloth was never likely to be useful for further sampling. Eventually I learned that five samples about five millimetres square had been cut out of the bandana for DNA testing, but otherwise it remained intact.

Meanwhile the sceptics were still telling me that allowing police to have control of trial exhibits as well as responsibility for the Innocence Panel was doomed to failure. A private researcher and DNA enthusiast, Michael Strutt, said that the panel would almost certainly fall at the first hurdle, and he predicted this would occur shortly after the next election. Strutt compared the Innocence Panel to the Royal Commission Unit set up following the Wood Royal Commission into the New South Wales Police Service. The unit found an entrenched system of corruption resulting in widespread police perjury and the practice of evidence planting to secure convictions. One purpose of the Royal Commission Unit was to receive and process applications from prisoners for assistance in overturning convictions involving police corruption. Although hundreds of prisoners made applications to the unit, less than 30 received any Legal Aid funding, and only a handful were successful in gaining a review of their convictions. The unit was disbanded in 1999 with the bulk of its funds unused and returned to consolidated revenue.

Rumours began circulating in August 2003 that the Innocence Panel was a time bomb ready to explode, and explode it did, spectacularly, leaving a crater in the law-and-order political landscape that surprised even hardened cynics like Michael Strutt. In the best of Westminster traditions, when a government justice initiative with bipartisan support self-destructed, announcement of the disaster took the form of a press release from the police minister expressing support for the victims of crime.

> *Minister for Police John Watkins today suspended the NSW Innocence Panel from taking further applications pending a review of the operations of the panel and draft legislation being prepared. Mr Watkins said he'd acted after discussions with the Innocence Panel chairman, former Supreme Court Judge Mervyn Finlay QC, which raised questions about the current process...Mr Watkins today said Stephen Wayne Jamieson, convicted over the rape and murder of Janine Balding in 1988, was one of the 13 applicants who had come forward since the Panel was created. Jamieson was convicted of murder by his own confession, and eyewitness testimony of his part in the horrific crime..."I'm suspending the operations of the Innocence Panel because I don't believe there are sufficient checks and balances to protect the victims of crime from further anguish. In this case, the Balding family has suffered enough and without legislation to underpin the Panel, the process just means more uncertainty and pain. This is distressing, and I believe the Panel needs legislative support to help it protect victims better.*

The first Stephen Jamieson or I knew that the Innocence Panel had blown up was a telephone call I received from Stavro Sofios at the *Daily Telegraph* in Sydney following publication of the police minister's press release. Sofios promised to fax me a copy of the ministerial statement. In the next 40 minutes, I logged 27 telephone calls from journalists on the message bank service of my mobile phone. I returned all the calls and answered the media questions as best I could with nothing more than the newspaper's copy of the press release to guide me. Sofios' article in the next edition of the *Daily Telegraph* was headed 'MP's hand of help for a murderer' and the story began with a clarion cry that was consummate tabloid provocation: *He raped and strangled a young bank teller 15 years ago in a brutal crime which forever scarred Sydney. But Stephen Wayne 'Shorty' Jamieson is still trying any legal trick he can to get out of the jail cell he is supposed to die in.*

I cringed at the next few paragraphs in the article, which quoted Beverley Balding as saying I disgusted her. *Why are you doing this to us? Why are you trying to help a criminal and not look after the people who need looking after? They [the killers] can rot in hell but let Janine rest in peace.* Mrs Balding was a strong advocate for the death penalty and she told ABC Radio, 'If the death penalty had been in, surely to goodness by now Jamieson wouldn't be around and he wouldn't be doing what he's doing today'. Jim Hanna from AAP rang just after I'd spoken to Stephen Jamieson on the telephone and I informed the journalist that Stephen was sorry the legal system had caused the Balding family so much grief. The prisoner was also concerned that the Baldings and the press were given the jump on the results of his innocence application in direct contravention of the confidentiality promised to applicants. Indeed, I still had no idea what aspect of the case caused such a furore, and when I called the Innocence Panel, the most they would say was that the testing results were in the mail.

By the time the mail arrived, the press had lost interest in the case, other than Richard Ackland, who was filing his usual Friday opinion piece in the *Sydney Morning Herald.* I now had the facts and passed them on to the lawyer turned journalist and publisher, who got the story right with an article headed, 'A question of guilt that's too hot to handle'. Ackland pointed out that Jamieson was one of the ten Never to be Released prisoners cemented in their cells by the Carr Government: *Their manoeuvrings through the legal system have considerable potential to traumatise the Government, apart from their victims. That is the reason applications to the Innocence Panel have been suspended.* In concluding the article, Ackland commented that the doors of the Innocence Panel may remain permanently closed unless the government could resolve the two grief problems: the grief caused to victims and their families, and the political grief for the government if Jamieson was the wrong Shorty.

Despite my urgings, nobody would print a rebuttal of the two big lies in the minister's press release. *Jamieson was convicted of murder by his own confession, and eyewitness testimony of his part in the horrific crime.* Neither of those statements was true. Jamieson was convicted of murder by a fabricated confessional record of interview prepared by police; and all credible eyewitness testimony identified Shorty Wells and not Shorty Jamieson as the boy named 'Shorty' at the Janine Balding crime scenes.

On 8 August 2003, the Innocence Panel wrote to me in my capacity as Jamieson's legal representative to coincide with the minister's press release. Most notably, the letter said that the rectal swab was the only item to disclose DNA of anyone other than the victim. This was extraordinary given my previous discussions with Robert Goetz and Michele Franco of the Division of Analytical Laboratories (DAL). Both forensic scientists said that previous testing was likely to have destroyed any genetic material in the swab. I wondered if the panel was talking about the same swab sample. The Panel's letter was a word salad.

> *As all searches and testing have now been finalised the Panel advises that all items found from such searches have now been subjected to DNA analysis by the Division of Analytical Laboratories. Such DNA analysis identified the rectal swab as the only item to disclose DNA of anyone other than the victim…It [the Innocence Panel] may inform the applicant, and does, that the applicant "is excluded as being a possible contributor to the DNA recovered from the rectal swab." So too the Panel may inform you, and does, that "the DNA recovered from the rectal swab originated from more than one individual. Assuming only two individuals contributed to the rectal swab, the DNA profile recovered is consistent with originating from" two known persons. The Panel is precluded by the Crimes (Forensic Procedures) Act 2000 from informing you of the identities of such persons, other than to say that neither of the persons so identified is Mark (Shorty) Wells, referred to in your correspondence.*

It was hard to know if this form of writing was legalese, or just bad English. After several readings, it seemed to me that the Innocence Panel had two DNA profiles from crime scene material—both excluding Wells and Jamieson as contributors. As to the bandana, a partial DNA profile of Janine Balding was identified in the centre of the garment consistent with it being tied in a knot and placed in the victim's mouth as a gag. No other DNA was found on the bandana. I assumed from the letter that the Innocence Panel had a reference sample of both Shorty Jamieson and Shorty Wells' DNA. How else could the two men be excluded? That was a big mistake on my part. It took another 20 years before I discovered that the DAL had no reference sample for Shorty Wells' DNA—and the government had no interest in looking for one.

The only reason the Innocence Panel was able to exclude both Shorty Jamieson and Shorty Wells from the 2003 DNA comparison tests was they got a match with two other people. I was left to guess which DNA profiles they had and which profiles matched the crime scene material. It seemed I should be consoled by the exclusion of the two Shortys. But I wanted to know who were the *two known persons* the panel had identified? And why the secrecy?

I guessed that the August 2003 letter was written in a rush, consistent with the Innocence Panel drawing stumps and abandoning its office in headquarters of the Police Service with such speed that Australia Post was unable to deliver further submissions to Judge Finlay's review of the panel. The review was unremarkable and listed the things that were wrong with the panel long before Stephen Jamieson put his name to an application. It was grossly unfair, I thought, that the government used Jamieson to scapegoat its own failure to properly resource DNA testing. I received an email from Michael Strutt saying he agreed with the government that the Innocence Panel as it stood left too many questions unanswered. *But how come they only just noticed that so far down the track?*

I called David Barrow, the head of the indictable appeals section of Legal Aid NSW, explaining that I'd done about as much as I could for Shorty Jamieson pro bono. What the bloke needed was a serious legal team backed by a Public Defender to approach the Supreme Court for another judicial inquiry into his conviction. Barrow suggested I fill out a legal aid application form and attach the new evidence including correspondence from the Innocence Panel. I explained that further testing of the headscarf for a male DNA profile was critical and Barrow promised to discuss the case with the Senior Public Defender, Peter Zahra SC, who happened to be a recognised legal expert on DNA testing and analysis.

After the initial flurry of interest from the commercial media in the demise of the Innocence Panel, the ABC's Quentin Dempster put together a television piece for *Stateline* in which he looked at police involvement in the collection of forensic samples from crime scenes and recommendations that police should be required to permanently retain the material. Currently the officer in charge of an investigation had final responsibility for deciding to retain or destroy forensic material at the end of legal proceedings. The decision to destroy material from crime scenes was often taken without proper regard for appeal processes and developments in DNA testing technology. Police Commissioner Ken Moroney issued police with a directive to retain all forensic material in January 2002, and the Finlay report found that the instruction was routinely ignored.

Dempster raised with Bret Walker SC, in his capacity as president of the NSW Bar Association, the question of the impact of the Innocence Panel on victims of crime and their families. The lawyer responded that conviction and sentencing are ongoing judicial processes and one part of the process is no less important than another. Few people would suggest abolishing the trial because of the impact on victims and families, and the same principle should apply to the procedures of the Innocence Panel. Walker said: 'Where one is talking about DNA technology...its benefits as well as its burdens ought to be available to everybody whose life can be affected by the outcome of criminal justice and those people must include those convicted of the worst crimes'. I remembered that Bret Walker was senior counsel in a High Court challenge to the cement law in the case of *Baker v The Queen* and I wondered if he could assist in Jamieson's case.

Journalist Katrina Bolton from Sydney ABC Radio presented a comprehensive study of the panel in a program titled, 'A Question of Innocence'. The Privacy Commissioner, Chris Puplick, was interviewed and said the panel struggled to work out its protocols and procedures because of the absence of a statutory framework. He complained that the panel had to make its own rules, 'but this is a job for the parliament'. (Separately to the program, Chris Puplick told me in a letter that Shorty Jamieson *is currently serving a sentence for a crime which I do not believe he committed.*) Bolton asked Beverley Balding, 'What if the DNA testing supported his [Jamieson's] claim that he wasn't there?' Janine's mother was unmoved.

> *Well, I think he should stay where he is as far as I'm concerned. How many more judges and how many more people have we got to bring into this to try and prove that he was innocent? What's he going to do, come out and commit another crime and kill another girl? Do we want that to happen to some other mother's daughter... so why bring all this up again?*

At the end of the radio program, Katrina Bolton spoke with Rob Warden who headed the Center for Wrongful Convictions in Chicago. Warden told the story of the Central Park jogger case currently working its way through the United States courts. A young woman was raped and beaten senseless as she jogged in New York's Central Park. Five teenagers were convicted and sentenced for the crimes, but an older man later confessed and his DNA matched forensic samples from the crime scene. Although there was no DNA evidence against the teenagers—who always maintained their innocence—the prosecutor was fighting to keep them in jail saying they must have committed the crimes in company with the older man. Warden said that the prosecutor refused to give up the teenagers' convictions even though the older man's confession excluded them absolutely, and there was no evidence they knew him prior to the attack on the young woman. 'Those are the kinds of tortured excuses prosecutors sometimes come up with to defend convictions'.

Chapter 25

OPERATION TRITON

Against the odds, Bronson Blessington was granted conditional leave in the High Court to appeal the severity of his sentence after I filed an 'in person' intervener application in the case of *Baker v the Queen*, the official Legal Aid sponsored challenge to the cement law. Alan Baker was arguably the 'worst' of the ten Never to be Released prisoners, a man whose crimes against Virginia Morse and Ian Lamb were so unspeakable the trial judge could not bring himself to describe them in any detail in his sentencing remarks accompanying the court's judgement. Arguably, the 'best' of the ten non-release prisoners for the purposes of legal argument in the High Court was Bronson Blessington given his youth and the fact he had the mental capacity of a nine or ten-year-old at the time of his crimes.

In October 2003, for the purpose of assisting with the Blessington facts that may be relevant to the *Baker case*, I was seated in legal chambers in a recycled art-deco bank building in Martin Place with John Basten AO, KC and Will Hutchins of the Prisoners' Legal Service when the telephone rang. I'd been in conferences with senior counsel on many occasions over the years and the phone never rang—suffice to say nobody interrupted senior counsel. I knew John Basten from a previous case in the Federal Court when I represented HomeFund borrowers in a class action against the State government.

"It's for you" said John Basten, handing me the telephone.

How embarrassing. Who in the world would even know I was in John Basten's chambers? Lyn Lovelock, the Deputy Clerk of the Parliaments, wanted to inform me that officers of the Independent Commission Against Corruption (ICAC) were executing a search warrant on my parliamentary offices—even as she spoke—and did I want to be in attendance? An agency of the executive government, the ICAC was known around the houses of parliament as the 'political police'.

I would not be returning to my parliamentary offices before the conference with Mr Basten concluded in half an hour or so. Lovelock handed the phone to my traumatised secretary and I apologised profusely.

The corruption commission is a public body that strikes fear in the hearts of politicians because ICAC officers operate in a way that is contrary to all the rules of due process. Unlike police investigations, no civil rights or rules of evidence apply to ICAC interrogations, and according to the enabling ICAC legislation, the commission *can inform itself on any matter in such manner as it considers appropriate.*

Light rain was falling as I emerged from the art-deco former banking chamber. The normally grey granite pavers of Martin Place were glistening black in the light rain. I treaded warily—with a sick feeling in the pit of my stomach—as I made my way back to Macquarie Street. A few weeks earlier, an anonymous scandal sheet had done the rounds of the Parliament House press gallery boxes alleging I'd misused my expense account by representing prisoners and writing books. The claims were so ridiculous that not one journalist called to ask what the scandal sheet was all about. But someone who shall remain anonymous sent a copy to the ICAC.

Upon entering my deserted and upturned parliamentary offices, I was shocked to read on a copy of the search warrant left on my desk that my use of parliamentary resources and allowances was indeed the object of the search and seizure operation. According to a handwritten note from Lyn Lovelock, officers from the corruption watchdog had removed from my office several boxes of files, correspondence, personal papers, the hard drives from two desktop computers and a laptop.

I'd not missed the parliamentary office raiders by more than just a few minutes and their body odours—mostly testosterone—hung foul in the air. The paintings on the walls of my offices were askew. An exquisite light-filled work by Brian Dunlop rested on the back of a couch, its hanging wire curled and broken around the frame. I could not imagine what I might be expected to hide behind wall pictures. A brief examination of the office filing cabinets revealed a random culling of the files. Several files were undisturbed, even though their contents revealed much more about my use of parliamentary resources than anything taken under the search warrant. The ICAC officers who raided my offices were not just foul smelling, but sloppy investigators. They called their investigation 'Operation Triton' after a demigod who lived in the depths of the sea.

On my desk under the search warrant, I found a ten-page document titled 'search and seizure record', which listed all the material removed from the offices. Some of the material was described in vague terms and I was unable to identify it, but one item jumped off the page: *Interview at Goulburn gaol*. The ICAC had taken a transcript of the tape recording of Shorty Jamieson explaining to John Bracey and me how he was verballed by police at Southport in Queensland and forced to sign a false record of interview. It was easy to become a bit paranoid when an agency of the executive government turned your life on its head, but even so, ex-police did work for the ICAC, and I was feeling vulnerable.

In contrast to the wheels of justice, the affairs of State move at breakneck speed, and within a few days, the Clerk of the Parliaments, John Evans, was guiding me through a claim for parliamentary privilege over the transcript. As luck would have it, I used the Shorty Jamieson papers for the purposes of preparing a speech in parliament about the irony of the legislature imposing a life sentence on an innocent convict. Advice from Bret Walker indicated that using the papers in this way may be sufficient to establish a breach of parliamentary privilege entitling the parliament to demand a return to the clerk of all material taken by the ICAC. The Legislative Council's privileges and ethics committee commenced an inquiry, received evidence and published its report in the twinkling of an eye. The ICAC initially resisted the findings of the committee but returned all the material to the Clerk of the Parliaments the day after the parliament ordered it to do so.

Instead of celebrating this first-round win over the investigators, I feared I'd added to my woes further down the track. It would be a pyrrhic victory if the parliament's decision served only to strengthen the corruption watchdog's resolve to justify its investigation. According to the scandal sheet, I'd falsely claimed an allowance for living in the country when my primary place of residence was the city; I'd wrongly used my parliamentary offices for political activities and for writing books; and I'd improperly claimed travelling expenses for visiting prisoners at Goulburn jail. My denials of any wrongdoing fell on deaf ears at the ICAC, and before long, I received notice to attend three days of private inquisition hearings. After that, I could expect to be the subject of an ignominious public hearing at which the ICAC exercised extensive coercive powers, including denying the presumption of innocence and the right to know my accusers.

I was genuinely shocked by the suggestion I'd acted corruptly and struggled to take the investigation seriously. ICAC officers had removed from my offices 130 documents covered by parliamentary privilege and they'd damaged beyond repair the hard drive of one of my computers. Between the documents lost on the computer and the ones left behind in the search and seizure operation, the investigators had no chance of following the paper trail of my affairs, and so I volunteered my duplicate records in the hope of getting a fair go. Every document I presented was met with silence. Nobody was burdened by the onus of proof at the ICAC and the case against a person was never officially stated. Investigators also used listening devices and telephone intercepts, which meant every spoken word had to be accounted for, and a person making inconsistent statements would be presumed by the narrow ICAC rules of engagement to be a liar.

The ICAC's private inquisition hearings began and proceeded uneventfully. I spent two days in the witness box under cross-examination by counsel assisting the investigation, and I was asked every conceivable question about my life and parliamentary activities. In effect, I was required to justify to the ICAC each day of my existence since my election to the parliament in 1999. Documents used to compile coloured charts of my daily comings and goings included the parliament's printed evidence of my travel claims, mobile phone and ATM records, bank statements and tax records.

Suddenly the assistant commissioner hearing the case, Justice Paul Stein AM, QC, was re-appointed as an acting judge of the Court of Appeal, and my lawyer, John Marsden, wanted to make a fuss—apparently there was a problem with a serving judicial officer working for an agency of the executive government. Under the Westminster doctrine of separation of powers the legislature, the executive and the judiciary must not confuse their roles in representative democracy (especially politicians sentencing prisoners, you might think). Anyway, Paul Stein stood down, and the case was back to square one.

I was not too pleased about losing Stein as judge and jury of my affairs, or the additional cost of starting the hearings again (you cannot recover costs in an ICAC case—win, lose or draw). On the positive side, the delay gave me time to prepare a proper defence to the ICAC's claims.

A new assistant commissioner, Peter Hastings KC, was appointed, and I knew nothing about the man except he was often briefed as a government prosecutor, which gave me heartburn and palpitations. Hastings wanted to cut to the chase and go straight to public hearings. Witnesses were summonsed, exhibits compiled and hearing dates advertised. Two weeks were set aside for the public hearings: one week for the witnesses to be heard and a further week for my responses. The substantive allegations seemed to be I didn't really live on the north coast and therefore I'd been wrongly claiming expenses for travelling to parliament in Sydney; I was inappropriately claiming an accommodation allowance for staying in Sydney even though I was engaged in parliamentary business; and I was using the parliament's resources to write a book and computer program. The complaint about spending taxpayer funds to visit prisoners seemed to have fallen by the wayside.

John Marsden was too sick with malignant cancer to represent me at the public hearing and barrister Michael Lee SC took over, instructed by solicitor Kara Greiner, whose father Nick Greiner was the former premier who lost his job as a result of a flawed ICAC investigation. At every chance, I took great delight in introducing my solicitor as 'Kara Greiner as in *Greiner v the ICAC*'. Michael Lee (known in my family as 'the Archangel Michael') had acted for Marsden in his high-profile defamation case against Channel Seven. Marsden won the case and was awarded costs of $8.2 million. Lee had a framed copy of the costs cheques on the wall of his chambers. The lawyers did a sterling job under the double burden of my press releases about progress of the ICAC hearing and Marsden's barking commentary from his St Vincent's hospital bed.

In the years since the ICAC was established, millions of public dollars were spent investigating politicians, and while several reputations were destroyed, no successful prosecution had emerged from the investigations as at 2004. (Twenty years later and more than 50 people had been charged and convicted of offences arising from ICAC investigations). Most allegations against politicians in the early days of the ICAC concerned misuse of parliament's resources and allowances and unlawful intent in that context was almost impossible to prove. In my case, I was a member of five parliamentary committees of the upper house, and pretty much flat chat on parliamentary business seven days a week. I said so on the first morning of the ICAC public hearing in a press release.

I spent the first 15 minutes of the public hearing in the witness box defending the press release and trying to rebut Peter Hastings' assertion that what I said may be a contempt of the ICAC. While I agreed with the proposition that I was hoping to influence press reports of the hearings, I was simply answering what the morning papers had said and making sure they had the full story. It was an outrage, in my opinion, that the ICAC was happy to brief the press with details of the allegations, and at the same time to ignore every question I asked about the case against me.

This exchange over the press release set the tone for my interrogation and I argued with the inquisitors about almost every proposition they put to me. Their case was based on a particularly narrow interpretation of the legislation and guidelines governing the use of parliamentary resources and allowances. Each year, the Parliamentary Remuneration Tribunal published a 'determination', which set out members' entitlements and the rules they were expected to follow when they spent those entitlements. Throughout the hearing, I tried to explain that investigators were on the wrong track.

At the end of the two-week hearing, I provided hundreds of pages of material answering ICAC questions. I followed the rules as prescribed by the PRT and the relevant documents were in my office when it was raided if only the ICAC investigators knew what to look for.

In the month before Christmas 2004, I received a call from the ICAC to inform me that a decision would be delivered to the President of the Legislative Council, Dr Meredith Burgmann, on Friday at 11.00am. The president had been one of my strongest supporters during the inquiry and a vocal opponent of agencies of the executive government having the right to raid the parliamentary offices of legislators. She also spoke out against the parliament passing retrospective life sentences on prisoners for the sole purpose of scoring cheap political points.

On the appointed day, I foregathered with my legal representatives on the red leather seats outside the president's office. The political police were already inside and I was unashamedly nervous. I'd prepared two press releases, one saying the ICAC was a sensible organisation making a useful contribution after all, and the other asserting that the ICAC and not me was the waste of taxpayer funds. I handed Michael Lee a draft appeal to the Supreme Court, and he began scoring through the various prospective grounds of appeal with his pen, which really put me on edge.

We waited nearly half an hour and then Meredith Burgmann emerged from her office with the Clerk of the Parliaments and the ICAC officers in tow. Everyone was smiling and the ICAC's solicitor, Roy Waldon, said there was no finding of corrupt conduct. I thanked him for a good decision and there was handshaking all round. I asked for a copy of the decision and was told it should be under my parliamentary office door. What about a copy for my solicitor? Waldon scratched around in a shoulder bag and begrudgingly found a copy of the 64-page report for Kara Greiner. According to the executive summary, I *probably* lived on the north coast, and the use of parliament's resources to write books and computer programs was within the rules but *inappropriate and ill-advised.* The result was always going to annoy me. If I didn't live on the north coast, I was the first homeless person elected to parliament, and a host of politicians before me had written books on the job. What I knew about computer programs you could write on the back of a postage stamp. I headed for my office where I looked forward to getting my parliamentary life back, although the reputational damage of an ICAC investigation was probably unrecoverable.

Chapter 26

BRET WALKER

In the shadow of the ICAC troubles, I visited the High Court in Canberra for the appeal hearing in *Baker v the Queen*. John Basten expected he would be given leave to intervene on behalf of Bronson Blessington as the *Baker* decision directly affected Blessington's liberty. Will Hutchens had filed a mountain of documents in the court making two broad arguments: the exercise of judicial power by a legislature to retrospectively vary a prisoner's sentence was inconsistent with the judicial power in the Australian Constitution; and the legislative scheme so enacted failed to distinguish between a child and adult offenders. Since the demeaning ICAC experience, I looked forward to attending a real court with real judges, who applied rules of evidence and other forms of due process that had evolved over nearly 800 years since the Magna Carta of 1215.

I arrived early at the High Court on the shores of Lake Burly Griffin, fully expecting breakfast or at least a cup of coffee after the three-hour drive from Sydney. The front entrance to the court was blocked by the media, jostling me with microphones and questions, and when finally I reached the inside of the box-like glass and metal building, I discovered that the canteen did not run to coffee until after the court opened at ten. Chris Reason from Channel Seven had followed me into the foyer of the court and I stopped for a chat after the disappointment of no coffee. The journalist asked if I would do a formal interview with the assembled media given that none of the lawyers acting for parties or representing interveners would talk for fear they might be seen as pre-empting their cases. I agreed on the basis that I acted for nobody and I enjoyed a good relationship with the press—or so I thought.

Standing in a media pack outside the front entrance to the High Court and surrounded by microphones, cameras and aggressive journalists, it was fair to say I felt a bit intimidated. As I attempted to explain my support for Blessington's intervention in the *Baker* case, I realised the reporters regarded me as representing all ten Never to be Released prisoners—Blessington's successful intervention may be sufficient to overturn the cement law and allow the other nine to secure a review of their legislated life sentences. I argued that each of the prisoners ought to have his sentence considered on its merits which the parliament had failed to do. Also, I said that the ten prisoners could be compared to the Australian prisoners David Hicks and Mamdouh Habib who were then incarcerated in Guantanamo Bay by the executive government of the USA. I was referring to punishment in the form of indefinite detention by way of executive and not judicial ruling, but the journalists were incensed by the analogy.

I retreated to the High Court building and found my way into the courtroom, which is built like a theatre with tiered seats for the audience, an orchestra pit for lawyers and a stage for the seven judges. Leaning across the brass railing that separated spectators from participants, I caught the attention of Will Hutchins who gave me the first instalment of a bad news day: the government was opposing Blessington's intervention in the case. I barely had time to process the information when the seven judges of the court filed out onto the stage and arranged themselves in front of the orchestrated lawyers and the rest of us. Chief Justice Murray Gleeson sat in the middle of the judges and indicated to the assembled lawyers to stand one at a time and announce their respective appearances.

Brett Walker informed the court that he appeared for the appellant Allan Baker. Michael Sexton, the Solicitor-General for New South Wales, said he appeared for the respondent (the Queen) and the Attorney General for New South Wales. The States of Western Australia and South Australia were also represented to protect the rights of their respective governments to pass any law they pleased so far as prisoners were concerned. When John Basten announced that he appeared for Bronson Blessington in support of the appellant, the Chief Justice asked Michael Sexton about his attitude to the proposed intervention. The Solicitor-General was opposed to the idea.

> *We would oppose the application, your Honours …Insofar as Bronson Blessington's case raises the same issues, in our submission, these will be fully canvassed by the parties. Insofar as they raise different issues because, for example, he was underage at the time of the offence, we would say these are matters for another day. In particular, it is our understanding that Bronson Blessington's primary position is that his application, which is on foot before the Supreme Court of New South Wales, is not governed at all by the legislation that is being considered by the Court in this case, that he is governed by earlier legislation.*

Blessington's application to the Supreme Court for a review of his life sentence had been outstanding for more than seven years because of first one law and then another introduced by the Carr Government to cement the prisoner in his cell. To say his application was 'on foot' was technically correct, but spurious in light of the fact that the young man now had to be in jail for 30 years before his review application could be dealt with, and basically he had to be on his death bed before parole was to be considered. Basten was given no opportunity to cavil with the Solicitor General. The Chief Justice told Basten the Court was not prepared to grant the leave he sought and that was the end of the matter.

I was heartened by the sonorous voice of Justice Michael Kirby AC, CMG. "I would have granted the application," the judge said. As in politics, you need the numbers in the law, and Kirby was the single dissenter on a conservative High Court.

The reason the court did not want to hear from John Basten was that the eminent silk was about to tell the eminent justices a few home truths. Of the approximately 250 life prisoners who had applied to the Supreme Court for a review of their sentences to a fixed term of years, Blessington was probably the least culpable on account of his age and mental capacity at the time of his crimes. Plus his review application was lodged with the Supreme Court *before* the cement law was introduced into the New South Wales Parliament. Proportionality in sentencing demanded he receive a sentence comparable to punishment for similar crimes committed in 1988. Using legislative power to manipulate judicial authority with retrospective additional punishment was par for the course for State parliaments but prima facie unconstitutional.

Another home truth was the High Court's previous decision in *Kable v Director of Public Prosecutions.* Gregory Kable killed his wife with a carving knife and had served seven years for manslaughter when, in 1994, the Fahey Coalition Government passed the Community Protection Act to keep Kable in prison. The High Court in *Kable* struck down the Community Protection Act 1994, which was former Premier John Fahey's last futile attempt to keep the conservatives in government after the unjust ICAC routing of Fahey's predecessor, Nick Greiner. Kable walked free and Labor under Bob Carr defeated Fahey in the State election of 1995. Greg Kable did not turn out to be the demon contemplated by the Community Protection Act and he became a useful member of society, running a mentor program for young prisoners.

John Basten remained stuck fast in the middle of the High Court lawyers looking restless and uncomfortable. Protocol demanded he wait for a break in the proceedings before exiting stage left. To his right, Bret Walker for Baker was standing at the lectern facing the judges and resting on one elbow as if he had exhausted the last of his arguments. Walker was dialoguing with Justices McHugh and Kirby.

> McHugh: *Mr Walker, the New South Wales Parliament, subject to the federal Constitution, could take any fact it liked as the basis of one of its laws. If it wanted to, it could have made it a condition of these applications that you are named in a particular newspaper on a particular day.*
> Walker: *I think the traditional example, to emphasise the point, your Honour, is to refer to colour of hair.*
> McHugh: *Colour of hair, yes...*

> Kirby: *If I could just say what I have in mind. We are now considering this issue in the new enlightenment of Kable, of what is appropriate, or what is permissible under the federal Constitution to impose upon judges of a later age by reference to what judges of an earlier age—some but not all—have said. It is a very arbitrary trigger, a very arbitrary trigger indeed. It is offensive to a notion of equal justice under the law because some judges would have said these things ['I recommend this prisoner should never be released'] and other judges would never have said them.*

The traditional view of parliamentary democracy was that limits existed on the law-making powers of a State parliament. While recognising the supremacy of the legislative arm of government over the executive and judicial arms—because the people elect members of parliament—it was never intended that parliamentary representatives pass any law that might take their fancy. Albert Venn Dicey (1835-1922) who refined the doctrine of parliamentary supremacy said there are many laws *which Parliament never would and (to speak plainly) never could pass.*

Over lunch in the High Court's canteen, Bret Walker confirmed his view that a State parliament could pass a law imprisoning all red-headed citizens—if it had a mind to do so—but the chances of those politicians who supported such a law getting re-elected would be seriously diminished. We had a memorable discussion about Thomas More, Chancellor of the Exchequer under Henry VIII. Did More die for his faith or pig-headedness? A good historical argument could be made either way, yet I'd no problem deferring to learned counsel, whose opinion was worth a king's ransom.

Chapter 27

OPERATION CERDUNA

On the way back to Sydney from the *Baker* hearing in Canberra, I called in at Goulburn jail to convey the disappointing news to a few life prisoners about Bronson Blessington's unsuccessful intervention in the High Court proceedings. Bronson himself was in Silverwater prison for access to his Sydney legal advisers, so the first prisoner on my list was Stephen Jamieson. I found him in the Multi-Purpose Unit (MPU), segregated and alone. Goulburn's MPU was two-star accommodation compared with the one-and-a-half star B wing. It was frequently used for disciplinary purposes. As we sat down at the table in the MPU's upstairs common area at the end of the cells, Stephen told me he wanted to return to his old digs. Two or three correctional officers—and others coming and going—could see us from behind a glass partitioned office across a narrow corridor.

I asked the prisoner what he did to land in the MPU and he said he was transferred to Silverwater prison in Sydney with Bronson for a couple of weeks, 'for operational purposes' which turned out to be an interview with the Police Integrity Commission, the corruption watchdog for police. According to the PIC annual report, *Operation Cerduna is an investigation into an allegation that police officers perverted the course of justice during the investigation of a murder.* Officers of the PIC wanted to talk to Stephen about the allegation that police had signed him up for murder, and they wanted to do it on their Sydney turf. When Stephen returned to Goulburn after the interview, his cellmate of many years, Rick, had a new cellmate.

I asked how he got on with the PIC officers and Stephen said they looked like characters from the movie *Men in Black* in their dark suits and ties and Percil white shirts.

"I asked 'em for a card and they said they couldn't give me one for security reasons. 'Don't worry, we're not coppers', one of 'em said. They showed me their badges and I'd never seen badges like that. They said if I wanted more information to go through the prison channels." He turned his head at an angle to one side and said, "That's about it."

Did they ask you about the murder?

"Yeah, I said I never murdered nobody."

Did they believe you?

"I dunno."

What about the people here at Goulburn jail? Do they believe you?

"I've told the screws here what happened, and they say I tell lies, but I never had no reason to tell lies."

Have you ever told lies about murdering someone?

"I'd know it if I murdered someone. I wouldn't be able to handle it. For some reason it's not in me nature. I'd be like one of these blokes who kills someone and then can't live with themselves."

What do you mean?

"I couldn't live with meself if I murdered someone. I'd neck meself ."

What happened when you came back to Goulburn?

"I was in reception and they said, 'You'll go into D wing for a few days'. I said, 'Me mate's holdin' me cell'. They said, 'No, it's taken'." Instead of placing the prisoner in the unpopular D wing, the reception officer arranged an escort to B wing where Stephen had previously shared his cell with Rick. This time he was placed in a cell on his own in B wing.

"After four days in the cell, I asked if I could go out in the yard. I was talkin' to Rick in the yard and the next thing I know this bloke 'Richie' comes up and king hits me. Turns out 'Richie' is Rick's new cellmate. Later I read on a report that I called his mum a slag. I don't even know his mum."

That was enough to get Stephen in the MPU and he told me he'd been "one out" in a cell on his own and "goin' nuts" ever since.

"If I was a lock-in in B wing I'd be happy. I'd have a shower and get out for a walk in the big yard. Down here in the MPU, the yard is so small you can't swing a cat."

I reminded him that the B wing big yard at the moment smelled like a sewerage treatment works from overcrowding and blocked toilets, not to mention the dangers of mixing with violent men in a confined space. He said he knew about violence—he wasn't allowed use the internet because of the violence. I laughed out loud. A prisoner in a cell near the MPU common room mimicked my laugh like a lyrebird hidden in the bush. Suddenly the place erupted in howls of mimicry.

The cries of the criminally damned were more than I could bear and I summoned one of the officers in the office across the corridor to let me out. As I pushed my chair back from the table and stood up, I told Stephen to watch the television news that night for a report of the High Court case.

We shook hands in the corridor, and as I followed the officer towards the stairs that lead outside, I heard Stephen talking with another officer.

"Any chance of a TV, chief?"

The reply was muffled in the cacophony of caged laughter, but I heard it clear enough. "Yeah, yours and Buckleys."

I caught up to the officer ahead of me and asked about arrangements for television sets. He told me that 95 percent of prisoners had their own.

"There's a couple of floaters, which are usually taken, but most of them have their own."

I asked how a prisoner got TV and he said someone had to put $279 in their bank account "which includes the cost of the co-axial cable." It dawned on me that Shorty Jamieson had nobody sufficiently interested in him to buy him a television. Later, I arranged for a television set through a prison welfare organisation.

The correctional officer placed me outside the heavy iron gate that guarded the entrance to the MPU building. Blinking in the bright sunlight, I looked around for my next escort—nobody moved inside the jail without an escort. I was thinking about the dilemma of *Operation Cerduna*. Like all the government watchdogs, the PIC was shrouded in mystery and secrecy, and if you tried to assist with their inquiries, you were immediately bound by their statutory silence provisions. For this reason, I declined an invitation to give evidence to the inquiry, telling the officer who contacted me that I knew nothing about the crimes against Ms Balding other than what was contained in the court transcripts. Being free to talk about the case without secrecy constraints was important if something needed to be said in support of a review application—especially if I hoped to secure media interest in Stephen's predicament.

Chapter 28

THE MURPHYS

Standing in the concrete courtyard outside Goulburn jail's Multi-Purpose Unit, I could feel the midday sun beginning to burn my forehead as I waited for my next escort. For the moment, I closed my eyes and raised a thin folder of papers above my head for protection from the sun. Next thing I knew, a correctional officer was standing beside me—the moon-faced fellow who met me on my first visit to Bronson Blessington.

Where have you been? I asked incredulously as I began to walk away from the MPU towards the main gate. My escort was not moving.

"I only work casual when I'm needed. If you come this way you can see the Murphys."

He headed towards the education wing adjoining the Circle offices and I took off after him.

On the way into the jail, I'd asked to see Les and Gary Murphy, both convicted with their brother Michael Murphy and two others—John Travers and Michael Murdoch—of the murder of Sydney nurse Anita Cobby in 1986. The things those men did to Anita Cobby are the most appalling and gruesome criminal abominations in the collective living memory of the people of New South Wales.

I wanted to see Les and Gary Murphy because many of the police who investigated the Anita Cobby crimes also happened to investigate the crimes against Janine Balding two years later. I'd read in Julia Sheppard's book, *Someone Else's Daughter: the Life and Death of Anita Cobby*, some striking resemblances between what Jamieson had said about his police record of interview and allegations made by Les and Gary Murphy at trial. Gary's solicitor, Leigh Johnson, was supposed to join us but cancelled at the last minute, so I was not expecting to see the Murphy brothers that day.

"Are you going to do something for the Murphys?" asked the moon-faced prison officer as we approached the education wing.

What could I do? The crimes of children against Janine Balding were bad enough, but the cruelty and inhumanity of what grown men did to Anita Cobby was incomprehensible. I explained that I did as much as I could for the Murphys with Blessington's failed intervention in the *Baker* case. Had the application been successful—based on the fact of Blessington's youth and his mental incapacity—then perhaps the cement law might have been set aside by the High Court for the benefit of all ten Never to be Released prisoners. To paraphrase one of the journalists who interviewed me in Canberra, what more could I do to incur the people's wrath than to help the worst of the worst get out of prison?

"You can write down the Murphy brothers' story."

We were in the doorway of the main office in the education wing with empty classrooms on either side. Les and Gary Murphy were standing in the reception room to the left of me, and to my surprise, Kevin Crump was standing to the right with his Legal Aid solicitor. While the three prisoners did not bear the same degree of responsibility for their crimes as their co-offenders, the murders of Anita Cobby, Virginia Morse and Ian Lamb were so outrageously violent and despicable it was hard to imagine any government having the faintest political interest in releasing them. For all that, their legislated sentences were grossly unfair—an insult to the principle of fair and equal justice. Kevin Crump and Les Murphy both had their sentences redetermined by the Supreme Court and both were in line for release on parole before the 2001 cement law came along. And Gary Murphy—like Shorty Jamieson—might be innocent.

Kevin Crump showed me a letter from the Parole Board denying him parole even though he'd served the 30 years of his redetermined sentence for his lesser part in the murder of Ian Lamb and the unspeakable crimes against Virginia Morse. The letter was written in unreadable English and I told him it meant he was stuck in jail so long as the cement law blocked his way out. Crump was a big man in his mid-fifties and he wore a Kairos wooden cross around his neck. He opened a folder of certificates he'd achieved and results slips of various courses he'd attended in anticipation of his release. In redetermining his sentence, Justice McInerney found that Crump had been a model prisoner and *made every attempt to rehabilitate himself in the difficult environment of maximum-security prison.*

I turned to ask the moon-faced correctional officer if he'd arranged for me to be ambushed, and once again the bloke was missing in action.

One of the officers on duty in the education office opened the door of the classroom to the left and directed the Murphys and me inside. Kevin Crump and his solicitor were hanging there in the reception room and I wished them luck. I was literally lost for words that might console Kevin Crump whose chances of getting out of jail in the foreseeable future were remote. The cement law said that *any* prisoner who had *ever* been the subject of *any* Never to be Released recommendation in *any* court was not entitled to parole except perhaps on their deathbed. Whatever the High Court might have said about the new law, it was a perversion of sentencing principles, and Crump's case demonstrated a particularly nasty aspect of that perversion. To retrospectively prevent by legislation any review of a sentence that had already been served seemed to me to be an exercise of legislative power sufficient to turn Albert Venn Dicey in his grave. For his part, Kevin Crump believed the 'error' in his sentencing would soon be rectified by the courts.

Leaving Kevin Crump in the reception room, I followed Les and Gary Murphy into the empty classroom and the officer closed the door behind us. Both men were wearing green shorts and green sloppy joes with white training shoes and white socks. I shook hands with the brothers and we sat at the laminate table. The tension between us was immediate and palpable. Les was suspicious of anyone interested in writing about the murder of Anita Cobby since "everybody who wrote about it got it wrong."

I could set the record straight if he explained his involvement. But what was the point in going over it again? He'd told the judge reviewing his conviction of his limited role in the crimes and the judge reduced his sentence. End of section.

Les Murphy is a small man, stocky, and he seemed to be both intelligent and persuasive. All the more reason, I thought, for him to tell me what happened to Anita Cobby in all its gruesome detail. The young woman was raped and brutalised so badly her physical features were barely recognisable. At the end of her torture, John Travers slit her throat from ear to ear with a butcher's knife, severing her jugular vein so that she bled to death like a slaughtered animal. Her desecrated and mutilated body remained in a paddock at Prospect in western Sydney for two days before a farmer found it when investigating the odd behaviour of his cows. I wanted to know what part Les and his brother Michael played in this horror before agreeing to help.

Gary Murphy is average height, a thin and gaunt man, his head pushing forward from stooped shoulders in an apologetic sort of way. He has a pronounced speech impediment and appears unable to explain himself or express ideas using clear and unambiguous language. I suspected he carried the burden of some kind of dyslexia. The two brothers shared a cell in B wing and Les said Gary suffered epileptic seizures about once a month as a result of being bashed by police. Julia Sheppard's book described Gary's arrest—as reported by a Channel Seven news journalist who interviewed witnesses in Tari Way, Glenfield, where the arrest took place.

> *One neighbour said, "The ungodly screams of that boy (Gary Murphy) I'll never forget them as long as I live... He just got laid into..." Another neighbour had looked over the fence into the yard. "They hit him with the butt of a gun first of all. Then they booted him... they had him on the ground, they had a foot on his back and he never fought back... they dragged him up the path, they didn't walk him up the path, they threw him against the tree... he was thrown down onto the ground. The police had their feet*

on him again and they laid into him. We're not saying he's innocent, we're not saying he's guilty, but you're supposed to be innocent until proven guilty. Three against one... no one needed to do that."

While Gary Murphy had always maintained his innocence of the crimes against Anita Cobby, few people heard his pleas or gave them any credence in the frenetic aftermath of the sickening crimes. The same page of Julia Sheppard's book describing the arrest also refers to Gary's unsworn dock statement in which he said he'd been drinking at the Doonside Hotel with his friend Ray Paterson on the night of the murder. He said he stayed at the hotel until closing time. *Me and Ray Paterson left together. I don't know where we went. I can't remember. It wasn't important at the time but I do know I was not at a rape or a murder. That's one thing I would remember.*

I showed the two men the passage in the book. Les said his glasses were in his cell and Gary said he had trouble reading. Anyway, they were not impressed with any stories written about the crimes against Anita Cobby. Les repeated that he'd nothing to prove since his retrial—the judge in the new trial didn't make a Never to be Released recommendation because of Les' limited involvement in the crimes. But like Kevin Crump, Les Murphy was still caught by the cement law because it covered all previous judicial determinations—even a determination where the earlier decision was quashed. The absurdity of the cement law knew no bounds as I tried to explain to Les.

The two men had initially refused to let me interview them when Leigh Johnson had pulled out of the meeting at the last minute.

I thanked them for changing their minds and agreeing to see me without their lawyer present, and I promised to do anything I could to help them. I would speak to their lawyers.

"Just be careful what you write," Les said in a smiling voice, and I was uncertain if he was making a joke or a threat.

They were entitled to make an application for a conviction and sentence review if fresh and compelling evidence pointed to an error in the case against them. I thought their best chance was to question the police records of interview which had to be a verbatim record of what they told police.

"I said I weren't there," said Gary ruefully.

I was surprised when Gary Murphy used the same words and the same intonation as Stephen Jamieson. The idea that two of the ten Never to be Released prisoners might be innocent was mind-boggling. Gary pushed his papers across the desk, and as I flicked through them, I recognised the same difficulties I'd seen in the Jamieson paperwork: the adverse comments in his case management file on account of his apparent obstinacy; the denial of small privileges until the prisoner acknowledged his guilt; and numerous suggestions that he could not be trusted to tell the truth. The Murphys had served nearly 20 years in prison, and if Gary was lying, he was a persistent liar.

Writing in *The Good Weekend* magazine published with the *Sydney Morning Herald* on Saturdays, Amruta Slee had alerted me to Gary Murphy's situation. Slee quoted the legal team of solicitor Leigh Johnson and barrister Sandy Wetmore in an article about the Anita Cobby murder that was published on 1 March 2003. Leigh Johnson described their first interview with Gary Murphy at Parklea prison.

He's not educated to a very high standard, and he was telling this convoluted story, carrying on about Les stealing a car and changing the numbers. And we were going, "Yeah, but what about the murder," and he said, "Well, I don't know, I weren't there." Sandy and I were in a state of shock because we'd assumed with the rest of the world that he was guilty, so then we pulled out each one of the other four boys [they were in separate cells] and interviewed them—and each one of them confirmed that Gary wasn't there. We got this in writing from all four of the others.

Julia Sheppard said in her book that none of the accused had contact with each other during their interrogation *so there could have been no collusion concerning their versions of events.* The article in *The Good Weekend* also reported that Gary Murphy told his lawyers—and he was telling me again—that he signed a confession "just to stop them bashing me." I showed him the news magazine article and a copy of a letter from Sandy Wetmore advising me that the barrister didn't have a copy of the police record of interview. I asked Gary if he had a copy and he told me it was lost in a flood at Leigh Johnson's office. I explained that Shorty Jamieson benefited from an application to the Innocence Panel as the resulting DNA evidence may assist him in establishing a judicial inquiry.

Gary confirmed he was at the Doonside Hotel with his friend Ray Paterson on the night of the murder. Initially, Ray supported Gary's alibi, but then changed his story.

Meanwhile Les Murphy was bouncing one leg impatiently on the ball of his left foot. I had a copy of Les' police record of interview with Detective Sergeant Kevin Raue and I avoided asking the prisoner why he signed it as the explanation was set out in his dock statement and recorded in Julia Sheppard's book. Les said was scared of Detective Raue and other police were treating him badly. Significantly, Les said in his dock statement that many of the questions in the record of interview were not even put to him, and he didn't give some of the recorded answers. I handed him my copy of the record of interview, which I'd obtained from his solicitor at trial, Marcus Solomon.

Why didn't the bloke who typed this sign it?

Les Murphy looked quizzically at the document. "I dunno. Nobody's ever asked me that before."

You've signed it and so has Detective Sergeant Raue, but not the bloke who typed it.

"I'll be stuffed," said Les, and he looked up quickly to catch me frowning.

Did Detective Raue type it himself?

"No, no, there was another copper. His name's not on it. He was a big bloke—bigger than Raue."

How did they conduct the interview?

"The copper doin' the typin' stopped typin' when I gave 'em an answer they didn't like. Then the other copper, Raue, would answer the question and the first copper would keep typin' as if I'd answered."

Did you read the record of interview before you signed it?

"What was the use? I knew what they were up to."

Can you tell me now which answers you gave and which ones you say Detective Sergeant Raue gave?

"I guess so."

Did Raue ask you if Gary was there?

"Yeah. About three times."

And what did you say?

"I told him Gary weren't there. And each time I said it, Raue kicked the chair out from under me, and I fell on me arse on the floor of the police station. Eventually I stopped sayin' it."

Detective Raue denied in cross-examination during the trial of the Murphy brothers that he had mistreated or threatened Les Murphy, or that he had been involved in recording a false record of interview.

Gathering up my papers, I promised to visit the Murphys again, and to help Gary with his application to the Innocence Panel if he so wished. I explained that the panel had been suspended as a result of privacy issues raised in Shorty Jamieson's application, but another panel would continue reviewing cases when the new legislation was in place.

Sandy Wetmore had informed me that without the police record of interview, Gary Murphy could not have been convicted by a reasonable and impartial jury that was properly instructed. The barrister also said there was no DNA evidence produced at the trial, although forensic samples were taken from each of the accused. I told Gary it was likely the Division of Analytical Laboratories at Lidcombe still had forensic material as Michele Franco had informed me that DNA swabs from crime scenes were held going back to 1986—the year of the Anita Cobby murder.

I called the guard and he escorted me from the education wing. When I reached the main reception area, I inquired about the moon-faced officer, and my questions were met with blank stares. Outside, I smiled into breathless blue sky. Anita Cobby's abduction, rape and murder were such appalling crimes that even a wrongful conviction was unlikely to arouse sympathy for the Murphy brothers. Sadly, vengeance ran deep for certain crimes, and a whole generation of citizens remained traumatised by what was done to Anita Cobby in the Prospect cow paddock.

Even so, it still bothered me that in every comparable common law jurisdiction outside Australia, Les and Gary Murphy could expect a judicial review of their sentences based on the right to equal treatment under the law and other due process rights in a bill of rights. They could also expect to be given credit for their good behaviour in prison. And a forum would be available such as a criminal cases review commission to test the extent of their involvement in the crimes for which they were convicted. All just wishful thinking on my part, perhaps, but I remained hopeful.

At the time of writing, Les and Gary Murphy had been in prison for the crimes against Anita Cobby for almost 40 years. Michael Murphy died aged 65 of cancer at Long Bay prison hospital in 2019, 33 years after his part in the crimes against Anita Cobby. In 2023, Kevin Crump died aged 74 of a heart attack in Wellington prison northwest of Sydney, 50 years after his part in the crimes against Ian Lamb and Virginia Morse.

Chapter 29

'AMANDA'

After the detour to Goulburn jail to visit the Murphys, the trip back to Sydney was a bit of a blur. I was happy to turn off my phone and enjoy the countryside. As I drove into the Parliament House underground carpark, I turned the phone back on and listened to an urgent message to call 'Amanda' (not her real name)—one of Bronson's welfare workers from a prisoner support group. The prisoner had been woken at six in the morning and told to pack his things as he was on escort from Silverwater to Long Bay jail. Two plastic tubs were tossed into his cell, and a few hours later a prison van lumbered out the gates of the prison complex headed to Long Bay jail at Malabar in Sydney's east. Amanda said Bronson was terrified of returning to Long Bay.

He must have known he would be moving about in the prison system when the High Court legal proceedings were concluded.

"But the legal proceedings are not over," she cried.

Well, I suppose that was technically true, but the authorities would know that Bronson no longer needed to reside at Silverwater in close proximity to his Sydney lawyers. The words were no sooner out of my mouth than I realised I'd done nothing to explain to Amanda that although Bronson's outstanding Supreme Court application for a review of his life sentence remained in the court list, it would not be heard for several months—and possibly longer.

"Bronson will be killed if he goes back to Long Bay," Amanda yelled into the telephone. "You *must* do something."

I'd never been good at doing what I *must* do, but I promised to do what I could. Before ending the call, the young woman told me Bronson had not confided in me the dangerous conditions of his incarceration at Long Bay jail. I knew he'd spent nearly seven of his then 17 prison years in strict protection—the modern equivalent of solitary confinement—in Sydney prisons, but I'd deliberately avoided looking at the conditions under which his sentence was served for fear of being disheartened by something I could never change. I was especially conscious of not using my position in parliament to get special treatment for prisoners.

A few days passed before I could get an appointment at the jail, and by the time I made the short trip from the city to Malabar, I found Bronson deeply traumatised and at the edge of despair. He explained that he'd left Silverwater after the High Court case and the Long Bay prison reception had allocated him to the Metropolitan Special Purpose Centre where another prisoner had vowed to kill him. His possessions had still not arrived from Silverwater and he'd been bunkered down in a strict protection cell without a change of clothes. He told me he was "goin' crazy."

What's the story with the bloke who wants to kill you?

"I've had a problem with this bloke ever since I first came into the adult prison at Long Bay. I was a bit green around the gills at the time and said some things I wouldn't say now. The bloke's been psycho ever since. Now I find he's still here—waiting for me according to a message I got."

What happened between you?

Bronson told me the story but asked me not to repeat it. When it was told, the prisoner was breathless and I was speechless. Life behind bars gave a whole new meaning to living on the edge. Most inmates had a list of dangerous associates recorded on their management files—some at the inmates' request and others determined by Corrective Services. I assumed the bloke Bronson was concerned about was on his non-associations list.

"He's not on me list."

Why not?

"I dunno."

The bloke wants to kill you and he's not on your list?

Bronson shrugged his shoulders and said he wouldn't give the bloke up for wanting to kill him, which was the only way to get someone on his non-associations list.

Suddenly I was irritated. I suggested that giving up this particular prisoner would be a good thing to do, despite the dangers. Bronson argued against me, saying I couldn't imagine what it was like to live with violent men, to be always looking over your shoulder, jumping at shadows and having no security. He could not afford to be known in prison as a 'dog'.

I reminded him that all prisoners lived in fear of reprisals of one form or another, constantly at risk of assault, exposed to drug dependence and mental illness, with no privacy or personal life beyond the occasional weekend family visit.

You've had more support than most prisoners—not to mention the reassurance of your faith.

"By the way, I've got a scripture passage for you," he said, unfolding a sheet of paper. "It came to me this morning."

I was about to upbraid him for changing the subject, but I read the scripture passage, which described the disciples' joy as they discovered that devils submitted to them when they used Jesus' name. Jesus reportedly said in response, *I have given you power to tread down serpents and scorpions and the whole strength of the enemy; nothing shall ever hurt you.* I folded the sheet of paper and handed it back.

I don't wish to appear ungrateful, but I think the passage is for you, not me. Besides, evil is to be found in the hearts of men (and fewer women), not scorpions and serpents. I'm not a supporter of treading down people—even bad people. More interesting to me was whether angels are real, and could the moon-faced prison officer be one? It was a rhetorical question since I'd first met him in company with other officers who obviously knew him. If the officer was an angel, I was the man in the moon.

"Angels are real, Brother," Bronson said confidently. Sometimes they speak to me when there's danger, like telling me to get out of the yard." He rattled off something from the writings of the Apostle Paul about welcoming strangers, *for by doing so, some people have entertained angels without knowing it.* Given the size of the universe, I was open to the possibility of all things angelic.

I called the nearest correctional officer and asked to be escorted to the office of the deputy governor who cheerfully looked up the inmate classification files on the prison's computer. Sure enough, the threatening prisoner was not on Bronson's list of non-associations. I explained the problem of the prisoner's safety to the deputy governor and he agreed to take charge of the situation. Blessington would be in the next prison van to leave Long Bay headed for Goulburn.

Chapter 30

MICHAEL WHELAN

Bronson Blessington's observations about angels and demons made me curious enough to contact theologian Michael Whelan and find out what an enlightened priest had to say about good and evil in the criminal justice system. Michael occupied a modest office in the old presbytery building in the grounds of St Patrick's Church in Harrington Street at Church Hill, the site of the first Catholic Church in Australia built on land donated by my Irish ancestor William Davis in 1839. The priest presided over Sydney's Aquinas Academy named after the Angelic Doctor of the Church, Thomas Aquinas (1225-1274), often cited by Christians as the primary authority for the teaching that the angels work together for the benefit of everyone.

I made my way up creaky stairs and along a narrow corridor in the former presbytery building until finally I reached Michael Whelan's office door where he waited with open arms. He shepherded me into the office which had a view over a courtyard and seated me in one of two comfortable lounge chairs with a coffee table between us. I placed my tape recorder on the table, and my host poured strong black coffee. Priests living alone did not run to cake and warm scones in my experience.

"Thomas Aquinas from the thirteenth century would say that evil is the absence of what ought to be" Michael said with a circular movement of one hand. "What ought to be, humanly speaking, is connectedness, care, and commitment to our fellow human beings. In that sense, evil is absence or emptiness of the good. Evil is a fragmenting or disconnecting force on society—and in my own being. It disconnects us from who we are."

Perhaps we can be aware of evil and simply avoid it like the plague?

"Although we speak of evil as an absence, we should not think of it as without influence. It's analogous to a vacuum in physics. For example, I can come to a group as the bearer of evil and diminish the moral life of the group. I can take away being. I can dismantle or destroy. I can disconnect."

I asked whether the existence of evil can diminish in any way the responsibility of the two boys who murdered Janine Balding? Is evil some external force or part of human nature?

"You've got to safeguard human freedom, as well as human culpability and accountability. But you're also asking the question, is there more to this than just two disturbed boys? Can serious crime committed by children be adequately understood and dealt with in a merely legal or psychological way? These are not easy questions to answer."

It seemed to me that evil in the form of unbridled self-interest—lacking in any measure of compassion—was well documented and could be identified in spades at the Janine Balding crime scenes.

"Evil is a very slippery concept," the priest said. "The problem is, our culture does not have a credible language or symbolism to speak of evil, unlike many other cultures—or even our own culture a generation or two back. Because we don't have the words to name it or the symbols and rituals to deal with it, we tend to dismiss evil as if it were not a factor in our lives."

I put it to the priest that evil is self-evident in some situations such as rape and murder. While not denying the proposition, he suggested that evil can sometimes clothe itself in the self-righteousness of the moral majority.

"More than 1,500 years ago, St Augustine of Hippo made the astute observation that evil needs goodness to achieve its ends. It cannot exist on its own—it needs something good to diminish or corrupt." He hesitated for a moment as if searching for the right words. "For example, I could not slander another person if I did not have the gift of speech or the ability to communicate. And there's a corollary to this principle: evil may actually appear to us as good. If I were in charge of evil in the world, I would come dressed as a bishop, or politician, or police officer or some other agent of good order. The greater my talent, the greater my potential for evil."

I wanted to know what Michael Whelan thought about the dynamic involved for the victims of crime when misfortune and tragedy seemed to take over their lives. He told me a story he heard from his friend, Terry O'Connell, a pioneer of restorative justice which brings together offenders and victims of crime. During filming of a program for ABC television, O'Connell interviewed Joan and Jack Anderson, the parents of Rosemary Anderson who was killed in a suburb of Perth in 1963. The young woman's 18-year-old boyfriend, John Button, was convicted of running her down in his Simca motor vehicle after a drunken party and he spent five years in jail for the crime. Button always protested his innocence even though he signed a confession after many hours of police questioning.

In May 2001, 38 years after he was convicted of killing his

girlfriend, John Button successfully appealed the conviction. A former police accident investigator, Trevor Condren, gave court evidence that he told investigating police there were no signs on Button's Simca it had collided with a pedestrian. At the time, investigating police dismissed Condren's forensic examination of the vehicle on the basis they had their confession. Following the successful appeal, Joan Anderson told Terry O'Connell she would never believe anyone other than John Button killed her daughter, even though Perth's notorious serial killer, Eric Edgar Cooke, confessed to the killing four months after Button was convicted. The story had a happy ending and Joan Anderson eventually let go of her suffering, admitting she found an identity through the pain and resentment.

"There's a difference between human weakness and evil," said the priest, "although our human weakness can provide an opportunity for evil to take over our lives."

The statement lingered in the air between us, and then the priest said, "I would ask the question: what is it about us human beings—and I think it's a universal thing—that we hang on to the pain and the grief? It's almost as if without it we won't be anybody, or we may stop existing if we don't have any hurt or emotional pain. I think this is behind the mentality that says put the bastards in jail and throw away the key."

I asked Michael Whelan about forgiveness.

"One of the things I say to people is *you* cannot forgive. It's a grace. It will overtake you. There's this awful saying 'forgive and forget'. Take for example someone whose child has been killed. Humanly speaking, we might expect them to take to the grave their sense of loss and sadness, maybe anger and resentment, possibly confusion and even guilt. Telling them to 'forgive and forget' is almost certainly going to add a further burden to their troubled life. They need to be heard in their pain and accompanied through that pain to something more life giving. That may, in some cases, include forgiveness of the one who has hurt them so deeply."

I mentioned the father of Anita Cobby, Garry Lynch, who wrote in his book *Struck by Lightning* about his experience of forgiveness. Lynch said he could see no reason to forgive those who killed his daughter. Perhaps he could forgive their souls but not their actions. How he dealt with his grief was another matter altogether. Lynch joined the Serious Offenders Review Council and became actively involved in the rehabilitation of serious offenders. Later he was involved in forming the Homicide Victims Support Group. Eventually he was forced to give up his work in the prisons. People have short memories. He tried to explain that long-term prisoners rarely re-offend after their release, but few people wanted to know about that. Plus he was getting too old to be constantly trying to justify his work.

At the end of our discussion, I asked the priest if he believed that evil may manifest itself in physical form such as demons and snakes. Although he had no personal experience of such things, he had read credible accounts of people bearing witness to their encounters with evil in other dimensions. I knew people who claimed to see monstrous depictions of evil whether in their minds or as apparitional phenomena.

"I'm loathe to go down that track" he said arrestingly. "Here again we have the problem of so few words and symbols to name evil and deal with it. It's difficult not to personify evil, and once we do, we almost always become distracted from its subtlety—its real power for destruction."

The priest referred me to the biblical statement that *the truth will set you free* from the bondage of lies.

"I think this teaching about lies goes to the heart of the matter. Whether it's lying implicitly or explicitly about some matter of fact in order to deceive or mislead people, or whether it's lying about the way I live—in denial of who I am. Conduct of this kind is promoting an absence of what ought to be. It's a movement towards non-being. We subtract something from the cosmos when we behave in this way. We're all responsible for maintaining a certain moral vision—a commitment to what is real and true. Otherwise, we have no sense of what is good and what is evil."

I thanked the scholarly priest for talking with me. He suggested a couple of books about the subject of evil such as Scott Peck's *People of the Lie*.

"There may be a copy in the Aquinas Academy library."

I followed him out of the office and into a vestibule elevator. On the next level down, the library filled the whole floor, and the priest somehow located the book amongst the thousands of volumes stacked floor to ceiling. In a courtyard just off Grosvenor Street, the Sisters of Mercy operated a coffee shop on behalf of the St Patrick's Church parish, and I settled into coffee and scones with lashings of Peck's book.

Like Michael Whelan, Scott Peck believed that evil is more likely to present itself as goodness and righteousness rather than something in the opaque world of the psychopath or sociopath—a world relieved of the burden of conscience or guilt. Sociopaths and psychopaths seem to be as happy inside jail as out.

> *This is hardly the case with those I call evil. Utterly dedicated to preserving their self-image of perfection, they are unceasingly engaged in the effort to maintain the appearance of moral purity. They worry about this a great deal. They are acutely sensitive to social norms and what others might think of them. While they seem to lack any motivation to be good, they intensely desire to appear good. Their 'goodness' is all on the level of pretence. In effect, it's a lie. That is why they're the 'people of the lie'.*

Peck says that evil is the misuse of political power and he uses his experience as an adviser to the American military to illustrate war as an example of group or public evil, which is ultimately the collective result of individual bad choices. Group evil has the potential to be much worse than the individual culpability of the people who make up the group. Peck explains the monstrous evil at work in the My Lai massacre during the American war in Vietnam as far outweighing the guilt or awareness of the 500 soldiers involved in killing defenceless women and children cowering in their villages.

The people he labels as evil are chronic scapegoaters and they're frequently found in politics which has degenerated into the art of blaming others in order to avoid responsibility for our own bad decisions. Group or public evil cannot be confronted except by influencing individual members of the group. With 22,000 registered lobbyists in Washington, the prospect of influencing individual group leaders is overwhelming. If access to the leaders is blocked then we must turn to the lowliest members of the group and seek grassroots support. Either way, we turn to individuals.

> *For the 'group mind' is ultimately determined by the minds of the individuals who make up the group. As a single vote may be crucial in an election, so the whole course of human history may depend on one solitary and even humble individual. This is known to the genuinely religious. It is for this reason that no possible activity is considered to be more important than the salvation of a single human soul. This is why the individual is sacred. For it is in the solitary mind and soul of the individual that the battle between good and evil is waged and ultimately won or lost.*

Working as a psychiatrist in some of America's worst prisons, Peck discovered that the vast majority of prisoners suffered from standard psychiatric disorders. Few of them could be described as evil. Even those inmates who kill are not necessarily evil. Peck says evil deeds do not an evil person make, otherwise we would all be evil since each of us has the capacity to do evil things. I was not so sure about that. Shorty Jamieson still said he couldn't live with himself if he killed someone. I know how he feels. To my mind, a person would have to be insane to want to kill a fellow traveller. Or, have the mental capacity of a nine or ten-year-old.

Chapter 31

JOHN DUNFORD

Several months after the trip to Canberra, Will Hutchins rang to say the High Court judgement in *Baker* would be handed down at ten on Friday morning. He regretted ruining my day, but the result was unlikely to assist Bronson Blessington. For this reason, the Prisoners Legal Service had arranged with the Director of Public Prosecutions to revive Bronson Blessington's application to the Supreme Court to redetermine his 'life' sentence to a fixed term of years. The most important question to resolve was whether the prisoner's 1996 sentence review application put him beyond the reach of the 2001 cement law passed by the parliament.

Unlike its decisions involving individual rights and freedoms, the High Court was ahead of the field when it came to modern technology, and the *Baker* decision was available on the internet simultaneously with the Chief Justice handing it down in Canberra. I received the news without leaving my Sydney office. In dismissing the appeal, the court had voted six judges to one—Justice Michael Kirby dissenting—to abandon the *Kable* principle that parliament should not recruit the State judiciary to facilitate a sentencing charade. In his dissenting judgement, Kirby referred to the failed intervention on behalf of Blessington.

> *At the time of the offence for which Mr Blessington was convicted and sentenced he was 14 years of age. He is now subject to the same legislation as that challenged in the*

> *appellant's case. He applied for leave from this Court to be heard as an intervener in the appellant's appeal because of the direct relevance of the decision in the appellant's case to his legal entitlements, which were pending. By majority, this Court refused that leave. As I indicated at the time of that refusal, I would have granted Mr Blessington the right to be heard. Principle, and an effective lifetime of actual incarceration, warranted our consideration of counsel's supplementary submission estimated to take less than an hour. That submission bore on the extreme nature of the legislation.*

Radio National covered the *Baker* decision on Sandy McCutcheon's *Australia Talks Back*. Chris Maxwell KC from civil rights group, Liberty Victoria, said the decision meant State parliaments had unlimited power to pass any law they pleased in the absence of a constitutional or statutory bill of rights. 'Our Constitution, sadly, doesn't permit any real consideration of the fundamentally objectionable nature of this kind of legislation.' Unsurprisingly, political leaders from the major parties declined to talk to McCutcheon on the implications of the decision, while they queued up to speak with the shock jocks of commercial radio. Major party politicians risked personal abuse from shock jocks and their listeners, but the upside was a forum to dole out vengeance instead of fair and just compensation for victims and the resources needed to educate and rehabilitate offenders.

Shortly after the *Baker* decision, the Supreme Court's Justice John Dunford KC was assigned to hear the Blessington application to decide the preliminary questions relating to the prisoner's sentence review. I didn't know the judge personally although at different times we'd been active members of the Thomas More Society, an irreverent gathering of papist lawyers. Dunford was the author of a speech titled, 'Looking forward: the direction of criminal law' which was given at a criminal law conference in Sydney in August 2004 and published in the October 2004 edition of *Bar News*. In the speech, Dunford talked about recent developments in the law and referred to certain police practices of the past. The words encouraged me to think the judge was fair-minded.

> *Other developments relate to the manner of police investigation, which has become much more sophisticated, particularly with the development of DNA evidence, telephone and listening device intercepts and controlled operations. Moreover, some of us can remember the old police 'verbals' which then gave way to the typed record of interview, both signed and unsigned. This was followed by the video recorded interview... Trials were much quicker when the main evidence in the Crown case was often the evidence of police officers reciting the verbal admissions allegedly made by the accused, and the Crown prosecutor would comment to the jury, as sometimes the judge would also comment, "Why would they [the detectives] lie?" No right-thinking person would regret departure of the old ways.*

The hearing of the preliminary questions before Justice Dunford in the Supreme Court took place on 3 December 2004, eight years to the day after the court acknowledged Bronson Blessington's application to review his life sentence. Dunford would decide whether the prisoner was still entitled to the review given the intervention of the 2001 cement law requiring life prisoners to wait 30 years and be on their deathbed before applying for a sentence redetermination. When the sentencing law was enacted, the government overlooked the fact that Blessington had filed his review application in 1996. A transitional law was hurried through the parliament to block retrospectively the prisoner's review application. But John Basten believed the transitional law did not achieve its purpose and the 1996 review application remained valid. Basten also said a strong argument existed that Blessington was no longer subject to the Never to be Released recommendation because of the remarks of Chief Justice Gleeson in the Court of Criminal Appeal to the effect that he did not support the idea of a trial judge seeking to influence future decision makers.

I arrived late and proceedings were already underway in Court 12 of the Law Courts Building in Phillip Street. John Basten appeared with Robyn Burgess for the applicant instructed by Will Hutchins of the Prisoners Legal Service. The applicant appeared in person in a grey suit, white shirt and silver tie—it was the first time I'd seen him in anything other than prison greens or a white boiler suit. He sat alone to one side of the court in close proximity to the press. The judge, a tall man with grey-rimmed spectacles, seemed to be observing Blessington's demeanour and it occurred to me it would be useful if the rules allowed the prisoner to say something. Seats were scarce and I edged forward and found a spot next to Howard Brown OAM, from the victims group VOCAL. Howard had a watching brief for the Balding family. Despite our differences on the issue of punishment versus rehabilitation, Howard and I always got along well.

John Basten was on his feet, explaining to the judge the constitutional issues in the case. Both the determination of guilt for a particular criminal offence and the imposition of a sentence for that offence were exclusively exercises of judicial power and therefore beyond the reach of parliament. To retrospectively vary a prisoner's sentence was another interference with judicial power. These intrusions were exacerbated where they gave legal effect to what was merely an expression of opinion by the sentencing judge. In addition, the legislative scheme so designed was fatally flawed in that it purported to operate uniformly to both adult offenders and children. And finally, the transitional law passed to block Blessington's 1996 sentence review application was a punitive measure directed solely at the applicant.

To my mind, none of the mental gymnastics required to follow John Basten's explanation of the way the Australian Constitution operated to enforce the separation of powers doctrine would be necessary if Australia had a bill of rights. In the rarefied air of constitutional interpretation, the ordinary citizen was well and truly out of the loop, and this suited the executive government. Sitting in the court and looking about at the blank faces in the public gallery, it occurred to me that the unambiguous language of a bill of rights would be a simple way to engage citizens in the legal system, and to recognise and respect their basic rights and freedoms. To argue the alternative proposition—that sufficient common law rights survived in our inherited English law—failed to recognise the extent to which the executive government had been extinguishing those rights since the States first agreed to federate under the Commonwealth.

Lawyers for the Crown asserted to Dunford that the intention of the Parliament of New South Wales was clear: to keep the prisoner in jail until he was in imminent danger of dying, or so physically incapacitated that he no longer represented a threat to the community. The judge wanted to know about "the prisoner who behaves himself and does his best to rehabilitate himself." On the Crown's view of the new law, the judge said, "the prisoner has no more chance of getting out than the person who makes no effort while in jail." Also of concern to the judge was "the person who committed just as serious an offence but in respect of whom the trial judge did not make a non-release recommendation."

John Basten confirmed these were legitimate concerns about the effect of the new sentencing law passed by the parliament. His Honour responded with a strong voice and laconic style: "Judicial restraint prevents me saying anything further." The words were judge speak for 'I can't say what I really think'—perhaps the most unpersuasive and controversial legal argument of all time for independent judicial officers whose primary role is to protect the people from tyrannical government.

As the judge stood to leave the bench, he informed representatives at the bar table that they should not expect his decision before Christmas. He seemed to me to be the sort of man who would not be easily dissuaded from a course mapped by his own intellect and experience. The moment the judge disappeared through the door to his chambers, I made my way across the courtroom and shook hands with the prisoner, complimenting him on his borrowed bag of fruit—and token appearance in the proceedings—before a court officer directed him through a discrete door adjacent to the press gallery and back to his waiting prison van.

Chapter 32

PETER ZAHRA

Soon after Easter in 2005—while I was reading the form guide for the election of the new pope [Benedict XVI when the ballots were counted]—Will Hutchins called to say Justice Dunford would be handing down his decision in the *Blessington case* on Friday at 9.30am. No sooner had I hung up the telephone when I received an email from the president of the Thomas More Society, John McCarthy AM, KC, KPO, KCSG, to inform me that Justice Dunford was retiring on Friday at 9.30am and members of the society were invited to attend his court and see off the good judge. I telephoned the judge's associate who informed me that the *Blessington case* judgement on Friday was His Honour's last after 12 years on the Supreme Court bench.

John McCarthy was Premier Bob Carr's personal lawyer and I might have a chance to talk with the learned counsel about the *Blessington case*. If the decision favoured the prisoner it would put some serious cracks in the cement law and there was no predicting how Carr might react. Having a chat with his lawyer seemed like a good idea at the time.

I managed to book the last seat on Friday's early morning flight to Sydney and rose at the ghastly hour of 4.00am. The Ballina airport coffee shop was open for business and stocked the morning papers. Professor Tony Vinson, the former Commissioner for Corrective Services, had given a Sydney University graduation address and an extract was published as an opinion piece in the

Sydney Morning Herald under the bold headline 'Punishing the hapless is the true crime'. The article began with Vinson suggesting that people respond better *to the opportunities afforded them than they did to threats and punitive policies.* People needed hope, the former prison boss wrote.

Vinson also contended that politicians had been battling with one another over who could be more punitive towards prisoners, and while this might serve their electoral interests, the war was phoney and self-serving, and intended to divert attention from the social neglect that sent large numbers to prison. It was not only abhorrent but also illogical, he said, for our political leaders to boast about the increase in prisoner numbers. Law-abiding citizens should draw no comfort from the fact that greatly increased numbers of offenders are behind bars. Although some people must be imprisoned for our protection, *the government cannot reconcile the fact that only 628 of the 9,000 prisoners behind bars are serious offenders.*

The next thing I knew, the plane was landing in Sydney. With no luggage to worry about, I headed straight for the airport rail service and I was in Justice Dunford's court well before the 9.30 start. The place was filling with horsehair and silk faster than the saddling paddock at Royal Randwick Racecourse. I offered the Public Defender, Peter Zahra, my seat and he declined with a twitch of his shivery grey moustache. Zahra was the foremost expert on DNA evidence at the Sydney bar and soon to become a judge himself. A court attendant called "All stand please" and then Justice Dunford entered the courtroom dressed in full criminal court robes—full bottom wig, maroon silk gown and grey fur trimming. He seemed to be visibly shocked at the large turnout for his final flourish from the bench.

Dunford took his seat, his associate called the matter of *Regina v Blessington*, and His Honour said there were seven questions to be answered. The answers were "Yes, no, no, no, does not arise, does not arise and no." With that, he handed the 17-page judgement to his associate and gestured to a court attendant who began distributing copies of the document to interested parties. There was a scrum at the back of the court around the attendant and Will Hutchins managed to get me a copy from a ruck position. Neither of us had a clue whether the case had been won or lost. Will drifted out of the courtroom surrounded by Blessington's supporters and I returned to my seat alongside the still standing Peter Zahra. I could not make head nor tail of the judgement. Part of the problem was reading the numbered paragraphs in answer to the seven questions while simultaneously listening to the farewell tributes to the judge.

His Honour stood and bowed to the court for the last time. After he left the bench, the assembled throng began to file out. I shook John McCarthy's hand as he was leaving, and then he was gone—long before I could get my head around the decision. I sat down and gave the 17 pages my full attention and soon discovered there was something in the judgement for everyone, which meant everyone would want to appeal. Bronson had succeeded on the primary question whether his application to review his life sentence filed in 1996 escaped the parliament's 2001 sentencing law and he would not be required to wait 30 years for a review. This meant the review of his life sentence could proceed immediately. But the judge had not addressed the question whether the prisoner was cemented in. The problem remained that Never to be Released prisoners were not eligible for parole until they were physically incapacitated to the point where they were no longer a threat to anyone.

Concentrating on the last paragraphs of the judgement, I was amazed to read that the judge was suggesting a course of action that was never argued by John Basten in support of the case. His Honour said that the non-release *recommendation* was not an *order* and consequently was not a *sentence* for the purposes of a criminal appeal. While a prisoner could not appeal a non-release recommendation, now that the parliament had turned the *recommendation into a sentence*, there may be an avenue for appealing the decision in the courts. Justice Dunford had found that the Blessington application for a redetermination of his life sentence to a term of years *remained on foot and could proceed accordingly.*

I wondered what John Basten thought of the decision, and then I realised I would probably never know. The learned barrister had just been appointed as a judge of the Supreme Court and was due to be sworn in next month. I pondered the unfortunate truism for prisoners: one door closes and another slams in your face.

Just a handful of lawyers remained in the court and Peter Zahra was one of them. He made no effort to leave and seemed happy for me to speak to him about the *Jamieson case*. I expressed my regret that the DNA implications of the case recently landed on the front pages of certain Sydney newspapers and he frowned inconsolably, lowering his horsehair wig onto a creased forehead. He told me we were living in the darkest of times so far as representing prisoners was concerned, and his office no longer engaged with the press for fear of public reprisals and vilification. If he must make a public statement, he would give journalists only two or three sentences so there was nothing for them to use against him or his clients. Victims and their families were acting as vigilantes and he had seen them physically attack prisoners in the dock and chase them downstairs to the cells. He was frequently abused and people in his office were harassed. Life as a criminal defence lawyer was increasingly problematic.

I asked whether Shorty Wells' black bandana needed to be sent to the USA or the UK for further DNA testing, or whether the facilities existed in Australia? It was a leading question—I really wanted the Public Defender to tell me why the testing for male DNA seemed to be stuck in limbo. Maybe the Victorian Forensic Science laboratory could do further testing, he said, but he wasn't certain. It was a matter for the Attorney General's Department and they would decide in their own good time. There was no rush as the department had still not decided what sort of statutory body should replace the police-controlled Innocence Panel.

My concern was that the government's real agenda was to avoid any review of the crimes against Janine Balding because that would inevitably lead to questions about the police investigation of the murder of Anita Cobby. The parallels between Gary Murphy's situation and that of Shorty Jamieson were impossible to ignore. Peter Zahra was thoughtful, even pensive, as he mulled over my assessment of the situation. Then he told me that Lord Denning had something to say about the importance of protecting the integrity of the justice system—there may be circumstances in which some questionable convictions should be left undisturbed.

My recollection was that Lord Denning had made scandalous comments about appalling crimes in the case of the *Birmingham Six*. In the foyer outside the court, the Public Defender was still lingering, and by the time I shook his hand and thanked him for speaking with me, I realised we were the last of Justice Dunford's farewell party to leave the precinct of the court.

Parliament House is a leisurely five-minute stroll down Macquarie Street from the Law Courts Building and the moment I reached my office I did a Google search for the *Birmingham Six case* in the UK. I was reminded that 21 people died in Birmingham pubs when a series of bombs exploded in the early 1970s. Six Irishmen living in Birmingham at the time were convicted in 1975 of the killings and spent 16 years in prison before proving their innocence. I learned that several books were written about the case including one by a British MP, Chris Mullin, titled *Error of Judgement*, originally published in 1986—five years before the convictions were quashed. The book included graphic detail of the way 'confessions' were extracted from the six prisoners. Mullin's book also covered the role of Lord Denning, who, as the most senior judge of the UK Court of Appeal in 1980, denied the Birmingham Six the right to sue the police who arrested and beat them. Lord Denning's words were chilling.

> *Just consider the course of events if this action is allowed to proceed to trial...If the six men win, it will mean that the police were guilty of perjury, that they were guilty of violence and threats, that the confessions were involuntary and improperly admitted in evidence and that the convictions*

were erroneous. That would mean that the Home Secretary would either have to recommend that they be pardoned or he would have to remit the case to the Court of Appeal. This is such an appalling vista that every sensible person in the land would say that it cannot be right these actions should go further.

His Lordship could not have imagined the reach of the internet and the extent to which his words would be used, not to protect the integrity of British justice, but to demonstrate its deficiencies. While Denning may have believed he was upholding the best traditions of English law, to the public he was denying the six men their day in court and making the justice system look ridiculous. The most respected judge in the country was saying, in effect, that it may be better for innocent people to serve life sentences than to let them go free and bring the law into disrepute.

Several commentators compared Denning's remarks to the idea of vicarious or utilitarian punishment put forward by author and social philosopher John Ruskin [1819-1900]. According to Ruskin, it might be possible to deal with unsolved murders by choosing an inhabitant of the place of the murder by lot and then hang the person to encourage the rest of the community to keep the peace. The idea found currency in the early colony of New South Wales when likely suspects were rounded up and flogged until someone confessed. And utilitarian punishment was behind the thinking that a person may be technically innocent, but they probably committed some other comparable crime, so justice has been served.

Checking the parliament's media monitoring service, I was

horrified to read AAP reporting Premier Carr as saying he did not agree with Judge Dunford's decision and his government would be seeking urgent legal advice. *In essence, I can assure the family of Janine Balding that we will do whatever it takes to see that this offender [Bronson Blessington] stays behind bars and dies in jail.* I suspected that the premier knew as much about the offender as I knew when I first visited him at Goulburn jail.

My parliamentary colleagues began calling to say Bronson Blessington must be a terrible fellow and I endeavoured to explain he was a model prisoner. The two representatives from the Christian Democratic Party in the Legislative Council, Reverend Fred Nile and Reverend Gordon Moyes, were particularly miffed as they'd previously lent their support to Blessington and now they were obliged drop him like hot candle wax as they dare not be seen to oppose the government on Laura Norder, a policy issue near and dear to their constituents.

The rest of the day was fairly unproductive as I watched the media monitoring service churn out one report after another, all with a slightly different take on the premier's intentions. I issued my own press release regretting the rush to judgement on Blessington and suggesting the courts should be permitted to exercise their role as the judicial arm of government. Sentencing was not just about retribution, but also involved questions of proportional punishment, rehabilitation and the individual circumstances of each prisoner. Politicians had no business usurping the work of judges. The decision to allow Blessington to re-determine his life sentence to a fixed term of years was common sense and consistent with sentencing principles in place when his crimes were committed.

That night I received a call on my mobile phone shortly after landing at Ballina airport. A night-watch shock jock wanted to know what I had to say about the Dunford decision and his producer placed me on hold. By the time I got to speak to the presenter, I'd walked off into a paddock adjoining the airport carpark, and I was gazing up into a sky filled with endless blinking stars. The presenter asked if I would have Blessington stay at my house and I told him the young man would be welcome anytime. This was too much for the radio waves and I was given short shrift. Once off the line, the presenter told his listeners that I was a mug, and a string of callers expressed similar sentiments. One or two wanted to talk about the extreme youth of the offender, his mental capacity at the time of the crimes, his prospects for rehabilitation and the idea of a second chance. The dissenters were cut off or faded to sotto voce before they had too much to say.

Chapter 33

THE TWO BOBS

Less than three weeks after Justice Dunford's decision to allow Bronson Blessington's 1996 sentence review application to proceed, the Bob Carr Labor Government introduced the Crimes (Sentencing Procedure) Amendment (Existing Life Sentences) Bill 2005 into the Legislative Assembly of the New South Wales Parliament. The Attorney General, Bob Debus, tabled the bill and said it would "protect the community forever" from Bronson Blessington. The Shadow Attorney, Andrew Tink, said the Opposition "strongly supports the need" for the bill. He hoped the Attorney really meant that Blessington would be in jail forever "because that is what I want to hear." Then the Speaker of the House called for a vote and the bill passed unanimously on the voices.

Sitting there in the Speaker's Gallery of the Legislative Assembly, shaking my head like some poor demented soul, I wanted to say nobody in the parliament knew anything about Bronson Blessington. Surprising to me was the blatant *ad hominem* nature of the legislation which would normally be regarded in parliament as overreach—usurping judicial power. In his second reading speech, Attorney General Bob Debus made no bones about what the government was doing.

> *A recent decision of the Supreme Court in Regina v Blessington has held that an offender with a section 13A application that was pending as at 8 May 1997 is not subject*

> *to the present rules for redetermination [of 'life' sentences]... The Government believes that the intention [of the cement law] was clear... The decision also canvassed the possibility that Blessington, and by extension any others who have not yet had their application determined, might now be able to appeal the court's recommendation that they never be released... But the people of New South Wales, and the Balding family in particular, deserve certainty... parole cannot be granted except when the offender is in imminent danger of dying, or is incapacitated to the extent that he or she [they were all men] no longer has the physical capacity to do harm to any person.*

I timed the reading of the bill, the debate and the vote in the lower house—it all took just 38 minutes. The following day, I had my chance in the Legislative Council debate to tell Blessington's side of the story. At the end of a three-hour speech, I was given leave to incorporate into *Hansard* a sample list of high-culpability life sentences for murder where the judges failed to impose non-release recommendations. Each of the listed offenders was much more culpable for their crimes than the 14-year-old Blessington. I managed to get support for my opposition to the bill from Greens members Ian Cohen, Lee Rhiannon and Sylvia Hale; Australian Democrat Dr Arthur Chesterfield-Evans; and the Unity Party's Dr Peter Wong. Government and Opposition members and the remaining minor party members (including the two Christian Democrat Party members) outnumbered us 29 votes to six.

As soon as the bill passed the upper house, the government promised it would receive Royal Assent the next day. And it did. Not one word of the passage of the new law through the parliament appeared in any news item. The record shows that the bill passed the Legislative Assembly on 4 May 2005, the Legislative Council on 5 May 2005 and received Royal Assent on 6 May 2005. A few days later the Legislation Review Committee of the parliament published a 14-page report on the bill including a list of 17 adverse observations. It noted that the bill breached international human rights laws to which Australia is a party and the government was expected to comply with those laws. *The Committee further notes that the separation of the legislative and judicial powers, while not an explicit requirement of the Constitution of New South Wales, is an important protection against political interference in personal rights, particularly in relation to criminal matters.*

A couple of weeks went by before I could visit Bronson at Goulburn prison. He was still a bit shell-shocked by the cruelty meted out to him in the name of the peace, order and good government of the people of New South Wales. I expressed my disappointment that Christian Democrat Party members of the upper house deserted him at the eleventh hour. I offered the thought that they regarded Christianity as their club and they didn't actually believe God worked outside the club—especially not in the prisons. The British Parliament, as well as being governed by a bill of rights in the form of the UK Human Rights Act, also had a sensible rule that ministers of religion were not permitted to sit in the Commons.

Bronson said he was grateful for any support he received, and he understood that people must move on, prompting me to ask whether he'd heard from John Basten before his swearing in as a judge. He produced a memo from the Prisoners Legal Service which included Basten's last advice. The eminent lawyer expressed the opinion that any legislation directed specifically at the prisoner was likely to raise a fresh set of constitutional arguments that the court would need to consider. And his final words in the advice were encouraging: *Would you please tell Mr Blessington how sorry I am that I cannot see his matter through to conclusion.* I told Bronson that the angels might still be working for him as Bret Walker had agreed to take over the case following the appointment of John Basten to the Supreme Court.

Just three months after Premier Bob Carr addressed the question of Bronson Blessington's sentence by adding more cement, he resigned as the leader of the Labor Government. History will remember Carr as a talented man who did good things for education and national parks, but squandered the opportunities presented by ten years of unprecedented economic growth to rebuild the State's ageing social infrastructure. The consensus was he left New South Wales in a mess and voters were waiting for him with a baseball bat.

In March 2006, Bret Walker appeared with Robyn Burgess before the Court of Criminal Appeal in Sydney and argued that the Never to be Released recommendation of the trial judge in Bronson's case was now a formal sentence thanks to the legislative intervention of the New South Wales Parliament and consequently the sentence could now be appealed. Included in the papers presented to the court were two psychiatric reports to the effect that the young man had recovered from the temporary mental disorder of early adolescence that afflicted him at the time of his crimes.

Bronson sat silently through the appeal, to one side of the bench and out of the line of sight of the three appeal judges. The prisoner was dressed in a dark suit, white shirt and paisley tie. Two corrections officers sat either side of him. Matthew Elliott was also there with the leave of the court after his lawyers successfully argued that Matthew's interest in the appeal was the same as Bronson's since they were both juveniles at the time of their crimes against Janine Balding.

Matthew Elliott, like Bronson Blessington, was still a young man in his early thirties even though he'd been in jail for 17 years—more than half his life. He was dressed casually in slacks and open-neck shirt and was seated between two more corrections officers. I was surprised how young and ordinary he looked, and I remembered Judge Peter Moss saying that Matthew was 'a very impressive young man'. As the head of the Serious Offenders Review Council, the judge's observation carried a good deal of weight. Like Blessington, Elliott had served a reasonable sentence, and one that was proportionate to similar crimes committed by adults in 1988.

Six months after hearing the government's appeal from the Dunford decision to allow Blessington and Elliott to redetermine their life sentences, the three judges of the Court of Criminal Appeal ruled that the two prisoners should remain in jail as determined by the cement law. *It would be an inappropriate exercise of judicial power to remove the legislative criterion upon the basis of which Parliament enacted constitutionally valid legislation.* In other words, the legislative arm of government trumped the judicial arm. Justice David Kirby in a dissenting judgement said there had arguably been a miscarriage of justice and leave to appeal should be granted. *By virtue of the youth of the offenders, their crimes could not be considered in the worst class. Accordingly, the life sentences imposed were manifestly excessive.* His Honour wanted to replace the life sentences of Blessington and Elliott with a non-parole period.

The two to one decision in the Court of Criminal Appeal was really the end of the judicial road for Blessington and Elliott. Legal Aid prepared an application for leave to appeal the decision to the High Court, but in 2007 the court said there was nothing new in the application and refused leave to appeal. I told both prisoners I was wrong about the angels—they appeared to have left the building. I was also wrong about the voters of New South Wales waiting for the Bob Carr Labor Government with a baseball bat at the 2007 State election. Although Carr had moved on, the Labor Party was re-elected with Premier Morris Iemma in charge. I regret to say it was me, not Labor, that voters batted away at the election, outraged no doubt at my persistent attempts to interfere with Laura Norder.

After losing my seat in parliament in March 2007, I continued to assist the prisoners Blessington and Elliott pro bono with applications to the New South Wales Governor for the exercise of the Royal Prerogative of Mercy. Also, I referred their case to the Human Rights Law Centre in Victoria where international law experts had expressed interest in the unfairness of backdating criminal punishment and sentencing children to life in prison—contrary to Australia's international treaty obligations. In the

International Covenant on Civil and Political Rights, Article 15 provides that no one convicted of a criminal offence shall be subjected to the burden of a heavier penalty *than the one that was applicable at the time when the criminal offence was committed.* Further, the UN Convention on the Rights of the Child was ratified by Australia in December 1990—three months after Blessington and Elliott received their judicial life sentences. Article 37(a) of the convention provides: *Neither capital punishment nor life imprisonment without possibility of release shall be imposed for offences committed by persons below 18 years of age.*

In a case lodged with the United Nations Human Rights Committee in Geneva in April 2010, the Human Rights Law Centre argued on behalf of Blessington and Elliott that natural life sentences for children breached international human rights law, as does sentencing a person to a heavier penalty than the one in force at the time of their offences. The United Nations Human Rights Committee ruled on 17 November 2014 that the State Party [Australia] had breached its human rights obligations to the prisoners. Submissions by the Australian Government to the Committee argued that the two prisoners' cases were without merit since they retained the possibility of release into the community, either on parole or through the exercise of the Royal Prerogative of Mercy. Unsurprising to me, the Human Rights Law Centre took issue with the government.

Here is the nub of the problem that allows State governments to get away with abusing the human rights of prisoners. Australia's penal history means State governments exercise legislative and executive power over State courts, power that preceded federation and State constitutions. It's a cozy arrangement that leaves most crime and punishment to the States with no real expectation that prisoners should be shown mercy for crimes that once attracted the death penalty. In effect, mercy is a faux remedy for serious convicts, allowing federal and State politicians to pass the buck on their responsibility for the human rights of State prisoners.

I wrote to the then prime minister, Tony Abbott, on 20 January 2015 applauding his plea for mercy on behalf of two young Australian men on death row in Indonesia, Andrew Chan and Myuran Sukamaran. I asked that the PM's mercy plea be extended to Bronson Blessington and Matthew Elliott, two other young Australians serving effective life sentences. Plus, I included with my letter a copy of the ruling of the Human Rights Committee in Geneva which was supposed to be binding on Australia as a signatory to the International Covenant on Civil and Political Rights. By the time the Department of the Prime Minister and Cabinet replied to my letter—referring me to the Attorney General for the State of New South Wales—Andrew Chan and Myuran Sukamaran were dead, executed by shooting for drug trafficking. In due course, I wrote to the State attorney of the day, Liberal Member for Wakehurst, Brad Hazzard, who advised that compliance with international treaty obligations was a matter for the Commonwealth, not the State.

Chapter 34

PETER O'BRIEN

Premier Morris Iemma finally introduced into the Legislative Assembly of the New South Wales Parliament the legislation to set up the new arrangements for DNA testing. He said the Crimes (Appeal and Review) Amendment (DNA Review Panel) Bill was an important mechanism for people convicted of crime *to have aspects of their conviction reinvestigated.* While the main point of the bill was to establish the DNA Review Panel to replace the now defunct Innocence Panel, the premier said the bill would also allow convicted persons to ask the new body to test biological material that may demonstrate their innocence.

> *[A convicted] person must point to biological material that, if tested, may affect their claim of innocence. For instance, a person convicted of sexual assault might identify a shirt left at the crime scene that the person alleges was worn by the real perpetrator and therefore could contain DNA and ask for that biological material to be tested. This could be relevant if their original defence was mistaken identity.*

I reckon that whoever wrote this section of the premier's second reading speech had a wicked sense of humour. By replacing the word 'shirt' with the word 'bandana' or the word 'headscarf', the example anticipated Stephen Jamieson's application to the DNA Review Panel. He completed and signed the claim in August 2007. The relevant question on the two-page pro forma application read: *Identify the specific items you think may assist your claim of innocence.* Stephen's answer could not have been more specific: *Headscarf owned and worn by Mark 'Shorty' Wells and used to gag the victim.*

You might think that a person's shirt left at a crime scene would have their DNA on it. Same goes for a bandana or headscarf, first worn by Shorty Wells around his neck and then around his head according to Bronson Blessington. Over time, the quality of any biological material on the bandana might become degraded, but DNA in a stable environment had been known to last for 7,000 years. And DNA testing had improved so dramatically that sophisticated testing equipment could now identify a person's DNA from just a few cells of biological material left at a crime scene—even just one cell.

Michele Franco assured me that the bandana had been in a stable environment at the health department's Division of Analytical Laboratories (later known as the Forensic and Analytical Science Service—FASS) since at least 2002. The forensic scientist had tested it for DNA in 2003, 2005, 2006 and 2008, reporting on each occasion that her attempts to extract DNA were unsuccessful. Meanwhile the DNA testing technology advanced in leaps and bounds to the point where the DNA Review Panel instructed FASS to carry out further testing of the bandana. In January 2014, just prior to the DNA Review Panel closing for business, Michele reported that *Traces of DNA from at least one other individual was also recovered.*

Legal Aid decided to fund additional testing at the Forensic Science Service in the UK, the government owned DNA testing laboratory at the coal face of Sir Alec Jeffries DNA research. The FSS had advanced technology called Low Copy Number (LCN) testing that could identify DNA from degraded biological material. When agreeing to do the testing, the FSS said that *any instruction to proceed should come from the DNA Review Panel.* After initially agreeing to assist in the LCN testing and to take responsibility for transport of the bandana, NSW Police had a change of heart—much to the chagrin of David Barrow at Legal Aid—deciding not to facilitate the UK testing arrangements.

Without fresh and compelling DNA evidence to support the proposed application to the Supreme Court for a review of Stephen's convictions, Legal Aid decided it could not continue funding the case. Stephen unsuccessfully appealed the decision to the Legal Aid Review Committee. *The committee disallowed the appeal because it is not satisfied from the material submitted in support of the appeal that the proceedings have reasonable prospects for success.* I could never understand why Legal Aid threw in the towel so early when the case was such an obvious injustice—the worst many people working on the case had seen.

Michele Franco's report from January 2014 revealed that FASS had tested the bandana for DNA against reference samples from Jamieson, Blessington, Elliott and Janine Balding. Chair of the DNA Review Panel, Ken Shadbolt QC, wrote to Stephen on 7 February 2014 attaching a copy of Michele's latest report, and advising the prisoner that further DNA testing would require payment of a fee. Also attached to the letter was a copy of the legislation winding up the panel and a copy of the Attorney General's second reading speech which outlined arrangements for police to carry out further DNA testing. According to the second reading speech, the government initially expected that the role of the panel would be replaced by routine DNA testing during police investigations.

> *However, it has since become apparent that DNA testing is a constantly evolving science. Even improvements between 2006 and today mean that DNA profiles may now be obtained, where previous tests yielded inconclusive results. These advances in technology mean that evidence capable of exonerating a convicted person may only become available a significant time after a convicted person has exhausted all avenues of appeal...The ability to facilitate testing by agreement [under section 97] will reduce the need for court-ordered disclosure. However, if police do not agree to provide information or arrange for testing, a convicted person may seek an order from the Supreme Court.*

The DNA Review Panel ended its unhappy life with the passage of another bill in the New South Wales Parliament—with the same name as the bill that brought it into existence seven years earlier. The panel closed its doors to prisoners wanting to review their convictions on 23 February 2014. In the seven years it had operated, the panel considered 31 applications and made no referrals to the Court of Criminal Appeal. During the same seven- year period, 69 applications were considered by the Supreme Court for conviction reviews under Part 7 of the Crimes (Appeal and Review) Act 2001. Five were successful. If Stephen Jamieson's experience was any indication of how other prisoners were treated, each of these review cases would have benefitted significantly from the expertise of an independent authority such as a criminal cases review commission.

I told Stephen I didn't know what else I could do to help him other than to lodge an application with the Governor asking for an exercise of the Royal Prerogative of Mercy. Hardly surprising, he said he was innocent, so why would he do that? Meanwhile, I had a few months off the job with a health problem, and Stephen was offered further pro bono legal support from O'Brien Criminal Law in Sydney. Peter O'Brien and Sidnie Sarang suggested a formal application for additional DNA testing of the bandana along with payment of the testing fee of $285. The testing resulted in another report from Michele Franco dated 4 December 2019—one that turned out to be much more useful than anything I'd helped to secure. An additional partial DNA profile was found using the Yfiler Plus System.

Statistical calculations were also carried out on the DNA recovered from the bandana using the PowerPlex21 System. The report was heavily redacted as to the likely contributors, but again, Stephen was excluded. Reading between the redactions, it seemed to me there were three possible minor contributors in the calculations. *The DNA from the minor contributors is not suitable for comparison due to the low level and complexity.* But these three profiles along with the Yfiler Plus profile could be enhanced using Low Copy Number testing technology.

What Stephen needed was a Supreme Court order to circumvent the unwieldy DNA testing laws which appeared to be designed to daze and confuse legal practitioners and unrepresented litigants alike. One subsection in the legislation said that nothing in the DNA testing law permitted police to provide information that may reveal the identity of anyone other than the convicted person—catch 22. Public law and criminal law were the two areas of expertise required to deal with legal conundrums of this kind, both above my paygrade. Peter O'Brien was considering the prospects of obtaining further Legal Aid assistance based on the results of the testing so far.

A couple of things then happened to draw me back into the case. One was a telephone call from Stephen who said that "the copper who signed me up for murder has gone to bloke upstairs" meaning that Detective Sergeant Kevin Raue had died. Could I still do that application for the Royal Prerogative of Mercy? Like all long-term prisoners who believed they were wrongly convicted, Stephen was exhausted by his efforts to get out of jail. If a mercy plea was the only way out, then that was preferable to a life in jail with no end in sight other than death.

The other thing that made me think again about Stephen Jamieson's case was the death of my friend and former judge, John McLaughlin. During the McLaughlin obsequies, I complained to mutual friends and legal colleagues about the difficulty of getting access to DNA evidence in the *Jamieson case*. Sydney lawyer Richard d'Apice AM, KCSG advised me to make an application under the Supreme Court rules for pre-litigation discovery seeking an order for the other Shorty's DNA profile, and an additional order for specialised DNA testing of the bandana to take place at the ESR laboratory in New Zealand.

When I made further inquiries of the FASS laboratory in Sydney,

I discovered to my horror that none of the Janine Balding crime scene material had *ever* been compared with reference samples from Shorty Wells. As well as DNA from the bandana used to gag Ms Balding not being matched to Wells' DNA, fingerprints from her car had never been compared with his fingerprints. For 20 years, I'd been under a misapprehension that crime scene material had been referenced to Shorty Wells.

It took a little time for these revelations to sink in. The clues were there when I looked back through my paperwork, beginning with the letter from the Innocence Panel telling me Wells could be excluded as a contributor to crime scene DNA. Wells was excluded because the Innocence Panel had already identified the limited DNA profiles available at that time. Later technology isolated additional profiles, but without Wells' DNA reference sample, every test for DNA from the crime scene was a waste of time for the purposes of advancing Stephen's case. Getting a match to Wells' DNA with one or more of the DNA profiles now available from the bandana was critical to securing a judicial review of the Jamieson convictions—certainly that was the attitude of Legal Aid if the services of the Public Defender were to be engaged.

In March 2023, I received an email from the Operations Director of the FASS laboratory in Sydney, Sharon Neville, formally advising me: *In relation to the homicide of Janine Balding, I am able to inform you that we never received or tested a reference sample from Mark 'Shorty' Wells… Also, under the Crimes (Forensic Procedures) Act 2000, we cannot access the DNA database to ascertain if a reference sample from Mark Wells was taken in relation to any other offence.* Independent inquiries of the database indicated there was no DNA record of Wells in any event—even though he'd been released from prison in New South Wales after a long stretch in the months before the murder of Ms Balding. Queensland Police eventually placed the Wells profile on the national DNA database as a consequence of crimes committed in Queensland in 2011.

I contacted two Queenslanders who knew more about DNA testing than anybody else I was acquainted with (Judge Peter Zahra had died in 2022 after suffering a stroke). One was Linzi Wilson-Wilde OAM who was CEO of Forensic Science Queensland; the other was Dr Kirsty Wright, the head of the Genomics Research Centre at the Queensland University of Technology in Brisbane. Both experts agreed that partial or degraded DNA profiles on the bandana could be enhanced using Low Copy Number (LCN) testing technology in New Zealand. Police routinely sent crime scene material across the ditch for advanced DNA testing at the ESR laboratory using technology that was unavailable in Australia. Kirsty Wright provided a pro bono report for proposed pre-litigation discovery proceedings.

> *In 2019 FASS used new DNA mixture interpretation and software to conduct statistical analysis [which excluded Jamieson]... newer technology now exists that has proven to be successful in obtaining DNA profiles from the bandana where initial testing failed. Additional testing as described above [in the report] provides a good probability of obtaining the DNA of the wearer of the bandana.*

Chapter 35

MICHELE RUYTERS

In the autumn of 2023, I lodged a claim in the Supreme Court on behalf of Stephen Jamieson against the Attorney General and the Commissioner of Police seeking pre-litigation discovery of Shorty Wells' DNA. Computer source code was found to be a 'document or thing' for the purposes of pre-litigation discovery so why not DNA? Secondly, I asked for an order that further testing of the bandana used to gag Janne Balding take place with the benefit of Low Copy Number (LCN) technology.

A few months later, in November 2023, I attended a forensic science conference at Darling Harbour in Sydney where 1,700 delegates from 70 countries exchanged information about the latest DNA testing and forensic science technology. One of the presenters at the conference was the FASS representative, Michele Franco. Over lunch we discussed the latest testing of the bandana, and the forensic biologist volunteered that she'd kept the bandana under lock and key ever since our first meeting at her laboratory 20 years earlier. I informed her that I'd just received an email from the government's lawyers informing me that the testing was now completed and outlining the test results. Michele was surprised by this news as her report—which would accompany the latest test results—had not been completed.

I'd long ago decided that the New South Wales Police Force was on a frolic of its own with regard to re-testing crime scene material for DNA on behalf of convicted prisoners. The forensic science conference simply confirmed my worst fears. Another presenter was Sallyann Harbison from the ESR Forensic Science laboratory in New Zealand. ESR and Sallyann were willing to test the bandana using the LCN technology following assistance with funding from Michele Ruyters of the RMIT University Bridge of Hope Innocence Project. Police forensics were considering our request for the LCN testing at the time of the conference. There were few surprises in the Jamieson camp when police decided not to allow further testing of the bandana in New Zealand—the same thing had happened in 2014 when Stephen tried to get LCN testing done at the Forensic Science Service in the UK.

The first problem for police was whether a courier to New Zealand could be trusted to ensure transport of the bandana while maintaining an appropriate chain of custody. My contact at the ESR laboratory told me that DHL and FedEx courier services delivered biological material for DNA testing by the truckload without any security or chain of custody issues. The second problem for police was that further testing might destroy or otherwise compromise the bandana. I explained that any further testing would slightly damage the bandana—including further FASS testing in Sydney—but it would not be destroyed or compromised in any significant way. My representations again fell on deaf ears, although I was comforted to know that police were anxious to preserve the bandana.

For me, the best thing that happened at the Darling Harbour forensic science conference was that a USA linguistics expert, Carole Chaski, who was due to make a workshop presentation and had a track record for getting convictions overturned in American courts, turned out to be a no-show. I'd engaged Dr Chaski to give expert evidence in the *Jamieson case*, and at her suggestion, I registered for a workshop that included forensic linguistics. When I aired my police record of interview woes with attendees at the workshop, they declared with one voice that the best forensic linguistics expert for a case like this was an Australian professor at the University of Melbourne, Dr Helen Fraser, who'd made a significant contribution to the justice system by undertaking research and casework related to the use of transcripts of spoken language as forensic evidence.

Another stroke of good fortune around the time of the conference was the swearing in of Ian Harrison SC as a New South Wales Court of Appeal judge and chief judge at common law. As I prepared for the hearing of Stephen's pre-litigation discovery application in the Supreme Court, I'd no idea the case was listed before Harrison—the kindest judge I'd ever known. If His Honour could sit on every bench in every court in Australia there would be no injustices and we really would live in the lucky country. Anyway, I was batting much further up the order of advocates than my usual artless spot down with the tailenders, and I was fully expecting a drubbing from counsel for the Crown. No sooner were we underway—handing up motions and proposed orders—when His Honour had a great idea. Why not avoid the complexities of the DNA testing legislation and the uncertainties of pre-litigation discovery and go straight to a judicial inquiry into the plaintiff's convictions?

As soon as a transcript of the proceeding was available, I walked a copy down Castlereagh Street to the Legal Aid offices near

Central Railway Station. Solicitor Karen Psaltis promised to attach a copy of the document to Stephen's latest application for legal assistance and to alert the head of Indictable Appeals to the latest development in the case. David Barrow had recently been appointed senior counsel and then to the District Court bench. I'd no idea who replaced him at Legal Aid. Stephen was soon given a grant of legal aid for the purposes of a new judicial inquiry into his convictions, which included the services of top legal counsel: Senior Public Defender, Richard Wilson SC, along with senior criminal law barristers Claire O'Neill and Slade Howell. Stephen would now get a fair go in the justice system with properly funded criminal law representation.

There was just one problem when the time came to hand over my files to Legal Aid. It was immediately obvious that I'd been working with the television program *60 Minutes* (with Stephen's verbal consent). But Legal Aid was opposed to talking to the media. As Peter Zahra was fond of saying, the media was death to the case of a criminal defendant. And while that may be true for somebody on trial, the media was a lifeline for a convict trying to prove their innocence in my experience. Working with the media was essential to getting public support for a convict.

Twenty years earlier when I first went into bat for Stephen, bad publicity was a nightmare, and yet every story would almost inevitably cause someone to come out of the woodwork who knew his case and had something constructive to offer—new information or useful leads to follow. Legal Aid was having none of that. They sent me a letter asking for *Stephen's written consent to be recorded by you and his signed waiver of privilege allowing release of the recordings to 60 Minutes.* All I could offer Legal Aid was an assurance from Channel Nine that they would not broadcast any audio or video material I'd obtained if Stephen had withdrawn his consent. None of this bothered me too much as I knew Channel Nine had plenty of material from other sources. At the same time, I was anxious to co-operate with Stephen's new lawyers appointed by Legal Aid.

The only person in the courtroom public gallery on the day Justice Harrison floated the idea of a judicial inquiry into the Jamieson convictions was the amiable *60 Minutes* producer, Amelia Ballinger, who'd been following the case since it was filed in court the previous year. Harrison explained that he'd given the Crown a timeline to convince him why cutting to the chase with a judicial review of the case was not the best outcome for everyone involved. Amelia was looking for a 'gotcha' moment to air her 'Get Shorty' program which was largely in the can. I assured her that the Harrison decision to hold a judicial inquiry was as 'gotcha' as the case was likely to get.

A few months earlier, I'd travelled to Melbourne with Amelia and award-winning print journalist Anthony Dowsley who was on loan to *60 Minutes* from News Limited. We met with Michele Ruyters who'd arranged filming in Victoria's Old Magistrates Court in Russell Street—the same courtroom, in fact, where Ned Kelly had been sentenced to death by hanging in 1880. When the sentence was pronounced, Kelly apparently told the judge he would *return from the grave to fight.*

I had my own fight to the death in Ned Kelly's courtroom when *60 Minutes* journalist Nick McKenzie interviewed me and "went hard" to quote Dowsley. McKenzie was using as a prop the contested police record of interview—giving it a level of credibility it didn't deserve—and after I asked the journalist not to use it, the direction of our interview turned south. His first question when the cameras began rolling was whether I was still in love with Shorty Jamieson. After that, we were all over the shop, and I expected, once again, to be trounced by the media when the program eventually went to air. Legal Aid did have legitimate concerns and I could only hope that most of my comments ended up on the *60 Minutes* cutting room floor. I'd happily do the interview again, of course, with or without the drama. Someone watching the program may come forward with new information. The alternative was to sit on my hands.

One classic example of people being unwilling to sit on their hands when faced with a wrongful conviction was the case of Kathleen Folbigg who was sentenced in 2003 to 40 years imprisonment (later reduced to 30 years with 25 years non-parole period) for the murder of three of her children and the manslaughter of a fourth child. After serving 20 years of her sentence, Ms Folbigg was found to be wrongly convicted and her convictions quashed on the basis that a recently discovered genetic disorder was the likely cause of the death of at least two of her children. It took 90 of the world's most respected scientists—including two Nobel Laureates—who all signed a petition to the Governor of New South Wales condemning the convictions before the justice system had another look at the *Folbigg case*. Some of the scientists appeared on the *60 Minutes* television program 'Reasonable Doubt' hosted by Tara Brown. Kathleen Folbigg was released from prison in June

2023 just a few weeks after Shorty Jamieson commenced his pre-litigation discovery proceedings in the Supreme Court. As in the *Folbigg case*, Stephen Jamieson argued that genetic science—DNA testing specifically—had developed to the point where crime scene material could be checked for further DNA profiles. DNA evidence probably existed that the bandana or headscarf used to gag Janine Balding was worn by Shorty Wells. Stephen and his four juvenile co-accused always said that police arrested the wrong Shorty. Four other witnesses identified a person who looked or dressed like Shorty Wells in the company of the juveniles on the night of the murder.

Unfortunately for Stephen, there was no opportunity for 90 scientists to sign a petition to the Governor in support of his innocence. But he did have two of the best forensic scientists in the country saying that the technology was available in New Zealand to enhance degraded DNA profiles from crime scene biological material. And the received legal wisdom was that a sufficient doubt or question about Stephen's convictions would be raised if DNA testing failed to exclude Shorty Wells as a contributor to the new DNA profiles. The prisoner also had a report from Dr Helen Fraser indicating his police record of interview should *raise significant disquiet in reasonable minds* as to whether he might be the victim of police 'verballing'.

The *60 Minutes* producers kindly provided Helen Fraser with a transcript of what she'd said in her television interview and then allowed her to withdraw anything that later caused her grief. The forensic linguistics professor was fabulous, of course, nailing the significant problems with the police record of interview that convicted Stephen. It could not have been a verbatim record of the exchange of words between the accused and police. Based on the timeline written by police on the document, parts of the text could not physically have been typed in the time indicated. Much to my surprise, the police record of interview went from being a prop in the hands of Channel Nine to an object of forensic analysis on screen with Dr Fraser explaining to Nick McKenzie the deficiencies in the document.

In the 2019 judicial inquiry into Kathleen Folbigg's convictions, the primary question for consideration was *What developments in genetics since Ms Folbigg's trial should be considered in any decision to either uphold or quash her convictions?* A similar question could be asked in any judicial inquiry into Stephen's convictions: What developments in DNA testing since his trial should be considered in any decision to either uphold or quash the convictions? Unfortunately for Folbigg, the judicial officer hearing her inquiry was Reg Blanch AM, QC, the former chief judge of the District Court who found that the convict's diaries were filled with *lies and obfuscations* rather than cries from the heart of a grieving mother—even though not one word in the diaries inculpated Folbigg in the killing of her children. I was reminded of Justice Newman's *tissue of lies* remarks when sentencing Stephen Jamieson,

In much the same way that the *Folbigg case* was rescued from the legal system by the *60 Minutes* program, I was hoping for a similar outcome in the *Jamieson case.* Anthony Dowsley was the journalist who exposed Nicola Gobbo, the undercover lawyer and police informant who also represented many of Melbourne's gangland criminals. The cover of Dowsley's book *Lawyer X* describes the affair as *the biggest legal scandal of our time.* Dowsley spoke with DNA expert Kirsty Wright as well as lawyers involved in the *Jamieson case.* The journalist was convinced that the other Shorty allegations had merit and there appeared to be deficiencies in the police investigation. At the same time, he felt the need to broadcast both sides of the story. I thought that the other side of the Stephen Jamieson story was a shameless public record long overdue for correction.

In the end, police, prosecutors and retired judges were unable or unwilling to justify the convictions on camera, so 'Get Shorty' went to air anyway—the last *60 Minutes* program broadcast in 2024. Nick McKenzie assured viewers that Channel Nine was not advocating for Jamieson or his release. *But convicted criminals deserve to have new evidence considered in exceptional circumstances.* The program was a cracker in my world

Chapter 36

THE CROWN

When asked whether police had acted corruptly, Helen Fraser pointed out to *60 Minutes* that the problem was the law—police could only do what the law permitted. Police inquiries were strongly oriented towards obtaining a confession given the ease with which a contested record of interview could be placed in evidence at trial. Once a jury got to see a record of interview, it raised the question 'Why would the police lie?' effectively reversing the burden of proof on the Crown to prove its case. From the defence point of view, a contested police record of interview without corroboration by a lawyer or other independent witness immediately raised concerns. The trigger for change was the Wood Royal Commission followed by the introduction of reforms requiring mandatory audio and video recording of police interviews.

Back in the day when safecracking was a popular crime, I was introduced to a retired policeman who bragged about planting gelignite at a crime scene and linking it to a known criminal he 'knew' was responsible for the crime. The case was complex and everybody involved has long since died. Unsurprisingly, police talk out of school—often over a few beers—and strangers will sometimes overhear what is said. In the *Beckett case*, I assisted Roseanne Beckett from the south coast to sue the State for malicious prosecution after she spent ten years in jail on evidence fabricated by police. The case began when police were overheard boasting in a pub about how they'd stitched up Roseanne.

Police are more circumspect these days, recognising the dangers of police culture and taking care to bring investigative skills to their workplaces. The Queensland Fitzgerald Inquiry (1987-89) and the New South Wales Wood Royal Commission (1995-97) exposed numerous cases of both police and political corruption. Politicians seem to be slow learners, however. The problem may well be the shrinking gene pool of people wanting to be members of mainstream political parties. Liberal, National and Labor Party combined membership in Australia was less than the numbers attending major football finals in 2024. Like church attendance, major political party membership has fallen off a cliff relative to the growth in the general population. Who would have thought that this year's Queensland State election could be won on the back of a dystopian slogan 'Adult crime adult time' despite all the evidence that children act impulsively and are treated differently in the justice system to adults who plan their crimes? Upping the ante on child punishment is nothing more than abandoning the child to adult crime.

In his political memoir *Run For Your Life* published in 2018, Bob Carr was still talking about his cement law as good Laura Norder policy. *If these criminals had extracted a specific sentence from the court system and later walked free then the victims' families would have felt betrayed.* Of the ten convicts sentenced retrospectively to life without parole by Carr's statute, 20 per cent were innocent convicts and 20 per cent were juveniles. Few victims of crime or their loved ones would be consoled by utilitarian punishment at this level of government. It follows that the real offenders in serious crime can get away with murder and mayhem so long as the police and prosecutors can find somebody else to blame—whether deliberately or accidentally.

When I last checked there were 105 prisoners serving natural life sentences without parole in New South Wales prisons. Based on my limited knowledge of these cases, I estimate that ten per cent of the prisoners are either innocent convicts, or their natural life sentences are excessive given the facts and circumstances of their crimes. If John Hatton AO were still an independent member of the Parliament of New South Wales, he would surely call for a royal commission into natural life sentences in the State. Or perhaps the former honourable member would ask for a standing review commission to give innocent convicts like Stephen Jamieson proper access to justice.

Bob Carr also said in his memoir that *we accept that life sentences must exist on the statute books as an alternative to capital punishment.* But the proposition is highly questionable, with due respect to the former premier. A natural life sentence for children, for example, may mean they could spend 60 or 70 years in prison when comparable crimes committed by adults in 1988 carried an average life sentence of just 13 to 15 years. Further, judges imposing natural life sentences for serious crime often take a very limited view of human nature, failing to recognise the possibility of corruption or human error in the legal process, as well as prospects for rehabilitation.

Judges too are part of the government—and a big part of the problem with wrongful convictions in my opinion. When Stephen Jamieson tried to have the evidence that convicted him reviewed by Justice Bruce James in 2001, the judge dismissed complaints about the police record of interview, ruling that the justice system should not expect police to keep pace with the exact words of the Jamieson interview given their limited typing skills. Detective Sergeant Raue who interrogated Jamieson told the court at trial that the words of the interview *were recorded exactly as Jamieson said it.* But the average speaking rate is 150 words per minute while a moderately skilled typist can type at best about 40 words per minute.

In Jamieson's failed judicial review, the judge seemed to have ignored the incongruity of the law requiring verbatim evidence from police while making allowance for police typing skills. Nearly four decades after his convictions and Stephen is still trying to convince a judge that there's something seriously wrong with a police record of interview when it bears no resemblance to the way he talks, or the way other suspects with the benefit of lawyers were recorded on police typewriters.

And then there's the thorny common law problem of *new* or *fresh* evidence which judges insist upon when the concept really has nothing to do with modern jurisprudence as judges learned to their shame in the *Kathleen Folbigg case.* Folbigg spent 17 years in prison while 17 superior court judges tried to fit the square peg of *new* or *fresh* evidence into the round holes that became known as the *CALM2 Genetic Variant in Sarah, Laura and Kathleen Folbigg.* Judges in Australia will struggle to keep up with science and technology in cases of unsafe and unjust convictions without urgent changes to the law.

Rather than deal with the technical medical issues in the *Folbigg case*, judges took the easy option of continuing to falsely assert that the convict's diaries spoke volumes of her guilt. The proposition was never true. One of the 17 Folbigg judges was the eminent jurist Michael Kirby who gave a recent presentation to the Sydney Institute in which he admitted that judges were swamped by appeal books no less than written and oral submissions. It's simply impossible to take in all the material, let alone apply any kind of independent thought to a case. In the same vein, few applications for special leave to appeal to the High Court are successful for one simple reason—otherwise the workload would overwhelm their honours.

On 14 March 1991, six months after Justice Peter Newman sentenced Stephen Jamieson to life imprisonment with a Never to be Released recommendation, the Birmingham Six walked free from the Central Criminal Court at the Old Bailey in London after spending 16 years in jail—wrongly convicted for the 1974 bombings in two Birmingham pubs that caused 21 deaths and countless injuries. The six Irishmen living in England were innocent convicts, four of whom were beaten and forced to sign fabricated police records of interview. Crown prosecutors spent the whole of the last day of the final appeal asking the court to distinguish between unsafe and unsatisfactory convictions—using rubbish arguments to the end to defend the indefensible. By the end of 1992, as many as 18 people were exonerated after being wrongly convicted for terrorist offences committed by the IRA in England during 1974. Of these, ten would have hanged had the death penalty still been in force according to Chris Mullin MP who spent years investigating the *Birmingham Six case* before securing interest in the proceedings from Granada Television's *World in Action.*

Following exoneration of the Birmingham Six and the scandal their case caused in the British justice system, the UK government established a Criminal Cases Review Commission, an independent statutory body to assist prisoners review their convictions. To date, the CCRC has referred about 850 cases to appeal courts, and around 550 of those cases resulted in convictions being overturned. Similar review bodies exist in New Zealand, Scotland, Norway and North Carolina in the USA. Canada is establishing a Miscarriages of Justice Review Commission. During his recent presentation to the Sydney Institute, Justice Michael Kirby suggested that a review body for innocent convicts was long overdue in Australia.

Bronson Blessington rang on his 51st birthday to say that a parole officer was reviewing his 37 years behind bars. Also, he was very proud of his new job in prison—training guide dogs. And the Senior Public Defender had apparently dusted off petitions to the Governor of New South Wales requesting the Crown exercise the Royal Prerogative of Mercy in favour of all three prisoners—Blessington, Elliott and Jamieson. A legal officer for the Crown confirmed that mercy petitions were now a live issue for the government.

Meanwhile the cavalry may have arrived. The Governor's boss, reigning monarch King Charles III of England, Scotland, Wales and other places, and *By the Grace of God King of Australia* (according to his proclamation) recently attended a function at the New South Wales Parliament, inspiring me to write to His Majesty. So far as I knew, the Crown had never shown mercy to a murder convict in Australia other than a woman who was the victim of appalling domestic violence before responding in kind to her tormentor by killing him. Whether His Majesty was concerned about an innocent man and two juveniles serving life without parole remained to be seen.

Space and time were limited so I was unable to say everything in the letter that bothered me about the new monarch being the boss of Australia. For a start, was Charles the King of the six States as well as the federal government in Canberra? The question raised a thorny legal issue about whether we're governed by a divisible Crown. To my mind, the answer must be that we are, otherwise the Crown could not represent Stephen through the Legal Aid office on the one hand, and on the other, brief the Crown Solicitor to defend the Police Force and the Attorney General against Stephen's wrongful convictions claim. For what it's worth, here's my letter to King Charles III.

JUSTICE REVIEW FORUM
PO Box 302
Bellingen NSW 2454
Australia
30 November 2024

His Majesty King Charles III
King of Australia
Buckingham Palace
London SW1A 1AA
United Kingdom

Your Majesty

It was great to see you in Sydney the other day, attending a luncheon to open an exhibition in the Parliament's forecourt, and helping us commemorate the 200th anniversary of the Legislative Council in New South Wales. I enjoyed your brief speech and the hourglass gift you described as a 'speech timer'.

Two hundred years ago, of course, Sydney was a struggling penal colony. The last of the prisoners arrived on board the *Eden* in 1840, some of them juveniles who never had the opportunity to return home to Britain. Here in the modern iteration of the penal colony, I thought you might like to know legislators still jail juveniles for life.

Of no less concern, judges still hand down life sentences to innocent convicts as directed by politicians, as if votes were somehow more important than justice. Securing a judicial review into wrongful convictions and unjust sentences in Australia is always a nightmare.

Given the common law history between Britain and the colonies, you might think we would have a rights bill to protect children from life sentences such as the UK Human Rights Act, or a statutory body like the Criminal Cases Review Commission to allow innocent convicts the opportunity to review their convictions and sentences.

I guess you already know, Majesty, that it's no longer necessary in the United Kingdom for the executive government to punish prisoners to demonstrate the respect due to British justice. Cases such as the *Birmingham Six* and the *Guildford Four* put an end to that nonsense. But I regret to say that State politicians down here are slow learners largely due to their unwillingness to let go of their penal colony executive authority over the courts and judges.

On a related topic, you might consider reminding your Australian representatives—six Governors and a Governor-General—that the life of every person, prisoner or free, is worthy of the King's royal prerogative of mercy and kindness. That would be a contribution up there with your efforts to draw attention to the dignity of all people facing the devastation of industrial scale climate change.

Yours sincerely
JUSTICE REVIEW FORUM

BUCKINGHAM PALACE

Private and Confidential

31st January, 2025

Dear Mr. Breen,

I am writing to acknowledge receipt of your letter which you sent to His Majesty The King.

It was thoughtful of you to take the trouble to share your views with His Majesty. However, whilst the strength of your feelings are understood, I must inform you that this is not a matter on which The King would personally comment.

Nevertheless, your comments have been very carefully noted, and I have been asked to convey His Majesty's warmest good wishes.

Yours sincerely,

Head of Royal Correspondence

Mr. Peter Breen

Chapter 37

CLAUDE ROBINSON

A few weeks ahead of the final Supreme Court hearing to determine whether a further judicial inquiry into Stephen Jamieson's convictions would take place, I attended a law and media conference at the Gilbert + Tobin law offices in a very tall building at Barangaroo on the Darling Harbour foreshore. Appearing for the law was the Federal Court's Justice Michael Lee, and representing the media was Channel Nine's *60 Minutes* host, Nick McKenzie. Attendees included open democracy supporters and advocates of free speech, most of whom seemed to agree that protecting the rule of law from secretive governments was the new frontier for journalists and lawyers. Nobody at the conference was surprised to learn that I was unable to get police to provide additional DNA information and undertake further DNA testing of crime scene material in the *Jamieson case.*

Peter Greste of the Alliance for Journalists' Freedom informed the conference that the *New York Times* identified Australia as probably the world's most secretive democracy, passing more than 100 national security laws since 2001. Michael Lee told a gaggle of ABC journalists that I was a rare political species in that I'd emerged from an ICAC inquiry with my reputation enhanced. May it please the Court, Your Honour. Quentin Dempster wanted to know if I was still woke. Cancelled more likely, Quentin. Former Attorney-General and High Commissioner to the United Kingdom, George Brandis KC, was interested to learn that the only reason Australia did not have a Bill of Rights was that the statutory instrument passed by the Hawke Labor Government in the House of Representatives stalled in the Senate in 1986.

According to Gough Whitlam who sent me a letter on the subject, debate on the Australian Bill of Rights Bill was hijacked by the then Western Australia Labor premier, Brian Burke, who informed Prime Minister Bob Hawke that there would be no money for head office of the Labor Party from Labor supporters in the west if the rights bill went ahead. Burke was concerned that the provision for one vote one value in the bill would put an end to Labor's gerrymander in the Parliament of Western Australia. After retiring as premier of the west, Burke became in quick succession ambassador to the Vatican and an inmate of Wooroloo prison for fraudulently misusing his parliamentary travel allowance. Another fraud conviction was quashed on appeal.

I chatted with Michael Lee about the *Phuong Ngo case* since I was aware it still troubled the judge. Ngo's conviction in 2001 and life sentence for the political murder of the Labor Member for Cabramatta, John Newman, was again under review. I'd driven for ten hours the previous day to visit Ngo and update myself on what was said to be new and/or fresh and compelling evidence. Sixteen years had passed since the disaster of Phuong Ngo's last conviction and sentence review. The man himself and none of his supporters were getting any younger. His father, Canh Ngo, had died a few months earlier aged 100 years. His mother, Hai Thi Pham, died in Vietnam in March 2001 three months before her son's conviction for political murder. Michael Lee had the onerous task of bringing the sad news to Phuong in prison.

Where was Phuong? How was he getting on?

Now 66 years of age and sporting a wispy chin beard worthy of a humble vegetable and watermelon grower, the prisoner was safely ensconced at the maximum-security Macquarie Correctional Centre in outback New South Wales. He'd transformed every spare patch of ground in his steel and concrete digs into an award-winning garden. His herbs and roses recently won first prize at the Wellington Show.

As legal counsel for Phuong Ngo, Michael Lee and Bret Walker had a running battle with prosecutors over secretive and indemnified Crown witnesses, covert audio and video recordings of ambiguous provenance and probative value, questionable transcriptions of evidence and the Kafkaesque practices of executive government agencies controlling the flow of information to the defendant—a battle the eminent lawyers and Ngo ultimately lost.

This far down the track in the *Jamieson case,* I don't want to bother you too much with the details of another case, but a few days after the law and media conference, I thought again about Phuong Ngo when I attended a book launch in the St Francis Xavier Hall at Lavender Bay, just north of the Sydney Harbour Bridge. Looking across the bay towards the city, the bridge was in full view, reminding me that in at least one of the three trials it took to convict Phuong Ngo, the prosecutor informed jurors that they should consider the evidence against the prisoner as if it were a jigsaw puzzle of the Sydney Harbour Bridge. Some of the pieces of the puzzle may be missing, but they could convict the moment it was apparent that the jigsaw depicted the famous bridge. The analogy was inappropriate in my opinion as it might trespass on the meaning of beyond reasonable doubt.

Anyway, retired judge Chris Geraghty was launching his last book before floating off into the cosmos, and Danny Gilbert of Gilbert + Tobin was doing the honours at the podium—plus the mandatory author Q&A afterwards. The hall was packed to the rafters with judges, retired diplomats, lawyers, former seminarians, friends, spouses and partners. Geraghty, a kind man who everyone loved, sold a couple of hundred books on my reckoning.

I collared retired Justice James Wood who was happy to talk about the importance of judges not talking about any of their old cases, especially the *Jamieson case* and the *Phuong Ngo case* (Wood was the judge in the first trial of Jamieson and the first and second trials of Ngo, but not the trials that convicted either prisoner). I wanted to ask the former chief judge at common law whether he thought the prosecution's Sydney Harbour Bridge analogy had the effect of reversing the onus of proof in the *Phuong Ngo* case? It would be a question for another day—perhaps the next review.

Geraghty's book, *Daydreams and Nightmares: the Meditations of an Ex-Priest and Retired Judge*, invited the reader to consider the best and the worst of judicial agitations and cogitations, changing names here and there to protect vulnerable litigants *from prying eyes and peeping toms* and the author *from baseless and expensive defamation claims.* Here's a paragraph I liked in the book.

> *I search to glimpse God's presence and power in my life, and in the world around me. I'm attentive to the soft sounds in the air, to the rhythm of my breathing, to the beauty out there of the world, and the loveliness of human contact. I give thanks. I ache for those in distress. Confused in the face of evil. Tormented by the suffering of the innocent.*

I had one more job to do before the Jamieson hearing and that was to visit Claude Robinson at Rainbow Lodge in the inner city, a halfway house for prisoners coming out of jail. Claude knew Stephen from Goulburn where they sometimes found themselves in adjoining yards. Claude eventually busted out of the prison cycle by dealing with his addictions rather than repeating the criminal behaviour they demanded. He was now running the Rainbow Lodge and he'd been nominated as a New South Wales Local Hero in the 2025 Australian Honours Awards. The lodge manager made me feel welcome.

We sat under a covered area at the back of the inner-city terrace accommodation, swapping crime stories, convict gossip and the horror of crime statistics. Crime and punishment cost the people of New South Wales a staggering $16 billion each year but finding a bed for a former convict was mind bendingly difficult. Almost 20,000 people left New South Wales prisons every year, but less than three percent of them could find a bed where they received support and professional care. Little wonder that half the prisoners released after serving their sentences went back inside after six months. Miraculously, Rainbow Lodge had a bed for Stephen if he needed one.

The last time Stephen appeared before Justice Wood on 23 October 1989 following the abandonment of the first trial over the other Shorty allegations, His Honour heard an application by barrister Ted O'Loughlin that his client appeared to be innocent and should have bail. In dismissing the application for bail, Wood said it might be appropriate to make a further application at some time in the future. I assured Stephen he could apply for bail a second time (albeit 37 years after the first) if Shorty Wells could not be excluded as a contributor to the DNA on the bandana. But he would need to demonstrate to the satisfaction of the court that he had somewhere safe to go since he had no family or relatives to help him adjust to life on the outside.

Chapter 38

DNA TESTING IN COURT

Stephen Jamieson appeared before the chief judge at common law, Justice Ian Harrison, at the Law Courts Building in Phillip Street on 13 December 2024. The judge would decide questions of DNA testing in the context of a formal application for an inquiry into Stephen's convictions filed in court by Legal Aid two weeks earlier. My application for Stephen asking the court to test the whole bandana for Shorty Wells' DNA using Low Copy Number DNA technology in New Zealand was effectively sidelined. Stephen did not turn up to court in person, appearing on a video link wall monitor in the courtroom. Like most prisoners, he hated travelling in the claustrophobic prison vans.

It was a stinking hot day and I knew the video link room at Goulburn jail was like a sauna with no natural light and insufficient fresh air. Normally a prisoner would spend half an hour or so in the room for a video conference before coming up for air, but Stephen was expected to stay there for the whole day awaiting the convenience of correctional officers to open the door and let him out for nature breaks, fresh air and a meal.

Stephen had no serious involvement in the proceedings beyond a narrow view of the judge and court staff who faced ten lawyers—five briefed by Legal Aid and five representing the Attorney General and the Commissioner for Police (enough lawyers to justify a criminal cases review commission, you might think). I was seated behind the real lawyers, cheek by jowl with other visitors in the public gallery, which consisted of two rows of chairs at the back of the courtroom. Immediately in front of me sat Howard Brown—formerly of the Victims of Crime League. Others assisting Janine Balding's family I recognised along with supporters of Stephen's wrongful convictions claim including legal academics and innocence project lawyers.

In his opening remarks, His Honour reminded everyone of the importance of a robust justice system that allowed convicts an opportunity to review their convictions and sentences in the light of fresh and compelling evidence without diminishing in any way the court's respect for the suffering experienced by the victims of crime and their loved ones. The judge insisted that the right to pursue an inquiry *is one that exists for any citizen in this State and it is in that context that these matters will be examined.*

Georgina Wright SC for the Crown made the announcement, surprising to me, that Mark 'Shorty' Wells had been located and given formal notice of the Jamieson proceedings. This was good news as some of the lawyers had been hassling me to hand over the Wells' biological material I'd picked up in Brisbane's Queen Street Mall all those years ago. I refused to give it to them on the advice of Kirsty Wright who said that for Stephen to attempt to do police work and get involved in DNA testing would be an own goal worthy of the bottom of the A-League table. Wells' DNA profile was now on the national database in any event.

Also surprising was the Crown's decision to call the new operations director of the Forensic and Analytical Science Service, Clinton Cochrane, to give evidence. His predecessor, Sharon Neville, who told me the FASS had never received or tested a reference sample of Mark Wells' DNA profile, had retired a few months earlier. Cochrane carried a laptop computer bag the size of a small briefcase to the witness box, and soon enough, he opened the bag to withdraw several pieces of paper.

In response to questions from the Public Defender, Richard Wilson, the forensic biologist used the paperwork to compare male DNA from particular parts of the bandana obtained in 2014 and 2019 with DNA from each of Stephen, Matthew Elliott, Bronson Blessington and Wayne Wilmot. All four were excluded as contributors. As Kirsty Wright had advised, DNA profiles could be compared to the bandana using the paper printouts of electronically recorded DNA information. The expectation in the courtroom was that the DNA profile of Shorty Wells was about to be compared to the unidentified male profiles from the bandana samples.

My concern about the evidence so far had been the apparent absence of electropherogram reports which were the subject of an amended Notice of Motion filed in Court on 27 March 2024. Without electropherograms, the witness could not say whether a particular DNA profile had multiple contributors. Indeed, Clinton Cochrane was asked whether Stephen's DNA had been compared to a combined PowerPlex profile, and the witness answered that Stephen could be excluded as a possible contributor *if that profile originated from a single individual*, allowing an unhelpful inference to be drawn that Stephen might be one of a number of unknown contributors.

I looked up to the video link monitor to see Stephen wiping away tears. Only Shorty Wells' DNA remained to be tested against the bandana samples. As Clinton Cochrane returned the last of the paper DNA profiles to his computer bag, Richard Wilson asked the judge if the court could take a short break. An academic lawyer seated in front of me in the gallery chairs turned and shrugged his shoulders. What's going on?

Twenty minutes later when the court resumed, the Public Defender asked further questions of Clinton Cochrane. The witness was referred to a redacted copy of Mark Wells' DNA profile already in evidence as an attachment to an affidavit. Cochrane said he could do a comparison of Wells' DNA profile to the bandana for exclusionary purposes if he had an unredacted copy of the profile. But under the appeal and review legislation, police could not provide DNA *information that will reveal the identity of the person other than the convicted person in connection with the offence for which he or she was convicted*. For this reason, the witness said, he could not provide further information about Shorty Wells' DNA profile even with the benefit of an unredacted copy of the profile.

Wells' DNA had escaped scrutiny once again, and since none of the ten lawyers in the proceeding made any objections, I assumed we were witnessing an understanding between the lawyers that the appeal and review legislation prevented police from revealing the identity of anyone other than those convicted of the crimes against Janine Balding.

As Clinton Cochrane left the witness box, I guessed that the impasse over the DNA testing would be resolved by a reserved decision of the judge, and that decision would probably be the subject of a Court of Appeal decision. The process was torturous, but I remained confident that the Crown's efforts to uphold Stephen's convictions would eventually fail. To me, no other outcome seemed possible.

Apart from the DNA evidence, Stephen would rely on the fingerprint case file to re-examine fingerprints taken from Janine Balding's car—Shorty Wells was a passenger in the car. Helen Fraser's forensic linguistic analysis of Stephen's police record of interview was also compelling. Always on the case, Helen introduced me to a forensic psychologist who would say something about the psychiatric evidence that helped convict Stephen. Plus there was the Police Integrity Commission report into the police investigation of the crimes against Ms Balding.

And finally, Kirsty Wright was available to give evidence about the DNA testing if only Legal Aid would brief her. The Queensland Government had recently appointed Kirsty to head an inquiry into DNA testing in the Sunshine State, recognising her competence and integrity. A report of the inquiry was tabled in the Queensland Parliament in August 2025. It found that poor science contributed to flaws in the Queensland DNA testing. Writing in *The Australian* newspaper, Mackenzie Scott said that Forensic Science Queensland knowingly provided courts and police with potentially inaccurate DNA results.

Chapter 39

UP THE CREEK

Justice Harrison's judgement (see *Jamieson v Attorney General for NSW* [2025] NSWSC 92) was delivered in the New Year of 2025, an unusual decision in that His Honour directed the parties to draft short minutes of order consistent with his ruling. It seemed to me the judge was ordering Legal Aid and the Crown to agree on the DNA testing regime rather than allow them to put it off until after the appeals process was exhausted—as if he were an inquisitor rather than an adversarial umpire.

Weeks went by as one adjournment followed another until the court fixed the Wednesday of Easter Week to hand up the short minutes of order. I travelled from the north coast a day early to visit Matthew Elliott and Stephen at Goulburn jail—an eight-hour drive each way—to avoid the holiday traffic heading north on my return. I had to be out of Sydney straight after the court case if I hoped to get home ahead of the holidaymakers.

Goulburn was noticeably colder than the north coast and the tell-tale signs of autumn appeared in the poplars, plane trees and the occasional pin oak along the road—splashes of green, crimson and gold across the countryside. I pressed the buzzer at the visitors entrance to the jail, and as I entered the perimeter fence, I noticed a stand of luminous autumn-coloured trees that had grown several metres in the two decades I'd been visiting the jail. Correctional officer Rick Czartowski identified them as ornamental pear trees as he escorted me to the legal visits area. He reminded me I'd served a long sentence at Goulburn jail—as long as some of the correctional officers.

I found Matthew and Stephen waiting for me in the visitors room and they seemed bright and cheerful as we shook hands.

"Sorry about the bad news," Stephen said casually.

What bad news?

"Tomorrow's court case has been adjourned, again."

Why?

"They couldn't get a match to Shorty Wells."

I looked at Matthew Elliott. What's Stephen saying?

"Legal Aid told him that Shorty Wells has been excluded as a contributor to the DNA on the bandana."

That can't be right. I sat heavily in the padded executive office chair while the two prisoners sat in the vinyl covered visitors chairs on the other side of the desk. What's going on?

Stephen said that one of the Legal Aid lawyers had phoned him to say they needed another adjournment to get more advice about a new report from the DNA testing lab.

"Apparently it's a 20-page report sain' they can't find Shorty Wells' DNA on the bandana."

It must mean they can't get a result from the samples they've tested. What about the rest of the bandana?

"Wells DNA must be all over it," Matthew said. "They found my DNA but not Shorty Wells'. I don't get it."

My attention was elsewhere even though the boys were on for a chat. They had few visitors so I was happy to indulge them. How was Bronson getting on at the Serco jail on the north coast? He was training guide dogs and teaching scripture. They thought that was an hilarious combination. Matthew said seriously that it was good for Bronson that he'd found God. Shorty agreed. Bronson once saved him from a bashing in prison, Shorty said, telling the prospective offender, another prisoner, to fuck off.

"Ephesians, I guess," said Matthew. Shorty said, "Genesis, I reckon."

You had to laugh.

Just out from Goulburn on the return trip home, my mobile phone rang. A recorded message from the Serco jail on the north coast switched me through to Bronson who wanted to know if I was ready for Jamo's court case tomorrow. I told him about the late adjournment. A new report from the government's DNA testing laboratory, FASS, found Shorty Wells' DNA was not on the bandana samples they tested.

"Sounds like corruption to me," said the prisoner.

Or a stuff-up—the government unprepared for advances in DNA testing technology.

"They're sittin' on their hands," Bronson said. "They just keep testin' the same bits of the bandana over and over again. I think they're havin' a lend of you."

You have to trust the process. Stephen's getting the judicial inquiry that will eventually get him out of jail.

Bronson's three-minute jail call clicked off the bluetooth car connection to my mobile phone as I pulled up at the rest-stop entrance to the Towrang Stockade near Marulan. I called the Legal Aid lawyers to facetiously thank them for the heads up on the court case—and a 16 hours' drive for nothing. Rather than provoke an argument, I asked for a copy of the 20-page forensic report that failed to locate Shorty Wells' DNA on the bandana. The report was confidential but I would get a copy after an independent DNA expert had assessed the test results. Could Kirsty Wright have a copy? Not at the moment.

Trying to control my anger, I walked off into the bush, and down the dusty track that led to the long-abandoned convict prison camp. Towrang Stockade is the former penal colony digs to about 250 convicts who worked on the chain gangs building the Great South Road in the 1840s. The foundation stones of some of the old buildings are still visible on a barren hillside overlooking the Wollondilly River. Dug into the earth and stone riverbank, a powder magazine is well preserved, hanging on stoically between the crumbling land erosion gutters where rivers of rain make brief and unseasonal appearances. Along the riverbank, I stumbled into a dry side creek festooned with brown gum leaves and grey branches fallen from the shanghai shaped river gums that towered overhead, a place so barren it had nothing to say of the changing season.

I hauled myself out of the creek bed and found a shaded log to rest and rage. How the chain gang convicts must have hated this place. And then the smell of burning incense filled the air. Looking about, I could not locate the source of the sweet-smelling aroma and wondered if I was having some kind of paranormal mystical experience. A brain explosion more likely.

Less than ten metres away was a fenced off area marking three graves so I made my way to a place where I could read the headstone inscriptions. Two smaller headstones marked the graves of Mary Brown, aged four years and one month, and Elizabeth

Whitaker aged 33 years who both departed this life in 1841 within a few weeks of each other. I thought about what misfortunes might have brought a woman and child to a convict chain gang camp and ultimately their deaths—punished perhaps by a brutal prison system designed and run according to the model for male offenders? Maybe the woman and child were innocent victims—the woman herself a prisoner. Women lived in fear and degradation in the colonial prisons and died young.

Staring at the bone-dry ground below the headstones, there was no escaping the thought that men treat women badly, and not just women prisoners, but innocent women such as Virginia Morse, Anita Cobby and Janine Balding—victims of the crimes of ordinary men who have it in them to dominate and to kill. And then for the hundredth time I checked myself, remembering that children, not men, had killed Janine Balding.

The larger headstone was sculptured from sandstone with scalloped edges and stylised engraved lettering that marked the resting place of John Moxly, a private soldier of the 80th regiment, who served for 22 years before his death in 1838 aged 38 years. His military comrades erected the monument as a mark of respect to *a good and deserving soldier.* The headstone included an inscription—words buried in dry lichen which were difficult to read. I made out the first part of it: *Remember me as you pass by. As you are now, so once was I.* Then I had to scrape away the lichen with my car key to reveal the last few words: *As I am now so you must be. Prepare for death to follow me.*

I walked back to the shaded log and sat down again. As I looked up and down the dry creek bed, the bush was perfectly still with the crisp autumn air afraid almost to move. Suddenly I let out a guttural scream that tore at my lungs and burned my throat. I did it again and again until I was coughing and spluttering. The bush remained unmoved. What made me so angry was losing control of the *Jamieson case* for a second time to Legal Aid and for the same reason as the first—insufficient resources to run the case myself. Only a properly funded criminal cases review commission would have access to crime scene material and the independence needed to properly re-examine evidence that put away an innocent convict like Stephen Jamieson.

I rang Anthony Dowsley who was back at the *Herald and Weekly Times* after his stint at *60 Minutes* and told him I was up the creek—the government DNA testing laboratory working on the bandana could not get a match to Shorty Wells' DNA.

"Maybe Blessington and Elliott are lying to you about Shorty Wells' being at the crime scenes," said the journalist.

Not a chance. If the government tested the *whole* bandana using Low Copy Number DNA testing in New Zealand they'd likely get a match to Shorty Wells' DNA. And I trusted the word of multiple eyewitnesses who were present at the crime scenes more than I trusted government DNA testing in Australia where police controlled what was tested and who got to see test results.

ACKNOWLEDGMENTS

This book has been taking shape for two decades and could not have survived the passage of time without the support of many people including some who are no longer with us, and others who prefer to remain anonymous. My librarian wife, Diane, has been looking at drafts and re-writes for all that time. Finally, the end of the book arrived simultaneously with Stephen Jamieson securing a judicial inquiry into his convictions.

Too many lawyers have helped with the case to make a full list, but I'm especially indebted to Richard Potter, David Barrow, Michele Ruyters, Will Hutchins, Gary Edmond, Peter O'Brien, Joanne Harris, Karen Psaltis, Richard Wilson, Slade Howell, Claire O'Neill, Richard d'Apice, Sidnie Sarang, David Giddy, Bob Moles and Kirsten Edwards. Over the years, the Law Society Pro Bono Scheme has also assisted me whenever I've needed a second opinion about legal issues affecting Stephen Jamieson.

Some of the lawyers I mentioned followed the emergent evolutions of the book and advised me along the way, while Richard d'Apice also checked for infelicities. Expert witnesses in the Stephen Jamieson legal action, Helen Fraser and Kirsty Wright, were generous to a fault with their time, and their feedback was invaluable. Michael Strutt and Michele Ruyters read everything I said in the book—on every occasion I said it. That said, the work is entirely my own, and I take responsibility for any errors or omissions, although I reckon there are none.

A final word of thanks to Michael and Jane Wilkinson at Wilkinson Publishing for lending their experience and skill to *Shorty* when they might have been nervous about a book that could be seen to support the wrong victims of crime.

ABOUT THE AUTHOR

Peter Breen is the author of several non-fiction books including *Advance Australia Fair* (1999); *The Book of Letters* (2002); *Murder Principals* (2010); *Protecting Reputation* (2015); *Candidates Disease* (2019); *Prodigal Pilgrim* (2022); *Dear Mr Putin* (2023); and *Letters to the Pope* (2025). He is a former independent member of the Legislative Council of the New South Wales Parliament. Before entering parliament, he worked as a senior human rights adviser to Queensland's Administrative Review Commission following the Fitzgerald inquiry into political and police corruption. His task was to draft a Queensland Bill of Rights. He supports the Alliance for Journalists' Freedom and practices as a solicitor specialising in defamation law—with an occasional dabble in crime for convicts who claim to be innocent. He represented Stephen Jamieson before Legal Aid NSW agreed to fund a judicial inquiry into the *Jamieson case*. Peter lives on the north coast of New South Wales between Bellingen and Byron Bay.

SELECTED BIBLIOGRAPHY

Bodey, Michael; 'Breaking the Fourth Wall', *Law Society Journal,* Sydney, Mar 2024.

Breen, Peter; *Candidates Disease: A Political Memoir*, Wilkinson Publishing Pty Limited, Melbourne, 2019.

Brennan, Frank; *Legislating Liberty: A Bill of Rights for Australia?* University of Queensland Press, Brisbane, 1998.

Brown, David; 'Breaking the Code of Silence: the Wood Royal Commission into New South Wales police – a brief overview', *Alternative Law Journal*, Vol 22, No. 5, Sydney, Oct 1997.

Byrnes, Andrew and Charlesworth, Hilary and McKinnon, Gabrielle; *Bills of Rights in Australia: History, Politics and Law*, University of New South Wales Press, Sydney, 2009.

Carr, Bob; *Run For Your Life*, Melbourne University Press, Melbourne, 2018.

Condon, Matthew; *Three Crooked Kings*, University of Queensland Press, Brisbane, 2023.

Conlon, Gerry; *The Story of Gerry Conlon of the Guildford Four,* Penguin Books, London, UK, 1994.

Dale, Amy and Ea, Henry; 'Trial and Error', *The Law Society Journal*, Sydney, Jul 2024.

Dowsley, Anthony and Carlyon, Patrick; *Lawyer X*, HarperCollins Publishers, Sydney, 2020.

Dyer, Ron; 'Review of the Crimes (Forensic Procedures) Act 2000', *Report 18*, Standing Committee on Law and Justice, Parliament of New South Wales, Feb 2002.

Fitzgerald, Tony; 'Commission of Inquiry into Possible Illegal Activities and Associated Police Misconduct', *Final Report*, State of Queensland, July 1989.

Fraser, Helen; 'Concerns about the authenticity of confession evidence in the 1990 convictions of Stephen 'Shorty' Jamieson', *Research Hub for Language in Forensic Evidence*, University of Melbourne, Oct 2024.

Friedman, Joseph; 'Miscarriages of Justice', *Law Society Journal*, Sydney, Nov 2022.

Geraghty, Chris; *Daydreams and Nightmares: The Meditations of an Ex-Priest and Retired Judge*, P&P Press, Sydney, 2024.

Grisham, John, and McCloskey, Jim; *Framed: Astonishing True Stories of Wrongful Convictions*, Hodder & Stoughton, London UK, 2024.

Hamer, David, and Edmond, Gary; 'Forensic Science Evidence, Wrongful Convictions and Adversarial Process', *University of Queensland Law Journal*, 38:2, Brisbane, 2019.

Kerr, John; *The Big Folbigg Mistake: A mother's fight for justice*, Kerr Publishing Pty Limited, Melbourne, 2022.

Kirby, Michael; 'A New Right of Appeal as a Response to Wrongful Convictions: Is it Enough?', *Criminal Law Journal*, Vol 43, Part 5, Thomson Reuters, Sydney, 2019.

Kirby, Michael; 'Suspect Convictions and a Criminal Cases Review Commission', *The Sydney Institute Podcast*, 2 September 2024.

McDermott, Quentin; *Meadows Law*, ABC Books (Harper Collins Australia), Sydney, 2025.

McMahon, Marilyn, and Fraser, Helen; 'Transcripts of indistinct audio recordings: time for reform', *Law Institute Journal*, Law Institute of Victoria, Aug 2023.

Mullin, Chris; *Error of Judgement: The Birmingham Bombings and the Scandal that Shocked Britain*, Octopus Publishing Group, London UK, 2024.

Peck, M. Scott; *People of the Lie: the Hope for Healing Human Evil*, Simon & Shuster, New York, NY, USA, 1985.

Porter, Chester; *The Conviction of the Innocent: how the law can let us down*, Random House Australia, North Sydney, 2007.

Ratzinger, Joseph Cardinal; *Truth and Tolerance: Christian Belief and World Religions*, Ignatius Press, San Francisco, CA, USA, 2003.

Ruyters, Michele, and Bartle, Jarryd; 'The problem of post-conviction review in Australia', *Alternative Law Journal*, Vol 49, No. 4, Sydney, Dec 2024.

Smith, Greg; 'The DNA Review Panel: Review of Division 6 of Part 7 of the Crimes (Appeal and Review) Act 2001', Attorney General and Justice, Sydney, 2013.

Wood, James; 'The Wood Royal Commission into the New South Wales Police Service', *Final Report*, State of New South Wales, Sydney, May 1997.

INDEX